I0814453

THE CRICKETERS OF 1945

THE CRICKETERS OF 1945

Rising from the Ashes of **World War Two**

CHRISTOPHER SANDFORD

First published by Pitch Publishing, 2024

Pitch Publishing
9 Donnington Park,
85 Birdham Road,
Chichester,
West Sussex,
PO20 7AJ
www.pitchpublishing.co.uk
info@pitchpublishing.co.uk

A CIP catalogue record is available for this book from the British Library.

ISBN 978 1 80150 757 8

Typesetting and origination by Pitch Publishing

Printed and bound in Great Britain by TJ Books, Padstow

Contents

Acknowledgements 11

1. 'Every Landing was a Close Shave' 17

2. Our Britain 48

3. Fun Among the Ruins 72

4. A Match for the Ages 104

5. Ealing Cricket Drama 140

6. High Summer 169

7. 'You've Had a Revolution' 198

8. Endgame 233

Source Notes 268

Bibliography 278

Index 280

Christopher Sandford is a regular contributor to newspapers and magazines on both sides of the Atlantic. He has written numerous books about music, film, sports and political figures, including a widely praised official biography of Imran Khan, as well as *Union Jack*, a best-selling account of John F. Kennedy's special relationship with Great Britain. *National Review* called it 'political history of a high order' and 'the Kennedy book to beat'. His book *The Final Innings* was the joint winner of the Cricket Society and MCC Book of the Year Award in 2020.

Also by Christopher Sandford

FICTION
Feasting with Panthers
Arcadian
We Don't Do Dogs

PLAY
Comrades

MUSIC BIOGRAPHIES
Mick Jagger
Eric Clapton
Kurt Cobain
David Bowie
Sting
Bruce Springsteen
Keith Richards
Paul McCartney
The Rolling Stones

FILM BIOGRAPHIES
Steve McQueen
Roman Polanski

SPORT
The Cornhill Centenary Test
Godfrey Evans
Tom Graveney
Imran Khan
John Murray
Laker and Lock

HISTORY
Houdini and Doyle
Summer 1914
Macmillan and Kennedy
The Man Who Would be Sherlock
John F. Kennedy and Great Britain
The Zeebrugge Raid
Summer 1939
Victor Lustig
Midnight in Tehran
1964

To Barbara Levy

Acknowledgements

THIS IS my first book written after the recurring house arrest imposed by the sanitary dictatorship devoted to the cult of health, as our political rulers here in the western part of the US became known at intervals from 2020–23, and for all I know may yet be again. Nonetheless, I hope the reader won't find any conspicuous falling off from the modest merits of the ones done during that great detention. I should mention two things upfront. First, this is not a statistical record of each and every individual cricketer, or cricket match, of the 1945 English season. Others, notably *Wisden*, have already performed that task admirably well. No slight is intended on the name of any player who might be missing, and anyone interested in reading more about the subject will find some suggestions in the bibliography at the back of the book. And second, it goes without saying that none of those listed here can be blamed for the shortcomings of the text. They are mine alone.

For archive material, input or advice I should thank, professionally: AbeBooks; *Acton Review*; Alibris; *America*; Rob Boddie; Bookfinder; Simon Brand; the *Brazen Head*; the British Library; British Newspaper Library; Cambridge University Library; Jane Camillin; *Chronicles*; John Connell; CricInfo; Cricket Archive; Cricket Australia; the *Cricketer International*; the Cricket Society; the *Daily Express*; the late Ted Dexter; Essex CCC; the late Godfrey Evans; the General Register Office; Dave Gilbert; Hampshire CCC; Nigel Hancock; the *Hedgehog Review*; the History Press; the late Robin Hobbs; Imperial War Museum; Imran Khan; Kent CCC; Leicestershire CCC; Barbara Levy; the MCC Library; Middlesex

CCC; the late Keith Miller; the Mitchell Library, Glasgow; Mitre House Hotel, London; *Modern Age*; the National Archives; National Archives of Australia; National Army Museum; Northamptonshire CCC; *The Oldie*; the late Jim Parks; Nigel Popplewell; the late Sir Oliver Popplewell; Derek Pringle; Public Record Office; Bill Reader; Tim Reidy; Renton Public Library; Neil Robinson, MCC Head of Heritage and Collections; Jane Rosen; Seaside Library, Oregon; Seattle CC; *The Spectator*; Surrey CCC; Surrey History Centre; Jon Surtees; Sussex CCC; Bruce Talbot; Derek Turner; USA Cricket Association; Vital Records; *Wisden Cricket Monthly*; Yorkshire CCC.

And personally: Wendy Adams; Leann Alspaugh; Rev. Maynard Atik; Pete Barnes; the late Lisa Betteridge; Danny Bonaduce; Rocco Bowen; Deputy Cy Brame; Robert and Hilary Bruce; the Burrough family; Lincoln Callaghan; Don Carson; Martin Chandler, Paul Darlow; Chris Davies; Monty Dennison; John Densmore; Chris Difford; the Dowdall family; Barbara and the late John Dungee; Steve Fossen; Malcolm Galfe; Lance Gibbs; James Graham; the late Tom Graveney; Jeff and Rita Griffin; Karolyn Grimes; Grumbles; Steve and Jo Hackett; Duncan Hamilton; Heart By Heart; Alastair Hignell; Charles Hillman; Alex Holmes; Hotel Magenta, Paris; Jo Jacobius; Julian James; Robin B. James; Bill and Morgan Johnson; Jo Johnson; the late Wilko Johnson; Lincoln Kamell; David Kynaston; Terry Lambert; Alex Larman; Belinda Lawson; the Lorimer family; Robert Dean Lurie; Somar Macek; Les McBride; Dan McCarthy; Matt McDonald; Lee Mattson; Jim Meyersahm; the late Jerry Miller; the Morgans; Harry Mount; the Murray family; Greg Nowak; Phillip Oppenheim; Valya Page; Robin and Lucinda Parish; Peter Perchard; *Plough*; Roman Polanski; the Prins family; the late John Riley; the late Malcolm Robinson; the late Keir Rothnie; the Rushbrooke family; the late Sefton Sandford; Peter Scaramanga;

Seattle Times; Fred and Cindy Smith; the Smith family; the Stanley family; Jack Surendranath; Nick Tudball; Derek Turner; the late Derek Underwood; the Villar family; Ross Viner; Lisbeth Vogl; Rogena and the late Alan White; Richard Wigmore; Debbie Wild; the Willis Fleming family; the late Aaron Wolf; and Bill Wyman.

My deepest thanks, as always, to Karen and Nicholas Sandford.

C.S.

2024

Peace is the only war worth waging.

Albert Camus

Summer afternoon; summer afternoon – to me those have always been the two most beautiful words in the English language.

Henry James

Somebody once asked me if I ever went out to bat trying to hit a six and I said, 'Sure, every time.'

Keith Miller

1.
'Every Landing was a Close Shave'

HE WAS a rather unlikely-looking hero. In April 1945, Bill Edrich of Middlesex and England had just turned 29, but seemed about ten years older. Edrich was only 5ft 6in, with prematurely receding hair and an upturned nose that gave him a vaguely mischievous, feral air – 'like a randy mole', as one woman put it. He also had false teeth and spoke in a high, chirpy voice. Despite these shortcomings, Edrich exuded an infectious self-confidence, not least when it came to his relations with the opposite sex. His basic courtship method was direct: he hugged, and then started undoing buttons. Although spurned as often as not, the sheer volume of his efforts brought him some success. By 1945, Edrich was on the second of what would become a total of five marriages. An incurable romantic, one of his later wives was to complain that at parties 'Bill never stopped checking the room for a pretty face, even when we were dancing together.' Edrich's son Justin remarked that his father had often inspired affection, among men as well as women, but that he wasn't well suited to dealing with the practical aspects of life. 'I think it's sad he spent so much time battling with various demons and never reached the stage where he was truly contented,' he told a biographer. 'Dad got his pleasure from short-term highs rather than overall fulfilment or peace.'

As a cricketer, Edrich's shining moment had come in March 1939, at Durban, when England were left a seemingly impossible target of 696 to win the final, and timeless, Test of their tour of South Africa. The batsman had managed only one run in the first innings, but he followed this with a knock of 219, made in seven-and-a-quarter hours, in the second. During the mid-afternoon break, Flt. Lt. Albert Holmes, the superbly pukka English tour manager, had poured the not out double centurion a large glass of champagne with the words, 'I hear you train on the stuff.' Edrich downed a second and a third glass as well but was then out in the first over after tea – if it could fairly be called that – having seen England through to 447/3. The match was eventually abandoned on the tenth day when the visitors' score stood at 654/5; the rain came down, everyone had had enough, and the Englishmen left to catch their boat home. Just as he was settling in for the train journey to Cape Town, where the mail steamer *Athlone Castle* awaited them, Edrich glanced out of the window of his compartment and saw a newspaper vendor's stand on the platform with a headline announcing that German troops had entered Czechoslovakia and that Hitler himself was now installed in the Royal Palace at Prague. 'At that moment, I knew that the world was fucked,' he later recalled with some emphasis.

To while away the sea journey back to Southampton, Edrich decided to throw himself a 23rd birthday party, even though this was at least a week early. He would remember 40 years later:

> There was a raging storm outside, and the heating broke down in the ship's restaurant, but that didn't bother me at all. I drank toasts with the manager and toasts with the players, and somehow I managed to notice that the skipper [Walter Hammond] had for company a well-upholstered young American lady who was wearing a low-cut frock and a diamond tiara, and telling him how much she wanted him to bowl a maiden over. I think we'd earned our night out, because it wasn't as if any of us got rich from the tour. When everything was added up, I put about 200 quid [roughly £4,000 in today's money] in the bank for my five months' work, so no wonder everyone enjoyed a lark when they could.

It's fitting to linger for a moment on Edrich as the English tour party crossed the South Atlantic, if only because he generally played his cricket like a sailor with a 24-hour pass. His drinking exploits were legendary, and he was judged even by Lionel Tennyson, famously able to hold his own in that area, to have 'overdone the Bacchic rites' while playing in a side Tennyson led to India in the winter of 1937/38. In time Edrich's England career would be rudely interrupted when he returned to the team hotel in the early hours of an ongoing Test match at Old Trafford and had to be helped to bed by the night porter. Unfortunately, his arrival there had woken the occupant of the next room, who happened to be the chairman of selectors.

When you add the fact that Edrich played pre-war football on the wing for Spurs, impressed no less than Ben Hogan with his golf swing when they played a round together, could bowl as well as bat on the cricket field with a furious, slinging action that brought him a total of 479 first-class wickets, held 527 catches typically standing close in, and later captained Middlesex with uncompromising belligerence, if only fitful psychological acumen (in an act of near-suicidal chutzpah, once informing his opponents' Fred Trueman that he was a nance, the signal for a terrifyingly fast delivery that bounced only once on its way to the sightscreen), it's possible to see how he was widely regarded as one of the renaissance men of English sport, and a bit of a lad to boot.

Perhaps under all the surface bravado Edrich concealed the soul of an ugly duckling, a boisterous and insecure perpetual adolescent eager to be liked. One or two of his discarded wives certainly thought so. But whatever the key to Edrich's character in civilian life, he proved an outstandingly brave man when the time came to fight. In early August 1941, a combined Middlesex and Essex side hosted one from Surrey and Kent at Lord's, in a match played in aid of the King George's Fund for Sailors. Thanks to the rain, there was only time for a single innings each. Batting at number five, Edrich scored 102 between lunch and tea on the first afternoon, at one point lofting a ball from the admittedly 54-year-old Test all-rounder Frank Woolley out of the ground and through a vent of the brick cooling-tower that then stood on St John's Wood Road, a carry of some 120 yards. Aiming to repeat the blow off the next ball he was stumped, retiring to the pavilion, said *The Times*, with a 'smile of unfeigned merriment on his face'.

Just six days later, Edrich, now in his wartime role as an RAF Bomber Command pilot, was at the controls of a twin-engine Bristol Blenheim on an 800-mile round trip, sometimes flying only 50 feet above the ground to avoid enemy radar, to attack the heavily defended German power station at Knapsack, near Cologne, a raid from which 12 of the total of 54 British planes failed to return. A crew of four sat within touching distance of each other in the domed glasshouse of a cockpit canopy at the front of the Blenheim, sometimes shouting to make themselves heard above the roar of the plane's engines, with one colleague, unable to wear a parachute because of his cramped conditions, crouched over a retractable Lewis gun in the rear turret. RAF bomber crews as a whole had a lower life expectancy than even an infantryman in the trenches of World War One. Historians have since competed to write more dramatic descriptions than each other of the obvious perils of such missions, but Edrich himself was more succinct.

'It was the bollocks,' he said simply.

'Flattened over the water, tucked in as close as I dared to the leader, I felt an exhilaration that swamped all other emotions. Low flying did not bother me a bit. I loved it.'[1]

---

1 The British government took a more hard-headed view of the events around Cologne. In a report to the Cabinet of 19 August 1941, 'the Chief of the Air Staff explained that the losses sustained by the bomber force in the recent and sustained attacks on Germany (107 machines lost since the beginning of the month) had been partly due to treacherous weather … our pilots had nonetheless shown extreme gallantry.' For his part, Hermann Göring, Reich minister for aviation (although he collected offices of state almost at will) was not pleased to be informed of the RAF's success both at Knapsack and the nearby power plant at Quadrath. He read the report of the twin raids while on board his private train, which, among other amenities, boasted two dining cars, a swimming pool, and a special compartment for the minister's pet lion. He, Göring, was visibly distressed by the news. In fact, his staff thought he might be suffering a heart attack as he embarked on a violent denunciation of his subordinate officers. The air force commander Ritter von Greim was one of those present and feared his chief 'might physically blow apart as his face and body swelled with rage, his cheeks a ghastly blue'. In the end Göring sank into a sort of torpor, and for some time after that the entire train was silent but for the muffled sounds of the hungry lion pacing back and forth in the next compartment. Bill Edrich was awarded the DFC for his role in the successful mission over Cologne.

Unsurprisingly, Edrich's front-line experience changed him, or at least served to reinforce his already strong belief that life was there to be lived. Among other things, the war left him with a strong impatience for delay and routine, a healthy disregard for most forms of officialdom, and a recurrent nightmare in which he would be back on the airfield waiting to take off in his Blenheim, only to look across to see another pilot as he stepped into his own plane, the man's face momentarily becoming a skull until it suddenly changed back again. 'He was always one of my pals who didn't make it home,' Edrich recalled. Perhaps it was no surprise that he seemed to be in a race with life or made no secret of his opinion of people. Even then blunt with an earthy vocabulary, Edrich had been both a popular and a slightly feared young man while growing up on his father's farm at Lingwood in Norfolk, where he prowled the nearby fields with a double-barrelled shotgun looking for rats, 'but also for trouble, too', a friend said.

In later life, Edrich developed a pronounced distaste for stuffy social protocol. One afternoon in 1945 he found himself wandering around Baker Street in central London with a pretty girl he had met only minutes earlier, 'longing to make love but unable to afford a decent room'. Like many people's, Edrich's basic courtship technique, impressively brisk at the best of times, had been charged with new urgency once the prospect of death had stalked the scene. In the end, he improvised with his new friend. 'There were fireworks up against a tree in Regent's Park.'

Plainly spoken and exuding strong Australian values, Keith Ross Miller was in some ways Edrich's natural counterpart. Born in the western Melbourne suburb of Sunshine, Miller was a versatile sportsman with matinee-idol looks and an innate aversion to authority. Like Edrich, he was mercurial and easily bored, with his performance on the field often depending on how hard he had partied the night before. He eventually scored over 14,000 first-class runs at an average of nearly 50 and took 497 wickets at 22 each, 170 of them in Tests, during an 11-year career, although it's absurd to judge such a player by mere statistics: you might as well review a book by counting the number of words in it. As a bowler, Miller could hurl it down at a distinctly lively pace off only a cursory run, gaining movement both ways. As a batsman he was essentially correct if tending to eschew the defensive in favour of the big hit. It was sometimes said that he struggled in England, where his commitment to the front foot could make him vulnerable to spin, although this failing does not seem to have been in evidence on his first-class debut in the country, at Lord's in May 1945, when he scored 105 in just over three hours at the crease in the first innings, and then characteristically ran himself out for a single in the second so that he could spend the late afternoon at the racecourse.

Miller was eventually appointed captain of New South Wales and, like Edrich, proved a modestly successful if unorthodox skipper with little time for the tactical nuances of the game. Once, on discovering that he had led an extra man on to the park at Sydney, his reported response was, 'One of you buggers clear off, and the rest scatter.' In later years it was thought that Don Bradman's more measured approach both as a player and subsequently a Test selector had thwarted Miller's seemingly inevitable appointment to lead Australia. It was possibly tactless of the latter to have once turned up for a meeting with the national board of control dressed in a white polo-neck jumper, ragged khaki shorts and a pair of wooden clogs. As Miller himself later put it, 'I was never Don's pin-up, and he rated only slightly below God when it came to Australian cricket.'

In August 1940, Miller, aged 20, enlisted in the army reserve before switching to the Royal Australian Air Force (RAAF) as Intake Number 410608. He served for a further five years before being honourably discharged with the rank of flying officer. In January 1943, Miller embarked on the USS *West Point* at Melbourne, which was to take him to Europe in readiness for combat duty. The journey included a stopover in Boston, Massachusetts, where he met a 25-year-old brunette from a wealthy stockbroking family named Peg Wagner, whom he took dancing. Relationships tended to progress quickly under the stress of war. The couple were engaged before Miller left three weeks later for the United Kingdom, a departure he described in almost lyrical terms:

> All the boats in line blew out this long mournful wail of their horns. They were the parting salutes of the doomed – of men who were going off to a foreign land to fight for their people's future, many of them never to return.

More prosaically, Miller, whose engagement to Peg perhaps strayed from the traditional monogamous ideal, wrote privately of one of the gratifying number of female Australian nurses on board the same vessel. 'Enormous honkers – like being smothered between two great pillows.'

Sent for flight training to the seaside town of Bournemouth, Miller had the first of several brushes with death that April when he was invited to play weekend cricket for an RAAF team in Dulwich, south London. While he was away a German bomb struck a local Bournemouth church spire, which then toppled over on to the pub where he typically propped up the bar each Saturday night, killing everyone inside. Later that year there was a characteristic difference of opinion concerning the correct form of address between Miller and his commanding officer, and the former spent three weeks in the brig as a result. In September 1944, a night on the town led to property damage and a black eye for a fellow airman. The following month, Miller, whose love of classical music matched that he displayed for fast women and slow horses, went AWOL to see Yehudi Menuhin perform in London. There was talk of a court-martial, although in the end his CO relented on the condition that he (Miller, not Menuhin) play for his unit's cricket team. Despite his various run-ins with authority, Miller was promoted to the rank of flying officer in November 1944. His new status did little to dampen his pervasive sense of contempt for the governing rules of military life. Described as the 'golden boy' of cricket, prompting the nickname of Nugget which stayed with him for the rest of his life, Miller was not one for the textbook approach to his duties. One of his biographers quotes a flying colleague as calling him brave but haphazard in his technique while at an aircraft's controls: 'Every landing was a close shave.'

In March 1945, Miller was deployed to the RAF base at Great Massingham in Norfolk, about a half an hour's drive from Bill Edrich's family farm. While there he continued to treat both the Axis forces and his own senior command structure with equal disdain. On 19 April, Miller's Mosquito squadron took part in a raid on a German V-2 rocket installation at Flensburg in Denmark, flying at treetop level for much of the three-hour outward journey. There were few casualties, mainly because the Luftwaffe was a spent force by that stage of the war and offered only token opposition, but it still took guts to fly a small, wooden-framed plane with 2,000 pounds of high explosive strapped underneath it over water in the dark. Some men in his position just accepted the risks as a necessary part of their job. Some rose to the occasion. Some lost their minds.

No one ever doubted Miller's essential courage, nor his lifelong propensity for insubordination. He was 'not infrequently impudent, with a strong – more accurately unorganised – will', one report noted. It was also said that Miller was given to unauthorised sightseeing tours while flying if he thought a particular part of the nearby scenery of sufficient interest, that he 'occasionally reports unshaven for duty', and 'reacts poorly to snafus in flight'. Despite his casual appearance, one RAAF colleague said of him that 'all kinds of admirers, and especially women, clung to him like bees to honey'.

As everyone knows, cricket is a reflection of life, and by and large cricketers answered the call of war in much the same spirit as everyone else. The records show that they volunteered at the same rate as other young men, and they died, too, in equal proportion. In all, some ten teams' worth of first-class cricketers were lost in the years 1939–45. Some, like Edrich and Miller, put their lives on the line, while others worked long hours in munitions factories or served in an administrative capacity. The two greatest Test players of the 1930s were among those thought to have had what was perhaps unjustly called a 'cushy' war. Born in 1903, England's incumbent captain Walter Hammond had joined the RAF at the outset, wanting to do his bit, but over the next five years found himself playing a good deal of sport, occasionally training new recruits, and coming to resolve a complicated home life that led to the terse Press Association report: 'A decree was granted to Mrs Dorothy Hammond, wife of the England star. Misconduct was alleged with a woman named Harvey.'

Like Hammond's, the war record of the peerless Don Bradman failed to win universal admiration in later years, when he was sometimes met by the taunt of being 'Last in, first out' of uniform. Even the greatest cricketer of his time – possibly of all time – had his critics. Initially joining the RAAF before transferring to the army, Bradman was invalided out again in June 1941. Then aged 32, the master batsman was suffering from a case of fibrositis, a nervous muscular complaint, while, to general amazement, a routine army medical revealed that he had 'distinctly sub-par' eyesight. The greatest athlete in Australian history was officially deemed physically unfit to serve his country. Later in the war, Bradman was further embarrassed when the Adelaide stockbroking firm he represented crashed due to fraud and embezzlement. Although there was no suggestion of any wrongdoing on his part, the scandal left what he called a 'rank smell of impropriety' clinging to him for years to come. Like many top sportsmen, of all nationalities, the Australian batting genius possessed an uncongenial personality. Monastically dedicated to the scoring of runs, he sometimes seemed oblivious of the disdain - if always tinged with professional respect – he inspired among his peers.

In a match later in the 1940s, it was said that Bradman threw Miller the ball, only for Miller to throw it back, refusing to bowl. 'I don't know what's wrong with you,' Bradman supposedly said. 'I'm almost 40, and I can do my full day's work in the field.' To which Miller replied: 'So could I, if I'd sat on my arse during the war.'

The protracted bloodbath of 1939–45 claimed its victims in the cricket world with the same callous indifference it showed elsewhere. Some of those brave individuals fell in front-line combat, others in a variety of war-related accidents. Chronologically the first Test-playing casualty, 37-year-old Geoffrey Legge of Kent and England, perished in November 1940 when the light training aircraft he was flying in his role as an officer in the Fleet Air Arm crashed in stormy weather into a field near Brampford Speke in Devon, killing him and his passenger. Eleven months later, a similar fate befell the 30-year-old Ken Farnes of Essex and England. Farnes was that unusual cricketer of his time who combined the attributes of a terrifyingly fast bowler with an interest in oriental philosophy, and more particularly the work of the Bengali poet Rabindranath Tagore.

As a result, Farnes lived by a different value system than that adopted by the typical English player of the 1930s, or for that matter of any other era of the game. Rather than go into a syncopated frenzy on taking a wicket, for instance, he often had some consoling words for the departing batsman. Len Hutton remembered that he had once had his middle stump uprooted by Farnes, and then been informed by the bowler on his way back to the pavilion that the names and distinctions that human beings apply to their earthly triumphs and disasters were merely an illusion. ('I thought he'd been drinking,' Hutton once told me.) Farnes died when, after joining the RAF, he went up in a Wellington bomber on his first unsupervised night flight from a blacked-out airfield near Banbury in Oxfordshire. Possibly disorientated by the absence of lights to act as a reference point on the ground, he crash-landed shortly after take-off. Farnes, who played 15 Tests for England, and who serves as a genetic fast bowling link between Harold Larwood and Fred Trueman, was buried at Brookwood military cemetery in Surrey. His headstone reads: 'He died as he lived, Playing the Game.'

George Macaulay of Yorkshire and England, who could boast the rare feat of taking a wicket with his first ball in Test cricket, was another impressively quick bowler (though he could cut his pace to off-spin if the conditions required) destined not to return from the war. Macaulay had immediately volunteered on the outbreak of hostilities, by which time he was nearing his 42nd birthday, and been sent as an orderly to a remote RAF base in the Shetland Islands. On 9 December 1940, he was admitted to the camp infirmary, where it was recorded that 'there was an alcoholic history for several years, that he had been drinking heavily during the past ten days, that he retired to his room in a comatose state and was moved to sick quarters at the request of the OC Station'. Macaulay died in his sleep on 13 December. *Wisden*'s obituary paid due credit to this versatile and relentlessly competitive player, who helped Yorkshire win no fewer than eight County Championships between 1922 and 1935, listing him as having fallen 'on active service'. Macaulay's death certificate put it more starkly: 'Cardiac failure three months. Chronic alcoholism, ten years.'

Perhaps the best-known of English cricket's wartime losses was that of Hedley Verity, the Yorkshire slow left-armer who had taken match figures of 15-104 bowling for England against Australia on a sticky wicket at Lord's in June 1934. As *Wisden* wrote, 'This amazing achievement could have been only possible for a man possessed of such length and finger-spin as Verity … the majority of the batsmen had no experience of such a pitch, and their efforts of dealing with it were, to say the least, immature.' It was the only occasion in the 20th century when England beat Australia at Lord's.

In the early hours of 20 July 1943, Captain Verity was at the head of the men of B Company of the Green Howards infantry regiment as they began their assault on the heavily defended plains of Catania, a normally placid resort overlooking the Ionian Sea. They were there as part of the multinational force spearheading the Allied invasion of Sicily, codenamed Operation Husky. Before dawn, Verity led his men up from their landing position, working his way with difficulty along an ill-lit, clammy dirt track until, panting from exertion, he reached level ground. A sign there emblazoned with a skull and crossbones told him he had just passed through a minefield. There were chaotic scenes as the remaining soldiers struggled uphill in the moonlight under attack from both German artillery and small-arms fire.

'We were more or less surrounded by the enemy,' one of the enlisted men reported. 'They were in front and on either side of us.' As a result, it was 'thunderously loud', and 'star-shells regularly burst overhead', momentarily turning the scene from night to day. The strobe-like flashes of light allowed the German defenders to open up at point-blank range, some of the British soldiers mown down as they advanced in columns, falling side by side, their uniforms cut to shreds. There were accidental clashes in the darkened intervals in between, and one soldier had crept forward to what he assumed was a group of his comrades crouched in a foxhole immediately in front of him only to retreat smartly on hearing German voices. Attempting to secure their position, Verity himself stood up again, signalling to his troops with his right arm, only to be hit in the chest by a burst of shrapnel. There was no practical way to help him as the rest of B Company withdrew. The last order he gave his men was 'Keep going.'

Although Verity was well enough treated by his German captors, his medical care was primitive. On 21 July there was an initial operation carried out in a tented Sicilian field hospital which stank of 'gore and sweat and human excretions'. The prisoner was then taken by slow boat across the Strait of Messina, and by train to a German military infirmary near Naples. There were some 400 casualties piled up in two rooms there, including men who had lost their arms or legs, and others whose stomachs were ripped open and who lay begging for death. Another hot train journey followed the next morning, when Verity was sent on to an Italian hospital at Caserta. A surgeon there operated on the victim's chest, removing part of his rib. Only a local anesthetic was used. On the Friday night of 30 July, Verity weakly signed a form presented to him by the Italian authorities in order to conform to Red Cross regulations. 'I am all right. I have only been slightly hurt,' it read, over the printed message *Saluti affettuosi*, or 'Affectionate greetings.'

That night Verity suffered the first of three successive haemorrhages. Some of his fellow British patients desperately looted the hospital kitchen and brought back ice cubes to try and staunch the bleeding. Their efforts were in vain. Verity died later in the afternoon of 31 July. He was aged 38 and was buried in Caserta with full military honours.

A gifted top-order batsman for whom cricket was all an adventure, Major Maurice Turnbull, also 38, was at the head of the men of the First Battalion of the Welsh Guards on the night of 4–5 August 1944 as they advanced on the small French village of Montchamp in the continuing Allied breakout following D-Day. With daylight there was fierce house-to-house fighting, and some of the troops became pinned down at the end of a narrow lane shrouded in a drifting, waist-high mist. With a hail of intense fire directed at them, they could only burrow deeper into the rubble. 'Resistance never let up,' wrote one of the Welsh officers, 'and we were soon faced by a line of Panzers grinding towards us.' When the moment came for the British forces to break cover, a sniper's bullet instantly felled Major Turnbull. In civilian life he had been the wavy-haired, blue-eyed, somehow quintessentially British all-round sportsman who captained Glamorgan from 1930 to 1939 and had the unusual distinction of playing nine cricket Tests for England and two rugby internationals for Wales. A short time later, a fellow serviceman was able to crawl forward to recover Turnbull's body and drag it away from the front line. He found a photograph of the deceased man's wife and three young children in his wallet and made sure it was returned to the family.

Perhaps the most poignant case among the 72 English first-class cricketers who lost their lives – among them no fewer than five former captains of Oxford University – was that of 32-year-old Flt. Lt. Gerry Chalk of Kent. Chalk had led his county to an eminently respectable fifth position in the last pre-war Championship table, an improvement of four places on the previous year. In the final fixture of the 1939 season, Kent, after being 80 behind on first innings, were left 382 to win on the last day of the match against Lancashire at Dover. The home team knocked off the runs in just over four hours. Chalk (94) and Arthur Fagg (138) put on 181 for the first wicket, the former, according to *The Times*, batting with 'a felicity that displayed savagery to the bowler but made no demands on the spectator, whom he charmed and beguiled'. This was to prove Chalk's last ever first-class innings. The newspapers had widely tipped him for England honours in 1940.

On 17 February 1943, Flt. Lt. Chalk took off with his fellow Spitfire pilots of 124 Squadron to provide cover for an Allied bombing raid on German shipping at Dunkirk. A high wind blew up as they approached their target, causing some of the planes to become separated from the main force. A group of 30 Luftwaffe Focke-Wolf 190 fighters then appeared in the skies above Ardres, a few miles south of Calais, where a British Wellington had just mistakenly dropped its load of bombs. As shells began exploding all around, a local farmer named Guy Haultcoeur hurriedly glanced up as he ran for cover. He remembered being both 'thrilled and appalled [*consterné*]' to see 'the long red and white trails spinning and looping and rolling, in a colourful and macabre dance' that ended only when the numerically superior Germans broke off and circled back to Dunkirk. Gerry Chalk was one of four British pilots who were officially listed as missing, presumed dead.

Forty-six years after these events, one of Guy Haultcoeur's successors on the farm at Calais came upon the partial wreckage of a long-buried British plane. The authorities were called, and in time the fragments were identified as Chalk's Spitfire. Word of the find reached the ground at Canterbury, and an honour party including the surviving members of Kent's last pre-war side went to France to pay their final respects. After the simple rustic funeral, the wicketkeeper Godfrey Evans, whom Chalk had brought into the team in 1939, was characteristically the first to offer a toast to his fallen skipper. Despite the solemnity of the occasion, the mood was essentially light-hearted. 'After all,' said Evans, 'that's the way we played it.'

This list of cricket's sacrifices is far from exhaustive, and no slight is intended on the names of the many players who are missing. It's enough only to add that for the years 1940–46 *Wisden* contained fewer than half the usual number of pages, and that a large proportion of these consisted of obituaries. They ranged alphabetically from Gunner Sidney Adams, Royal Artillery, who was 'killed, aged 40, with Allied forces – he was a council clerk and leg-spinner who took wickets with his first two balls in cricket [including that of Samuel Beckett], playing for Northamptonshire against Dublin University in 1926', to 'Mr Denys Witherington, killed while serving as a private in the Loyal Regiment – he captained the Leys School, and showed such capital form as a batsman and wicketkeeper that he played in the Public Schools match at Lord's.' The fast-rolling phrases, so compelling in their simplicity and repetition, could only hint at the individual scenes of horror and sacrifice: 'Died of wounds received ... Killed in France ... Perished at sea ... Fell in fighting in North Africa ... Downed on air operations ... Previously reported missing, officially stated dead.'

No less grim, perhaps, was the fate of those cricketers condemned to spend what might otherwise have been the most productive years of their lives as enemy prisoners of war. On the same day in June 1942, the Test players Bill Bowes of Yorkshire and Freddie Brown of Surrey, the latter a future England captain, were among some 30,000 troops captured following the Allied surrender at Tobruk. Tall and bespectacled, with a shock of wavy blond hair, the fast-bowling Bowes looked more like a gangling Nordic university professor (and, it was unkindly said, sometimes batted like one) than a professional sportsman. He represented his country 14 times before the war and just once afterwards, having lost over four stone in weight in the meantime. Brown similarly reported that he felt 'graver and more decrepit' by the time he was liberated three years later by American troops advancing on Oflag 79, a camp located in a former German army barracks near Brunswick. 'My old cricket clothes hung off me like a sack,' he noted.

The 29-year-old Wilf Wooller, a Welsh cricketer and rugby all-rounder serving with the Royal Engineers, was one of those unfortunate enough to be taken by the Japanese. This was widely considered a fate as dire as anything the war had to offer. Wooller entered captivity as a strapping 6ft 2in, 14-stone athlete and eventually went home again 60 pounds lighter and suffering from crippling stomach pains. The Welshman was physically ill the first time he tried to play rugby on his return, and rarely did so again, although his first-class cricket career lasted until 1962. It was said that in later years he consistently declined to use Japanese-made calculators due to his treatment as a POW.

Wooller shared some of his detention with Acting Major E.W. 'Jim' Swanton of the *Daily Telegraph* and Bedfordshire Yeomanry, who later spoke of a daily routine characterised at least at first by boredom and hunger as much as by the psychotic cruelty we tend to associate with the Japanese camp system. 'The guards weren't always brutal or sadistic, but they were invariably stupid,' he told me. Swanton had to wait until August 1945 for his own release, and, like Wooller, maintained a robust attitude towards the Japanese race for the rest of his long life, during which he found religion, married, and gradually came to wield as much influence on the game as any cricket pundit before or since. Perhaps only a thundering W.G. Grace in his prime carried as much clout at Lord's as Swanton did in the second half of the 20th century. In general, he wasn't a man given to excessive self-doubt. Writing of his eventual liberation, Swanton said:

> The allied invasions [of Japan] were planned for early September, so our expectation of life was roughly a month when the atom bombs fell on Nagasaki and Hiroshima. Any [delay] must have cost many more thousand allied lives, including in all probability our own, so in the arguments on the moral side of dropping the bomb some of us find objectivity difficult.

When Swanton finally returned to England from the war, his father walked past him at the station, having failed to recognise his own son.

The Australian cricketers Keith Carmody and Graham Williams were similarly held in German POW camps and resumed their playing careers after the war. Carmody developed claustrophobia, and Williams reported feeling 'a heightened fear of crowds' and a dislike of whistling, as 'everyone had done this in the camp, and it [brought] back painful memories'. We will return to both these players later. For sheer drama, though, neither man's experience could top that of their 19-year-old future Sheffield Shield colleague Ernest Toovey, of Queensland, whose ship HMAS *Perth* was torpedoed during the Battle of Sunda Strait, off Java, in the early hours of 1 March 1942, with the loss of over half her 682-strong crew. Toovey later left a diary account of the event:

> As I hit the oily water I felt a sharp pain to my right knee. I had hit some very hard object in the sea. This was to plague me for years to come. As I had left the ship right aft I may have just touched a part of the stern or some heavy object wrenched loose.
>
> The sea seemed bottomless. Then suddenly I shot to the surface with lungs ready to burst.
>
> It was all over, except to stay alive and try to make the shore. Peering into the starlit sky – oddly, a really beautiful night – the land appeared to be not too far off, probably three or four miles.
>
> Floating around in no particular direction I spied a 44-gallon drum, with a large plank attached. It must have been some sort of raft, originally, but had been smashed. Soon there were about a dozen sailors clinging to it, and we were exchanging names and making enquiries about our mates. They were from various parts of the ship; some were hurt but none too badly. My leg ached considerably,

> but the oil in my eyes was the major worry, as it was with all of the men.
>
> Strange situations cause strange things. Silly as it seems to have had an argument about sport while floating around amidst the blood and wreckage of the *Perth*, that was what happened. My ship mate Keith was a disputatious bloke, and I guess he being from the south and me from Queensland, this had formed the basis of a difference of opinion. The subject of the dispute was the choice of our Test team's stumper. I firmly told him that Don Tallon was the best man for the job.
>
> At least this discussion kept us awake, as it was so easy to just close the eyes and slip beneath the unfriendly water. Many men did.

The three subsequent years in captivity were to be a harrowing enough ordeal for Toovey. He spent them in a series of Japanese camps where, among other things, he was forced to resist a surgeon's repeated proposal to amputate his injured right leg. ('I have to play cricket for Queensland,' he told the doctor.) Toovey admitted that he never really recovered from the experience, in body or mind, but in later years he was always most struck by how it had all begun: floating half-choked with oil amongst the shipwrecked flotsam of the Java Sea, while debating the merits of the ideal candidate to be his nation's Test wicketkeeper.

* * *

Another of those players to swap their whites for a soldier's uniform was Stewart 'Billy' Griffith of Surrey, Sussex and ultimately England. Griffith served as a decorated officer in the Glider Pilot Regiment at the 1944 Battle of Arnhem, where he fought alongside his county colleague at Hove, Hugh Bartlett. Bartlett was an attacking batsman whose stays at the crease tended to be brief but often memorable affairs, but whose Test career was thought to have suffered after he had fallen out with his captain Walter Hammond over a woman in whom both were interested. Bartlett saw action as a pilot successively at Normandy, Arnhem and in the Rhine crossings, and like Edrich was awarded the Distinguished Flying Cross (DFC). Legend has it that his hair turned grey in a single night after he flew his sortie into Arnhem. Certainly, he was never the same strokeplayer again after the war.

Twenty-three-year-old Len Hutton, already a cricket world record holder for his Test innings of 364 against Australia at the Oval, had promptly signed up to fight in 1939. Like a number of peacetime sportsmen, he was assigned to the army physical training corps. Fifty years later, Hutton remembered that he had wanted to be 'in the heat of it, [but] instead spent most of my time sitting around in barracks with a lot of rather gloomy buggers drinking tea and listening to the war news on the radio'. One day in March 1941 the now unhappy warrior was exercising in an army gym in York when a mat slipped under him and he fell heavily on his left side. X-rays revealed a severe fracture just above the wrist. Hutton's active war, such as it was, was over. He underwent three operations before the end of 1941, separated from the service the following summer, and eventually emerged with a left arm almost two inches shorter than the right one. Forced to use a schoolboy-sized cricket bat for the remainder of his career, Hutton played a further 66 Tests for England, twice leading the side to series wins against Australia in the process.

The fates of other English cricketers ranged from those who fought, or fell, in action, to others whose job was to keep the bureaucratic machinery ticking over rather than to kill Germans. Many of these same players later remarked that it had helped that 'everyone was in it together'. The entry of the Somerset and England batsman Harold Gimblett into first-class cricket at the age of barely 20 in May 1935 had been the stuff of legend. He was already on his way home from an unsuccessful trial at Taunton when the home county found themselves a man short for the match that started the following day, with Essex at the Agricultural Showgrounds in Frome.

Gimblett was hurriedly sent for, hitchhiking the last part of the way in a passing lorry. He went out to bat shortly after lunch on the first day, with Somerset on 107/6 and pondering the advice of his captain to 'watch Peter Smith – he's bound to slip you a googly first ball'.

Gimblett had never actually encountered a googly in his limited experience of school or club cricket, and had only heard the term spoken of in the haziest terms. Nonetheless, he successfully blocked two balls from Smith, himself a future veteran of the desert campaign, and England Test spinner, and hit the third one for a single. All three deliveries had indeed been googlies. A few minutes later, Gimblett smashed Smith for 15 runs in an over and from then on raced to his fifty in just 28 minutes, bringing it up with a six. He required only 35 more minutes to complete his century. Gimblett had by then faced 71 balls and he made his runs out of 130 scored while at the crease, where his partner for much of the time was Arthur Wellard, one of the biggest hitters in the game. The debutant eventually made 123 in 79 minutes, including three sixes and 17 fours, playing throughout with a borrowed bat. Somerset beat Essex by an innings.

The question everyone asked – including Gimblett – was whether it had all somehow been an aberration, or a kind of glorious fluke? The player seemed to settle the issue beyond doubt when he top-scored with 53 in his second Championship match, against Middlesex on a turning wicket at Lord's. Just over a year after appearing in the middle order for Watchet in the Somerset leagues Gimblett found himself opening the innings for England in the first Test against India at Lord's in June 1936, where he scored 11 and 67 not out. It proved to be the most numerically successful match of his brief international tenure, during which he steadily lost ground to Hutton in the pecking order as England's first-choice opening batsman. He finished with an aggregate of just 129 Test runs at an average of 32. Over time, Gimblett's Somerset career similarly became one of fits and starts, with long stretches of relative anonymity punctuated by a furious eruption – a reflection, some believed, of his inner personality – rather than any pretence of Hutton-like consistency. At his best, he batted as if he was the ringmaster of a show that would be brought to an end only at his, not the bowler's, discretion. When the moment came Gimblett volunteered for the RAF, but was posted instead to the fire service, where he saw duty in badly blitzed towns such as Plymouth and Bristol. His county colleague Frank Lee became an umpire after the war and occasionally stood in matches where a 'very changed' Gimblett appeared.

'Harold looked just like a scarecrow. He must have lost 20 pounds since I'd last seen him … he told me about being on duty in Bristol one night and described a row of houses with a little park in front of them, and every time a bomb fell there was a lovely, pink glow and it blew up a piece of someone.'

Gimblett continued to play first-class cricket until May 1954, when, after scoring 0 and 5 and complaining bitterly of being poorly treated by his county committee over his request that they send him on a therapeutic ocean cruise, he stormed out of the Taunton ground forever. In its way it was as dramatic a farewell to cricket as his arrival on the scene 19 years earlier. Professional English sports clubs at that time tended not to have the large and imaginative public relations staff they enjoy today, and the Somerset authorities limited themselves to a statement noting that 'We shall not be calling on Gimblett's services again.' Unlike them, we will return to the player later.

Denis Compton of Middlesex and England, who shared Edrich's and Miller's second-star-to-the-right-and-straight-on-til-morning credo even before the war, signed on as a special constable, among other things responsible for evicting over-indulging drinkers from London pubs ('a case of poacher turned gamekeeper', Compton himself genially allowed) before being commissioned as a sergeant in the Royal Artillery and sent to India. In general he enjoyed life on the subcontinent, 'where you played a bit of cricket and then went up into someone's palatial estate in the hills for the weekend'. Before shipping out, Compton was based in the less exotic surroundings of an army barracks outside Chichester in West Sussex, where one night he went out drinking with a young serviceman named Ernest Ridgers. Ridgers has left a diary account of what followed:

> When we were in the pub Sgt. Compton wouldn't let me pay for anything, and after a while one or two of our other chaps came in and he bought them all drinks, too. One boy was black, and there were some Americans in the place as well. Well, two of the Americans went up to this black boy and told him to clear out as they didn't want to drink with blacks, so Compton said to him, 'Stay put, son.' Then the two Americans came back across and walked the black boy outside and the sarge and our chaps followed, and they caught hold of the Yanks and whacked them.

While some critics later found fault with Compton's outspoken views on the racial divisions in South Africa, there's no reason to doubt Private Ridgers's account that he was genuinely offended by this treatment of a fellow British serviceman at the hands of some boorish Americans, nor that he waded in to 'whack' them in the soldier's defence.

Godfrey Evans, arguably England's greatest wicketkeeper, also joined up early in 1940, despite being just 19 years old at the time. He spent most of the next 12 months square-bashing at an army Service Corps barracks in Ossett, West Yorkshire. One wet night in September his platoon was on a 24-hour exercise under 'actual battlefield conditions', which meant sleeping as best they could in a waterlogged ditch, when a stricken German aircraft came screaming out of the sky to drop its high-explosive bombs on a nearby poultry farm, killing some chickens, before crashing a few miles away from their position. Evans and his unit were hurriedly deployed to the scene, where they found the enemy pilot still strapped into his cockpit, 'burned to a complete crisp … the flesh was bubbling on what remained of his face'. The young Kent stumper would remember how quiet the other men in the group had become at the sight, and the sergeant who then spoke up: 'Now you buggers will believe you're in a war.'

Nearly 50 years later, reminiscing on the cricket scene of 1945, Evans, on the surface the least introspective of all sportsmen, chiefly remembered two things. First, the collective spirit of army life had understandably been strong for several years to come, 'meaning that in most county dressing rooms players still addressed each other as Major, or Corporal, or Sergeant, etc, while the clubs themselves were run exactly as if you were back in uniform. It didn't really matter how good you were at batting or bowling. What counted was whether or not you had that air of authority that came from being an officer.' Laudable as this last attribute was, it was not necessarily the best qualification for the crucial work of restoring English county and Test cricket after its six-year hiatus.

The second thing to which Evans drew people's attention was that 'All of us went a bit potty, one way or another, after the war was over. Some people seemed to have a double charge of life to them, like Bill Edrich, and others shrank back like poor Harold Gimblett. I'll tell you this, though,' Evans added, often tapping his listener's chest for emphasis – 'most of us were almost mad with impatience to start again.'

* * *

Daily life during the war began early for the young Cambridge University and Hampshire batsman John Blake, who had joined the Royal Marines at the age of 21. In September 1940, Blake had taken part in a joint services operation codenamed Operation Menace. This was a scheme to land a force of 8,000 marines and infantry troops under cover of darkness at Dakar on the coast of French West Africa (today's Senegal), then somehow to rouse the native population to overthrow the pro-Nazi Vichy French administration in the colony, replacing it with a more congenial one led by General Charles de Gaulle, before liberating the locally stored gold reserves of the Banque de France to London. That done, the raiders would take their leave of the area as swiftly as they had come, while several specially equipped Lancaster bombers circled overhead and dropped smoke bombs to mask their departure. If it all sounds like a luridly melodramatic James Bond plot, that may in part be because Ian Fleming, Bond's creator, had interested himself in Operation Menace while serving as an operative with British naval intelligence, and later used some of its broad detail in *Goldfinger*.

It was a fantastic scenario, which to succeed would have required outstanding organisation and phenomenal good luck on the part of the raiders, and extraordinary incompetence on that of the enemy, none of which had been much in evidence in the general drift of the war to that point. Sure enough, the ensuing mission did not go smoothly for the British. The 8,000 men duly went ashore, but were unable to locate the French gold, let alone to harangue the indigenous population sufficiently for them to depose the municipal government. The British armed trawler HMT *Stella Sirius* was sunk as she lay off waiting to receive the returning troops in Dakar harbour, and several other vessels came under sustained attack from the shore batteries before withdrawing into the night. 'A total shambles,' Blake was left to rue of the affair, remembering how he and his men had run for the gangway of their departing ship under heavy small-arms fire, while the sound of explosions had boomed towards them. The reports came from across the bay, in the general direction of the *Maison des Esclaves* (House of Slaves), a former island prison since refurbished into an armoury and gun emplacement that lay just outside the mouth of the harbour, on a direct line of retreat for the Allied convoy. 'They were throwing everything they had at us as we hared for the ship,' Blake later wrote. 'One of the aft magazines was hit by a burst from the shore, and flames immediately shot up and lit the dark sky like a ghastly Bonfire Night. The crew were yelling at us to run faster as the gangway was being lifted back to the deck. It was a vision from a nightmare. In the bedlam I heard one Irish voice shout out, "Everything's going to blow up. We're *fooked.*"'

Nonetheless, Blake somehow emerged from the chaos of Dakar, and by early 1941 was back training at a barracks in Eastney, near Portsmouth, where he typically rose following reveille at five each morning for a full day of drilling, marching and 'mind-numbing' lectures on the theory and practice of a conflict he had already seen at close quarters for himself. For many recruits, the combination of tedium mingled with occasional terror of warfare destroyed their initial enthusiasm for the life, but not in Blake's case. He remained a super-patriot, never complaining aloud of the boredom and danger, and displaying an almost excessive sense of duty, so much so that some of his fellow marines good-naturedly ribbed him for sounding like a recruiting poster. 'I still thought the whole exercise worthwhile,' he wrote. For at least some volunteers, it had taken the war for their country to give them the opportunity to show what they were worth.

When the training regimen allowed, Blake was sometimes able to drive the 20 miles to the cricket ground at Southampton. It was here, one day in April 1941, that the young soldier-sportsman experienced what he called a 'startling bolt of truth, los[ing] at least some of my more innocent feelings about the war', when he called in to collect some post the Hampshire club was keeping for him. Although it was a sunny spring afternoon, with no blackout provisions in effect until later in the day, Blake noticed on entering that all the blinds were pulled down in the county secretary's office.

> It was a very gloomy atmosphere, like stepping into an undertakers, and Mr MacLeod, the secretary, was sitting there at his desk with a single candle burning. He had a black armband on. A few days earlier his friend John Butterworth, a good opening bat, had been killed flying for the RAF somewhere near London. I later found out

> that Butterworth's younger brother had also died in the Dunkirk affair. Now I knew Alister MacLeod. He was a tough old bird who had fought in the first war. But he was really broken up on account of that family. And in those early days of the war the way you dealt with something like that was by drawing the curtains and sitting there with a solitary candle and a black armband. And so every time you went in to talk to him the whole idea of death was somehow brought home to you in a quiet cricket pavilion in Hampshire even more powerfully than when you were running for your life amidst the smoke of shellfire in Dakar.

Alister MacLeod was obliged to put on his black armband several more times before it was all over. On the night of 17 June 1941 his county's prolific left-handed batsman and occasional wicketkeeper Don Walker was shot down over Best in the Netherlands while on his way with the RAF to bomb a target in Germany. He was just 28 at the time of his death, and widely tipped for future England honours at both cricket and rugby union. Following that, MacLeod's family friend Gerald Seeley, who played a single first-class game for Worcestershire while still a teenager before becoming one of the many young cricketers to join the RAF, was shot down and killed in a raid over the Belgian coast. MacLeod wrote in his diary late that July: 'Here are the first terrible fruits of this war with the Germans, and the prospects seem every bit as dreadful as the great bloodbaths of the last one.'

In time, the Hampshire players Francis Arkwright and Norman Bowell both fell on duty, the latter while a Japanese POW, aged 37 and 39 respectively. *Wisden* had remarked of the county's only mixed playing record in 1939, 'Unpalatable as it may be, the truth is that the team lacked real fighting spirit.' It is not a judgement that would seem to apply to those same individuals over the six years that followed. As MacLeod later wrote of the steadily accumulating losses he was forced to record in his club's book of remembrance:

'Nowadays the ring of the young messenger on his bicycle is to be confronted by the angel of death.'

In the end even John Blake himself, the dashing young soldier-cricketer who had called in to collect his mail at the county ground that sunny spring afternoon in 1941, would fall while fighting with the Marines in Croatia. The citation for the Military Cross he won shortly beforehand read:

> For outstanding gallantry and leadership while serving with the 43rd R.M. commando in the attack which led to the capture of Mt. Ortino on 3rd February 1944. On reaching the top of the Mount through heavy machine gun fire, without hesitation and heedless of the danger from grenades, he led the forward section of his Troop in a bayonet charge on the enemy and captured 20 prisoners. Later in the day during a strong enemy counter attack, this gallant Officer moved from position to position, encouraging his men and directing their fire.

John Blake was aged just 26 at the time of his death.

* * *

Before moving on, it's worth remembering that few of these individuals, while all undeniably heroic, were entirely free of humanising contradictions. Keith Miller, as we've seen, was supremely brave in his own right, able to inspire others to feats of courage they never dreamed possible, and also engagingly blunt when it came to dealing with life's pompous authority figures. But like most of us, on occasion he could be domineering, selfish and plain rude, particularly to those he thought guilty of wasting his time or paying insufficient heed to his service both in and out of uniform. Although there's not the least suggestion that Miller ever boasted about, let alone embellished, his impressive war record – and we should always bear in mind his deathless remark when asked to compare them: 'Pressure is a Messerschmitt up your arse, playing cricket is not' – it's fair to say that a certain amount of hyperbole later attached itself to his time stationed at the RAF's 169 Squadron (motto: 'Hunt and Destroy') in Great Massingham. Miller's total of 600 hours at the controls of a combination of so-called 'nuisance raider' Mosquitos and Beauforts were spent in cramped, poorly heated aircraft that lacked all but the most basic defences, on the sort of missions that were often likely to end in disaster through bad weather, mechanical failure or both, quite apart from the prospect of enemy fire. The fact remains that relatively few of the sorties Miller flew while based in Norfolk in the spring of 1945 brought him into direct contact with the Luftwaffe. The official RAAF archive summarises his time as follows:

* 19 April 1945: Mosquito VI 626 – Bomber support – Patrol in target area, uneventful.
* 23 April 1945: Mosquito XIX 676 – Bomber support – Spoof patrol Travenuinde 15,000ft, uneventful.
* 2 May 1945: Mosquito VI 626 – Bomber support – Low level attack Schileswig-Jagel airfield, carrying two 100 gal Napalm drop tanks. One tank hung up and brought back to base – otherwise uneventful.

There were no further combat missions after that, although Miller did continue to fly occasional sorties over western Germany in order to inspect bomb damage in the area, and once to detour over Bonn so that he could look down on Beethoven's birthplace, breezily whistling the *Eroica* symphony as he steered the plane through a sudden thunderstorm. None of these excursions, even those primarily for sightseeing purposes, was for the faint-hearted. Taken as a whole, the prospects of survival for most night-flying wartime pilots were matched only by those of submarine crews. But perhaps it's fair to say that in Miller's case at least some of the dangers were mechanical, or self-imposed, rather than enemy-related, such as the affair, mentioned above, of the malfunctioning napalm tank which had jolted loose on his plane's landing at Great Massingham, then rolled 100 yards off the end of the runway and come to a stop in an adjacent field, where it miraculously failed to explode. None of this exactly qualified as a 'cushy' time in uniform. Even when strained through the sieve of nostalgia, Miller's war record remains that of an outstandingly brave young man who consistently put his own comfort second to serving in a cramped, smelly workplace operating in a larger environment that remained pitch-black unless or until it erupted in flames, at an age in life when his modern-day equivalent might be more concerned with his social media posts than in doing anything positively constructive, let alone dangerous, for humanity.

In short, Miller was one of nature's born scrappers, whom the actual war made into a hero; and it does nothing to diminish the fact to say that, like many of us, he could also be short-tempered, overbearing and on occasion insufferable; that he came to take an increasingly flexible view of his wedding vows; and that he perhaps masked his constant belief that something bad was always about to happen with a certain amount of bluster, aggression and exhibitionism. If it's true that he fought gallantly for the Allied cause, it's also true that his fellow airmen, alluding to their colleague's tendency to emerge unscathed from his various clashes both with authority and the enemy, referred widely, and sometimes satirically, to 'Miller's Luck'.

Similarly, it's not in any way to belittle the obvious horrors of life as a guest of the Japanese state from 1942–45 to quote E.W. Swanton's own account of an existence characterised by extreme tedium, but leavened by moments of absurd humour.

'About three one morning,' Swanton writes, 'some Jap guards were surprised to hear raucous noises coming from one of the nearby houses, and on entering found a British soldier in fine fettle. Next morning he was brought before the commandant [and] after a long lecture the sentence was pronounced. A board was hung round his neck with the legend: "I took whisky. This very bad thing." Then the POW band – an accordion and a trumpet – was called out, and ordered to play the prisoner round the yard.'

In broadly the same spirit, a torn scrap of scorecard records that on 6 February 1945 a 'hearty' cricket match was played between two sides of prisoners on the grounds of the Mulo camp at Palembang, 300 miles south of Singapore, with an Australian and an American standing as umpires, and an RAF mechanic named James Pennock, from Streatham in south London, keeping score. Or that a Royal Artillery officer named William Bompas, captured by the Germans early in 1943 and locked up in Oflag 79, wrote of his experience there:

> Cricket was played on four or five afternoons each week in the summer on the asphalt down the centre of the yard, with 6 and more or less out when the ball was hit onto one of the flat roofs. Bill Bowes (Yorkshire), Freddie Brown (Surrey) and John Bowley (MCC) and a lot of club cricketers regularly took part, and the standard was really very good.

Cricket in these surroundings was not only an important way to keep fit, but also a means of preserving one's identity, for men to remember the lives they had led and might hopefully lead again. It was a widespread practice throughout the German and Japanese camp systems, and right to the end of the war the Red Cross regularly included supplies of bats and balls alongside such commodities as tea, cocoa, butter, fresh socks and, above all, cigarettes in their care packages to inmates. In 1940, a 26-year-old Anglo-Irish writer-turned-soldier named Terrence Prittie was captured by the Germans in the retreat from France, and while in captivity smuggled out essays on cricket, later composing an entire waste-paper manuscript called *Mainly Middlesex*, about his favourite first-class county, which was published to acclaim after the war.

Keith Miller was in some ways the incarnation of classic Australian values as they were tested by war, and exemplified by men known for their raw courage, selflessness, loyalty, bluntness of speech and a lack of deference – almost a point of Antipodean honour – that could grate with the traditional British officer class. It must have been an almost surreal experience for such men, and their like-minded allies, to go overnight, as some of them did in 1945, from flying combat missions over enemy territory to playing a leisurely afternoon's cricket for their local team. Bill Edrich would never forget the incongruity of being stationed back in Great Massingham, where he and his colleagues sometimes unwound in between bombing raids with a spirited limited-overs match staged on the baize-like lawns of the nearby manor hall. 'Every now and then would come the old accustomed cry: "Owzatt?"' Edrich recalled. 'And then one's mind would flicker off to the briefing room, to joking with a pal … and one saw again his machine cartwheeling down, flaming from nose to tail.'

Keith Miller was later accorded the status of an Olympian god among mortals, whom no less a judge than Neville Cardus once called, a little breathlessly, 'as masculine as Tarzan, a young eagle among crows and daws … the supreme champion every boy would want to be'. In 1945, men like Miller and Edrich seemed to be constantly pushing at a revolving door between relative tranquillity and mortal peril. In later years, Cardus continued to believe that such individuals had possessed 'heroic, almost semi-divine' qualities. But he admitted that the thought had also crossed his mind that 'they were fully human, too, with all that implies, and that was what made them so interesting'.

2.
Our Britain

'THE PRESENT stage of the war is dour and hard, and the fighting must be expected on all fronts to increase in scale and in intensity. We believe that we are in the last lap, but this is a race in which failure to exert the fullest effort to the end may protract that end to periods almost unendurable to those who now have the race in their hand after struggling so far. Our resolve is more than ever unshaken ... our hearts kindle the flame of heroism, the flame of creative initiative in all fields, in all the realms of our rich, our many-sided life, in this, our God-endowed land, to which at length our burnished warriors will repair in glory ...'

When Winston Churchill made these remarks in October 1944, he echoed those of his predecessor in office 26 years earlier in assuring the British troops that they would be returning to 'a land fit for heroes'. In both cases, it proved a hard promise to keep. Even, or especially, after victory in Europe was declared in May 1945, the average British citizen found everything was either in short supply or else small: the recommended size of the much-heralded new family homes promised to appear in a 'great dynamic rush' that summer was just 900 square feet for a three-bedroom house. George Orwell wrote affectingly of 'a derelict, half-ruined community where the trains are black with grime ... shoeless children with hair close-cropped to avoid nits or lice playing among bomb-scarred lanes'; and that was in the relatively refined areas of central London.

Quite apart from the ravages of enemy damage, much of urban Britain remained a sad, soiled place, gloomy and neglected, its streets piled with sandbags and frequently obstructed by broken glass, crockery, furniture and other debris, while the ubiquitous blue tarpaulin stretched over broken or missing roofs kept up a kind of demented beat as it successively broke itself loose and flapped wildly in the wind. That July, the government announced a 25 per cent cut in the already modest clothing-coupon allowance, while with peace they were soon compelled to impose bread rationing at home, an expedient that had been avoided during the war. The meat quota of 1sh/2d. worth a week was to be maintained, but now one-seventh of it was to be taken in the form of tinned bully beef, while the household allowances for bacon, ham, sugar and cheese were all further slashed. One egg per person per fortnight remained the general rule. While rationing continued, so did the Ministry of Food with its raft of regulations enforceable in the courts. For years after the war, 'snoopers' were officially encouraged to report anyone suspected of the Babylonian luxury of enjoying a good meal. When Churchill's burnished warriors returned home at intervals in that summer of 1945, they did so to notices like this pushed through the letter boxes of their front doors:

> The new ration book will be issued from 28 May onwards for food purchases from 22 July. When you collect it, you must have your present Food Book and Identity Card (giving your present address in full) with you. You must clearly write this address in block capitals on the front cover of the Food Book, as well as your name, address and National Registration Number on the front of the Clothing Book. You will be told when you can use the Clothing Book. Until then none of your existing coupons is valid.

Even being bombed out was a bureaucratic business. The government booklet *After the Raid* advised householders who had been 'incommoded' by the Luftwaffe of the proper procedure for lodging a claim, which they should do in triplicate by means of Form C1 (1945), generally available from their local town hall – unless it, too, happened to have been razed – although this applied only to the 'exterior masonry of the domestic edifice so affected'. For claims involving furniture and other interior fixtures and fittings, the applicant's attention was drawn either to Form PCS (3) or PCS (4), which should similarly be filed at the applicant's town hall or council offices, which would in turn forward the particulars for the attention of the competent body constituted under the terms of the 1940 War Damage Commission. By June 1945, more than a million such claims had been lodged in Greater London alone, and such was the volume of the paperwork that an entire four-storey office building in Leeds was specially requisitioned to house it all.

Nor was the new post-war order as a whole always quite as munificent to those same gallant warriors so movingly eulogised by Churchill. A west country club cricketer named Joseph Hazel, serving as a lieutenant colonel with the Royal Artillery, entered captivity at the notorious Tandjong Priok camp in Batavia, Java, following the fall of Singapore in February 1942. This was among the most brutal outposts of even the Japanese wartime penal system. Among other horrors of his time in custody, Hazel had seen a fellow British POW bayoneted by a guard so that the man's intestines had fallen out as he lay in the dirt vainly trying to push them back in, as well as other scenes of a 'medieval barbarism' he later preferred not to dwell on. In July 1945, Hazel came home again to the wife and two children he had left behind in Taunton, only to then endure an 'almost equally bloody awful year' spent in increasingly acrimonious discussion with organisations such as the Inland Revenue and the War Office over relatively small sums of money. The latter body wrote to him on 20 July 1946:

'As you are now released from Army service you are not eligible for the refund of any furniture-removal or transportation expenses under any circumstances.' Another returning POW from Batavia was told: 'In connection with the claim presently under consideration, arrangements are being made for you to be medically examined by the Post Office doctor nearest your home.

After examination you should pay the doctor the fee of 21 shillings. There is no provision made for the expense of any travel or fuel allocation involved.'

The successor governments to Churchill's still deem it best to shield their citizens from direct access to any detailed national census data until 100 years after the event. But we can nonetheless hazard certain facts about daily existence in Britain in 1945. For one thing, there was an unprecedented emphasis on the paternalistic role of the state in its subjects' lives from which we're arguably yet to recover. The ministerial page-turner *Food Fact Essentials: A Realistic Book of Recipes for Comestibles and for Life*, issued to every British household, perhaps lacked the folksy charm we might expect from our political rulers today. 'In our straitened circumstances, when we must all continue to concern ourselves with basics, and to discard things that do not truly matter,' it began, in the tones of a somewhat irascible schoolteacher, 'it is necessary at all times to remember these two points: 1. What we *can* get is good for us; 2. A great deal of what we *cannot* get is quite unimportant.'

Even the latter-day Soviet Politburo at its most vigilant might not have been ashamed by the sheer amount of government supervision of the smallest details of its citizens' lives. According to the terms of the Board of Trade's provisions on the subject as published in April 1945, all British men's jackets were to be single-breasted, with 'a maximum permitted quota of three pockets, and three or less fastening buttons at any point ... waistcoats may display a total of two pockets, neither to descend beyond 3½ inches from top to bottom. The circumference of the trouser legs shall not exceed a total of 19 inches [unless] properly documented medical requirements dictate otherwise.' The strictures applying to women's fashions can readily be imagined. A popular cartoon in *Punch* of mid-1945 showed a shabbily dressed father interviewing a prospective son-in-law. 'Young man,' read the speech bubble above his head, 'are you in a position to supply my daughter with 20 clothing coupons every six months, as *I* have had to do?'

Perhaps it's no wonder that a man like Keith Miller, who somehow always seemed to resemble Errol Flynn sauntering off to the nearest nightclub, attracted quite as many admiring, and also possibly envious, glances as he did.

Central London itself, where much of our story is set, was a 'pretty bleak spot to operate in', Miller later confirmed. Even in summer it seemed to be permanently cold and foggy, its many blitzed houses caked in soot, with great sprays of weed flowering through cracked pavements, and pervaded by a smell of damp coal smoke and human decay. This was a stark contrast to Miller's earlier life. As we've seen, he grew up in the evocatively named Melbourne suburb of Sunshine, the youngest of four children of a sports-loving civil engineer, where his family had a large, red-bricked terraced house with a back garden big enough to accommodate games of 'toey', or French cricket. Even as a child, Miller spent a good deal of time at the nearby Caulfield racecourse, often missing school as a result, and on summer afternoons preferring to scour nearby Altona Beach for empty beer bottles, redeemable at a penny apiece. 'I loved my home life,' he later declared unambiguously.

While Miller's childhood had been idyllic, the same couldn't be said of his basic working environment in 1945. For most of that spring and summer, he was either 'strapped to a tiny seat, with a couple of unsmiling crew-mates and a freezing Elsan toilet for company', flying hair-raisingly low over the North Sea, or else walking around towns where everything was 'buggered about', the transport system typically in disarray due to fuel shortages, and street lights extinguished during the war only now gradually returning to provide soupy, 'dim-out' conditions on most night-time roads. Prostitutes – one commodity of which there was a surplus – continued to shine a torch on themselves as a means of soliciting. Once-elegant city squares and gardens lay converted to cabbage patches. Blast damage had destroyed windows and torn the leaves off trees. In London, the chamber of the House of Commons itself, a symbol of the way of life Britain had been fighting for, had been levelled by an incendiary bomb in May 1941 and now stood as a derelict, weed-filled grotto. Taken as a whole, urban Britain was then 'one of the most distressed places on earth, and I also saw Germany up close in 1945', Miller noted. This experience of the sheer squalor of life in his adopted home deeply affected him, increasing his conviction that it was a 'lousy' world which it was his lot to enliven as best he could. 'I sometimes caught myself thinking, "And we *won* the war ..."' Miller remembered. 'As I saw it, the job of those of us who played a game like cricket was to bring a bit of joy back into people's lives.'

Miller was never a martyr to introspection. In later years he preferred not to dwell on his exploits in helping to lift the morale of a war-weary public, even as he acknowledged that aspects of British life of 1945 had struck him as 'a bit rough around the edges'. Like most people of the time, whether or not in uniform, he was instinctively patriotic. Many of those individuals had rallied to a cause summarised in the wartime slogan: 'Our Britain – Fight For It Now'.

But which Britain, exactly, were they to fight for? The one that still operated much like a private gentlemen's club, where BBC radio announcers read out even the most harrowing war news of the day in the fruity tones of an elderly stage actor, often while clad in a smoking jacket for the occasion; or something more like the land envisioned by the ideologues of the 1930s, appalled by fascism and entranced by the possibilities of economic redistribution and a fairer, more egalitarian state? The positive encouragement of freewheeling social mobility does not seem to have been among the UK government's top priorities, at least until the political earthquake of July 1945. It's of course a caricature to say that the country was filled by a cadre of effete snobs on one hand, and of unpretentious, horny-handed yeomen, who actually did much of the work, on the other. But like most clichés it contains a grain of truth. Even today it's still mildly odd to read press reports about Wally Hammond's batting or Keith Miller's bowling set amongst all the advertisements for butlers, maids or chauffeurs ('Rolls Certificate and discreet service essential'), or the lingering accounts in *Wisden* devoted to public school cricket, which tended to be both more protracted and fulsome than they are today.

As a symbol both of the British class structure and the strength in depth of the nation's cricket, it would be hard to top the annual Gentlemen v Players match. Its last pre-war flowering, at Lord's from 5–7 July 1939, brought together for the 134th time what E.W. Swanton called 'everything fine in the land', epitomised by the contrasting parade of wage-earning professionals on one side, and what Fred Trueman later characterised as 'twats in cravats', nominally claiming only expenses, on the other.

Despite the drenching rain – another staple of the fixture – a mile-long procession of cars and carriages had snaked its way up St John's Wood Road before the start, and the old ground itself was decked out with a ring of fruit and sweet stalls, picnic areas, tea tents and champagne bars attended by liveried waiters and young women in starched white aprons. Some of the Gentlemen wore striped ties around their waists as they took the field, with one or two salmon-pink scarves peeking out under all the Panama hats and other multicoloured headgear. It was a scene not so much indifferent as oblivious to the march of time. The whole spectacle lacked only its Renoir.

It's true that in due course certain English first-class counties came to take such initiatives as allowing their professionals and amateurs to eat lunch at the same table, or even on occasion to share a dressing room, but in general the *ancien régime* proved as tenacious in the immediate post-war era of socialised medicine and the atom bomb as it had in that of the exquisitely well-bred young rakes whose essentially Victorian air of country-house hauteur tended to exceed any technical playing merit, or even aptitude, on their part.

In 1945, there were still county captains who if necessary preferred to communicate with their batsmen in the middle by way of a telegram transcribed at the local post office, and then brought back to the ground to be ceremonially presented to the player or players involved on a silver tray extended to them in between overs. The master–servant composition at the heart of most organised English cricket teams was strong enough for the secretary of MCC to have left his office following stumps one day in July 1945 in order to rebuke one of the representative Australian players appearing there for the impossibly tasteless offence of having left the visitors' dressing room to stroll down the pavilion stairs without having first troubled to put on a blazer. Such players might be idolised by tens of thousands of impressionable schoolchildren and widely admired, too, by their fathers; they were all eminently respectable, grown men, and in many cases combat veterans to boot; but in the brutal language of social class of the time, they were in 'trade'.

'It was all pretty feudal,' Keith Miller (not on this occasion the party guilty of the sartorial lapse) confirmed of the prevalent mood of top-flight cricket in 1945. Nor could it be characterised as over-burdened by political correctness, or even basic sensitivity, as defined by modern standards. 'CRICKET UNDER THE JAPS by E.W. Swanton' the first post-war edition of *Wisden* advertised in bold print on its front cover, quite possibly an arrestable offence today.

In many of its essential features, then, daily life in that immediate post-war summer would have been instantly familiar to most men and women of 50 years earlier. The same sense of suspended time hung over much of first-class cricket as it did other recreations. In 1945, four million British adults went to licensed dance halls each week, and there were 141 registered working men's clubs in greater London alone. Rural life could have been as depicted by Constable, with flails and wooden hoes, and fruit hauled to market on horse-drawn carts. In its notes distributed to American servicemen in Britain from 1942–45, the US War Department offered the following sketch:

> The British are often more reserved in conduct than we … so if Britons sit in trains or buses without striking up conversation with you, it doesn't mean they are being haughty and unfriendly. They don't speak to you because they don't want to appear intrusive and rude.
>
> Don't be misled by the British tendency to be soft-spoken and polite. If they need, they can be plenty tough … 60,000 British civilians – men, women and children – have died under bombs, and yet the morale of Britain is unbreakable. A nation doesn't come through that if it doesn't have plain, common guts.
>
> Britain may look a little shop worn and gray. But the Brits are anxious to have you know that you are not seeing their country at its best. There's been a war on since 1939.
>
> Above all, the British of all classes are enthusiastic about sports. The great spectator games are football in the autumn and winter and cricket in the spring and summer. See a 'match' of either of these whenever you get a chance. Cricket, for sure, is something to behold … If anything sums up the spirit of the country, it's this strange affair that seems to resemble nothing so much as our own baseball, except that in cricket one batter can score more runs in a single outing than some baseball teams manage in a couple of months.

* * *

Top level English cricket had stopped dead in its tracks on the Friday afternoon of 1 September 1939, the fateful day on which the German battleship *Schleswig Holstein* fired the opening salvo of the war on a Polish military depot at Danzig. But this didn't prevent the return of de facto first-class matches in the following five seasons, especially those played for charity. A London Counties side, for instance, was drawn up from amateurs past the age of military service, players on leave from the forces, or former greats like Kent and England's venerable Frank Woolley. At Lord's on 10 August 1940, the Counties hosted a British Empire XI for which Robert Nelson, the fresh-faced Northamptonshire captain then serving with the Royal Marines, scored an even-time 44. No fewer than 13,865 spectators paid at the gate to see the one-day match, and a collection raised £152 for the Red Cross. The Empire side won by 53 runs.

Just two months later, the Italian air corps sent a squadron of Fiat BR.20 bombers, each painted a brilliant green and blue, and flying in perfect wingtip formation, to attack British military installations around the Kent coast. After damaging part of the main London–Dover railway line, the planes circled back over the English Channel by Deal, dropping their remaining bombs, whether deliberately or not, on a row of identical wooden huts separated by a parade ground that marked them out as a barracks. One of the bombs crashed through the roof of an outlying building where 2nd Lt. Robert Nelson had just sat down to dinner, killing him instantly. Nelson had just turned 28, and his parents Robert and Mary, themselves only middle-aged, asked that his gravestone bear the inscription: 'A Lover of Cricket, He maintained in his Life the Spirit of the Game.'

A few nights later, another throbbing of engines was heard over Deal, almost too slow to be that of aircraft. These were Italian CANT Z.1007 bombers, nicknamed 'the buses' for their bulk and stately speed, and a local resident named E.A. Daugherty recorded that there was 'some little satisfaction' when one plane was brought down by ground fire close to the Marine barracks. 'The Italian pilot bailed out and landed near the railway bridge in Telegraph Road. I never learnt what fate befell him, but I should not personally have cared to be in his shoes after what had recently happened to the well-liked Lt. Nelson.'

The same carry-on spirit as at Lord's and MCC also prevailed at lesser cricket clubs throughout the war. There were charity matches at many of the county grounds, as well as a competitive round of league fixtures in the north. English village cricket, the pure and original manifestation of the game, sputtered on fitfully during the war, and David Blake, the younger brother of Hampshire's John Blake – and himself a future county player – remembered turning out for Wickham against Botley one warm day in August 1944 on a half-mown field in nearby Southampton.

'At the end of the match everyone trooped off for the evening to the Bald Faced Stag in Edward Road and our skipper stood up and made an emotional speech about the brave people of Poland and the evil Reds, and someone else started a fight on the subject, and I woke up with the first major hangover of my life.'

Being England, there were also numerous examples of cricketers' dogged perseverance in adversity, and of glorious improvisation amid all the gloom. At Kent, for instance, the club yearbook noted that a total of 138 incendiary bombs fell on the wicket at the St Lawrence ground, Canterbury, in the years 1944–45, although they had apparently caused little hardship – 'in fact, their ingredients appeared to be good for the grass'.

Other clubs and grounds experienced the war with much the same show of élan. Trent Bridge in Nottingham managed to host roughly a dozen well-subscribed charity matches each year, while serving successively as an army hospital and post office. It emerged relatively intact, although the county president Major Tom Barber remembered that at one point air-raid warnings had become so common that some of the spectators on the ground began to ignore them. It was a 'very English sight' to watch the unhurried progress of a cricket match while sirens wailed in the street all around.

There was more of an obvious struggle for survival at Lancashire, but the same insouciant attitude on the part of the county secretary when he came to describe the state of the Old Trafford ground in the club's minute book. Since 1941, there had been 'several surprises', he wrote, including a 'not insignificant' bomb crater at the front gate, while the groundsman's hut, two of the stands and the tiles on the pavilion roof had all caught a packet. 'We have a water cart standing before Talbot Road, and that is generally our only supply for daily use. The toilets are deplorable. Most of the playing area is in a distressed state.' In south London, the Oval was disfigured by a maze of wire cages and concrete blocks erected on the field in preparation for captured German parachutists who never came. The county yearbook would say, simply and expressively, of the war years: 'We got through', which was about the best any professional English club could hope for.

Stripped of its pavilion valuables and packed with sandbags, Lord's itself suffered a number of near misses, including a bomb that hit the playing area in October 1940 that failed to explode but, when dismantled, emitted a geyser of hot oil along with a photograph, wrapped in polythene, of a young German officer and the slogan 'With Compliments' written across it in English.

Nearly four years later, Godfrey Evans was playing for the Army against the RAF at Lord's when a German V-1 rocket cut out immediately overhead. There was a long silence, followed by a whistle, Evans remembered. 'We could hear it coming closer. The players and umpires threw themselves flat on the deck. People in the stands were hiding under their seats, although I can still see one old boy in a straw hat sitting bolt upright in front of the pavilion gate, glass in hand, looking for all the world as if it was just an ordinary day out for him.'

In the event the bomb fell about 100 yards short. 'We felt the place shake,' said Evans, 'and after that a loud cheer went up round the ground. Everyone picked themselves up again and Jack Robertson hooked the next ball he faced for six, straight into the road, which he did to the accompaniment of patriotic songs from the stands.'

* * *

Almost everyone who continued to comment or write on cricket seemed to agree that the game that emerged after the war should be what they called 'modern'. It should share in what contemporaries perceived to be general worldwide technological improvements and cultural advances. The days of the captain's telegram ceremonially presented to the batsman in the middle would be over. There was even once-unthinkable talk in the MCC committee room about some 'prospective review' of the long-standing distinction between gentlemen and players, although in the end the crisis was delayed by a further 17 years, or of tinkering with the format of domestic matches in search of the elusive 'brighter cricket'. This is the kind of talk every long-term lover of the game knows wearily in their bones. For now, the forces of tradition remained sufficiently potent for the young Denis Compton to remember that, on matchdays at Lord's, the amateurs' dressing-room attendant had continued to 'lay out the gents' flannels and bring them the day's freshly ironed newspapers on a tray', while, by contrast, 'we existed in a little upstairs cubby-hole that ponged of old socks and stale fag smoke'. Reviewing the prospects in *Wisden* of a resumption of first-class play shortly after the final victory in Europe, 'Crusoe' Robertson-Glasgow wrote:

> While the fate of the world was being determined, the game has been the scene of an interesting little battle, which for now has ended in a rout of the 'hustlers' and the triumph of conservatism over the heresy that progress and speed are synonymous. The defeat of the *soi-disant* progressives, with their programme of one-day and time-limited matches, was a certainty so long as the issue of debate rested with the majority opinion of practising cricketers ... Perhaps the reformers should be more honest about their aims. They talk much about improving cricket, in the same way some do about improving the breed of racehorses. But what they are really speaking about is money.

In the end all the bracing talk about limited-overs matches and a domestic knockout competition also took a further 17 years to materialise, and when representative cricket came to resume in

1945 it was in much the same format as it had been in 1939. (The experiment of the eight-ball over, introduced in the last pre-war English Test season, was abandoned.) Although there was no County Championship that summer, cricket of almost every other stripe returned to play its part in the nation's recovery, from a de facto Ashes Test series down to a large number of matches at the game's headquarters somewhat below the first-class: Beaumont v Oratory, for instance, or a keenly-fought affair between 'C' Division, Metropolitan Police, and St George's Hospital.

Although the idea of reviving international cricket had first been discussed the previous winter, it began to take more definite shape when in March 1945 the RAAF took a lease on the Saffrons ground in Eastbourne for the rehabilitation of their returning POWs. In time the unit's commanding officer, Capt. John Mallyon, decided that some form of organised sport might be in order for his men. Luckily, he was an old New South Wales club cricketer. An issue of bats and balls duly arrived from London, and at the first intramural game at Eastbourne on 7 April 1945, Lindsay Hassett, already the holder of four of his eventual 43 Test caps, scored 128 in just over two hours, while an enthusiastic crowd steadily built up at the pavilion end to applaud and shout appreciative remarks at the sight. The effect on Australian morale was considerable.

In due course, Mallyon made contact with 71-year-old Sir Pelham Francis Warner – 'Plum', to intimates – the former Middlesex and England captain who had regained the Ashes for his country in the early days of King Edward VII's reign. Also a former England manager and chairman of selectors, during the war Warner would be appointed deputy secretary of MCC, a title that somehow fails to convey the sheer scope of his activities, which ranged from the periodic review of members' dues to the personal selection and often supervision of very nearly every top-flight side to appear at Lord's, as well as acting as the players' effective travel agent, hotel booker and accountant. He was, simply put, the grand old man of English cricket.

In 1945, Warner lived, sometimes alone, sometimes with his infirm wife Agnes, in a five-room serviced flat on the top floor of a London mansion block behind the Albert Hall, which visitors reached by way of an antique, cage-like elevator manned by an ex-soldier with one arm who pulled on a rope running through a hole in the top of the lift attached to a pulley in the roof of the building. The living room of Warner's flat, which smelled obscurely of boiled cabbage, was furnished by a set of canary-yellow *Wisden*, a grandfather clock in the shape of a wicket, and a wall full of framed Spy cartoons of his turn-of-the-century playing colleagues. Though not teetotal, the Warners drank little, and never succumbed to extravagance. Plum himself was impeccably mannered, diminutive, bald, somewhat jug-eared – with a passing resemblance to the actor Martin Clunes – and not conspicuously one of cricket's modernisers, having once declared that the 24 consecutive Gentlemen v Players matches he had either watched or personally played in were 'the pinnacle' of a career that had seen him retire with a batting average of 36 from his 521 first-class matches, including 15 Tests.

In his day, Warner had been an all-round athlete, with a passion for golf and real tennis, and was articulate and well read, even if his earlier academic performance at Rugby and Oxford University did not indicate a particularly reflective or enquiring mind. Something of a devotee of hard-boiled American gangster films, he sometimes surprised visitors by announcing 'Stick 'em up, copper' in the tones of Jimmy Cagney. In 1945, Warner was also a practising journalist and editor, a competent author, chairman of several cricket sub-committees, an occasional umpire and reigning *éminence grise* at Middlesex. All in all, 'Plum's opinion was only slightly less exalted at Lord's than the voice of God,' wrote E.W. Swanton, who could conceivably have made a strong bid for third place.

Although the Australian servicemen based at Eastbourne would provide the nucleus of a representative side to play England in 1945, the idea for a series of international matches that summer had crossed Warner's mind earlier in the year. On 1 February, England's captain Walter Hammond had written to Lord's:

> Dear Plum,
> I was delighted to have your letter of January 29th … I would be grateful if you would pass to your Committee my sincere appreciation for their having asked me to play this coming summer in three 'Test Matches'. Naturally, I accept, subject, of course, to my being fit, which at the moment I certainly am not. However, I can advise you at a later date as to how I progress … I am not altogether certain how much cricket I shall be able to play if fit, as now that I am out of the R.A.F. I have a little work to do …

The summer's plans evidently advanced over the next few weeks, because on 19 March Warner in turn wrote:

> My dear Walter,
> I hope you are going to play here at Lord's on 19th and 21st May, England v. Australia; on June 2nd, England XI v. West Indies; on July 14th, England v. Australia and on August 6th and 7th, England v. Australia. I hope you are flourishing. Please do all you can to play in these games.

Like everything else, cricket was clearly in a state of flux in 1945. While men like Walter Robins, who captained Middlesex both before and after the war, reaching the rank of squadron leader in between, was widely proclaiming it 'a chance to sweep away the grouse-moor image' and speaking of his vision of an 'exciting new era' for the game, there were others – including Pelham Warner, in some people's opinion – who seemed to have stepped fresh from the pages of some bucolic P. G. Wodehouse tale, if not to have actually slipped through a crack in the space-time continuum. But even Warner was far from the most conspicuous embodiment of cricket's past. The structure of the game in 1945 was still able to accommodate a figure like 55-year-old Lionel Tennyson, more formally known as the 3rd Baron Tennyson, the poet's grandson, who had captained Hampshire through the 1920s, but was still playing competitively past the point of Hitler's downfall. A devotee of the turf, Tennyson had once managed to lose £12,000 – around £350,000 today – in the course of a week at the races. He owned five horses himself, some of which he rode in point-to-point events, and another of which, in an attempt to recoup his losses, he once entered in the Regulation Plate at Newbury. It finished last. The long-serving Hampshire treasurer Bernard Harfield would remember of his county captain:

> He had no regard for money, none. One summer when he was with us he lost more money on the casino tables and races than a professional player would make in his career. You would have needed dynamite to get him out of the Tweseldown course by Aldershot when they were racing there. [Tennyson] was a fanatic all-round sportsman, with a lot of beautiful equipment. He had to sell an antique billiards table once just to get out of Tweseldown. That's how much money he lost.

For his part, the future Surrey and England spinner Jim Laker, then just emerging from the army, would say: 'One man really summed up all that was wrong with the English cricket world in 1945. That was Surrey's captain Errol Holmes. He very nearly made me leave the game before I got started.'

Holmes, then aged 39, was a recent Royal Artillery officer who made no noticeable distinction between his leadership style in the army or on the sports field. He had a muscular military face, hard, narrowed eyes and an upper-class accent so fruity his men could barely understand his commands, along with a travelling wardrobe when playing in away matches that included both a black and a white dinner jacket. His slightly self-important manner went well with his oiled hair and upturned moustache. He captained Surrey on and off from 1934 to 1955, sat on several committees, and helped select the England teams in the summer of 1945, during which he was lucky enough to himself be picked to play for his country in the second representative match of the series, at Sheffield, where, batting in the middle order, he scored 6 and 2. Whatever else you could say about Holmes, he was not noticeably the voice of the future. Jack Hobbs once said of him that 'he cut a fine figure in the field' and 'would not tolerate anything shady or underhanded'. Set against these qualities, there were those, like Laker, who thought Holmes, with his piping voice and extended vowels, an 'anachronistic and frankly ludicrous sort' in the post-war world, and perhaps just a touch too keen on maintaining certain bygone mannerisms, such as his habit of addressing his subordinate players while in the field as 'My good man' – with a habit of adding the words 'Chop, chop' to each exchange – and avoiding their company entirely at all other times.

At the other extreme of the game there were men like Derbyshire's 34-year-old all-rounder George Pope, one of three sporting brothers, who also represented England in the summer of 1945. A tall, sallow-faced league and county professional with receding hair, piercing black eyes and a mordant sense of humour, Pope was one of those (usually apocryphal) cases of a young northerner emerging from down a coal mine to become a world-class fast bowler – in this case who could bat a bit, as well – with no apparent intermediate learning curve. With little top-class competition to speak of in the area, Pope seized the opportunity to establish himself as England's first choice with the new ball, which he did to particular effect in that same match at Sheffield, with figures of 5-58 and 3-69. Off the field, he had little time for authority in general, and in particular for Pelham Warner, whom he once dismissed as 'living in a garden party'.

After breakfast on Wednesday, 20 June 1945, while helping his wife do the washing-up in their terraced home in Shirland Street,

Chesterfield, and before setting out for the first of his two weekday jobs as a travelling dried-fruit salesman for the Liverpool-based firm of Leatherbarrow and Company, Pope heard the sound of footsteps racing up the cobbled street to the front door. A breathless friend burst in. 'Haven't you heard the wireless this morning?' he panted. 'You're playing for England.' This came as news to Pope, who, apart from being in indifferent health, would consistently present a challenge to Warner and his fellow selectors when it came to his willingness to represent his country that summer. For now, the Derbyshire man had only one thing to say about his dramatic call-up: 'Who's going to fix this with old man Leatherbarrow? Those high and mighties at Lord's never think about the rest of us having to make a living.' After letting that sink in for a moment, he added the rhetorical question: 'Why is that? Stupidity or ignorance?'

George Pope was far from the only individual in English cricket that year concerned about making ends meet. As Robertson-Glasgow had said in *Wisden*, the perennial debate about reforming the game after the war mainly came down to a matter of money. The MCC treasurer in 1945 was 63-year-old John Lyttelton, 9th Viscount Cobham, a Boer War veteran and former Conservative MP who had briefly played county cricket in the mid-1920s. Like Pope, he came from an extended sporting family, but that was perhaps where the similarity ended. Hagley Hall, the Lytteltons' ancestral seat in Worcestershire, was a magnificent, neo-Palladian pile with Chippendale furniture, Venetian windows and a row of flag-bearing turrets shaped like witches' hats designed by Inigo Jones, lying among 350 acres of landscaped deer park near Stourbridge. Maroon velvet banners with Cobham family crests spanned the building's entrance hall, which could have housed a reasonable game of indoor cricket. In all, Lyttelton presented to the world a brilliant image of dynastic wealth and power accumulated over the centuries. But his role at Lord's forced even him to confront certain hard truths. In keeping with other institutions, MCC had been 'sadly reduced' by the war, he wrote, with gate receipts 'sharply in the descendant in [light of] both a limited programme of matches and only modest entrance prices thereto' – either nine pence or a shilling to members of the public, with all serving members of the forces admitted free of charge. As a small reflection of the club's straitened circumstances in 1945, it was noted that while any troops stationed in or near Lord's 'might avail themselves of the baths on the top floor of the Tennis Court building, the coke used should continue to be paid for by the units concerned'. In another footnote to the minutes, the treasurer added: 'Any outlay in connection with the proposed new bakery must remain suspended.'

Individual cricket clubs also strove to adapt to the trying circumstances. There was a struggle for survival at most of the first-class counties. At Derbyshire, a letter went out to members appealing for contributions to a 'Grand Reconstruction Fund' of £10,000, 'without which [it] is uncertain if facilities for cricket can be adequately maintained'; while at Gloucestershire the club secretary admitted that 'after occupation for five years by home forces, the ground at Bristol requires urgent capital attention'. At Surrey – a club that boasted the king as its patron – the secretary wrote that a balanced budget was beyond his reach in 1945, and 'at present only a distant dream'. In Hampshire, they were down to just 587 dues-paying members by the spring of 1945, less than a quarter of the pre-war total. Like his counterpart at Derbyshire, the Sussex secretary Sir Home Gordon wrote to members asking them for 'supplemental funds in order [to] meet the club's essential commitments'. The response to this appeal was 'muted', Gordon was forced to admit.[2]

---

2 Sir Home Seton Montagu Gordon, 12th Baronet Gordon of Embo, Sutherland, to give him his full due, was another character from cricket's storied past. Then aged 73, he generally favoured the classic Henley ensemble of white flannels and striped blazer, with a red carnation in the buttonhole, adorned by the honorary Sussex cap voted to him by the county committee, his pride in which was certainly not untainted by an implied, though unjustified, aspiration to first-class status. In addition to his administrative duties, he also wrote under Pelham Warner's editorship for *The Cricketer* and other outlets. Home had first gone to Lord's as an eight-year-old boy in 1880, when he met W.G. Grace, an event he revisited frequently in print.

Meanwhile, there was well-founded concern in *Wisden* that the government might see fit to levy an entertainment tax on gate receipts, thus 'adding a further drain on revenue, all the more serious now when the counties face the heavy cost of renovating their grounds and rebuilding blitzed pavilions and stands, with improved accommodation necessary to meet the requirements of the large crowds which are certain to assemble'. Perhaps the one exception to the dismal rule came at Lancashire, where the committee decided that Old Trafford had simply been so badly damaged that it would effectively have to be rebuilt from the ground up and launched a £100,000 appeal fund accordingly. By October 1945 nearly a third of the total was in hand, and the following spring's *Wisden* carried an arresting artist's sketch of the proposed new pavilion, a vast, three-tiered affair under a red-rose flag, with two brilliantly lit pagoda-like towers at each end that all soared up over the field like a gaudily-iced wedding cake, little of which survived in the ancient ground's final refurbishment.

Lancashire's Cyril Washbrook, born in 1914, was one of the few men who could ultimately boast of a first-class playing career that linked the Jack Hobbs era, when certain English gentlemen cricketers still took the field clad in a hard straw hat and a monocle, to that of the post-modern world of the 1960s. He represented England in all five of their home internationals in 1945. A stocky, but superbly agile man, Washbrook despised notions of false modesty and clearly thought himself integral to England's fortunes, and with some reason, finishing the 1945 series with a batting average of 47, second only to Bill Edrich in the list.

Washbrook was another of those cricketers to have served in the RAF, though like his captain Walter Hammond his war duties were largely restricted to the physical training of new recruits. He was also one of nature's born administrators. Washbrook was appointed a Test selector in 1956 and made a surprise but successful England comeback that summer against the touring Australians at the age of 41, although it was always said that he had excused himself from the room when his name came up for discussion.

Bob Bennett, a future Lancashire chairman, and ironically at one time responsible for the England team's discipline, first turned out for his county as an amateur when Washbrook was the side's manager. The excited debutant bought a cream shirt and a new pair of flannels for the occasion. 'I thought I looked pretty smart,' Bennett said, 'and I folded the shirt cuffs back a couple of inches. As we left the dressing room I was confronted by the manager. "Where are you going?" he snapped. I mumbled something about going on the field. "On the field? Well, roll your bloody sleeves up. You're going out there to work, not to ponce about."'

If Washbrook was one of those cricketers who remained anchored to the game's pre-war conventions, his county and Test colleague Bill Roberts, a left-arm spinner, took a more contemporary approach to his duties. Also born in 1914, Roberts was a slim, blue-eyed type with a mop of wavy brown hair and the habitual expression of a schoolboy having just run away from ringing some grown-up's front doorbell. He had first played county cricket in 1939, taking seven cheap wickets against Northants in late August, but then immediately signed up for an infantry regiment on the declaration of war. Impatient with cricket's existing class structure, Roberts generally addressed his colleagues as 'mate', irrespective of status, while in the field. In later years he frequently recalled the occasion in June 1945 when Errol Holmes had chased the last ball of the afternoon session down to the distant long leg boundary at Sheffield. Roberts had then watched with sardonic amusement as Holmes proceeded to stroll the 100 yards back across the ground to the pavilion gate, where all his professional teammates were dutifully lined up waiting for him before they could go in for their tea. 'As matters stood in 1945, you weren't allowed to leave the field before an amateur.'

Roberts played in three of England's five representative matches in 1945 but managed a total of just five wickets at 27 apiece, while, when the time came, batting much like what he was, a specialist bowler. He returned to Lancashire for a few more seasons but his health broke down and he died in August 1951 at the age of 36, after a relapse following an operation. One of his bon mots had been to call Pelham Warner 'just a grandiloquent juggler who threw people in and out of the side at will, and like Washbrook always wanted you well-groomed on parade. With Plum, the cricket seemed to come second to how you deported yourself, although I do recall him watching us practice once in the nets at Lord's and shouting out, "*Bowled*, sir!" with real gusto when I knocked over Bill Edrich's castle.'

* * *

Perhaps the actual results of the 1945 matches weren't as important as what they signified about cricket's ability to survive. That resilience was visible in the way individual English clubs adapted to the challenges of six years that in many cases saw them deprived of facilities and income, not to mention of some of their finest players. The men who returned tended to divide into those who looked for fundamental change to the game's existing set-up, and others who convinced themselves that only they stood between the febrile social atmosphere of the day and total anarchy. There was a third group, too, perhaps best epitomised by Keith Miller, who in 1945 really lived in two parallel worlds. There was Miller's civilian life as a mercurially talented young all-round cricketer, likely at any moment to suddenly release the brakes and drop in a screaming bouncer, or, when the time came, to crash a six into the top-tier seats of the pavilion, and in general to exude the air of a schoolboy in the midst of an extended summer holiday. Then there was the world of the hardened fighter-bomber pilot, a precarious existence in which he became increasingly inured to the idea of sudden death. Miller could take the Mosquito up on another nerve-shredding mission far over a ravaged but still far from undefended enemy homeland, with 2,000 pounds of napalm strapped just a few feet under his seat, and then come home and change clothes and go off to play cricket as if nothing particularly dangerous or disturbing had happened. This same slightly schizophrenic air, of shadow and light, surely lay at the heart of the cricket played that summer.

In the meantime, there was the irrefutable lesson behind E.W. Swanton's account of the match improvised in his camp located on the Thai–Burma railway, played after a desultory lunch on Christmas Day 1942.

'It was perhaps the very fact of our so occupying the afternoon that caused our guards to receive subsequent requests to play cricket with suspicion, as having some religious significance and therefore being good for our morale,' Swanton wrote, of a sport that became not only a mental escape, but in its way the nervous system of the whole camp. When no further live play was possible, he added, 'there were occasions when we could lecture, and be lectured to, about the game … It was a subject that filled countless hours in pitch-dark huts between sundown and the moment that continued to be euphemistically known as lights-out. And it inspired many a fond daydream, contrived often in the most gruesome setting, whereby one combated the present by living either in the future or the past.'

Part of cricket's charm surely lies in the way it continues both to renew itself, and to release successive generations from a captivity that in some senses might be said to bear comparison even with Swanton's.

3.
Fun Among the Ruins

VISITORS BRAVING the ascent in the hand-drawn lift up to Pelham Warner's flat in the Kensington mansion block would have been greeted on arrival by an interesting character, or perhaps characters might be nearer the mark. Like many of us, Warner was something of a study in contrasts over the years: imperious and yet often considerate; antiquated and yet a great champion of youth in sport; vain and yet sometimes humble; a figure steeped in the racial attitudes of the colonial 1880s (and the grandson of a slave owner), and yet anxious to 'bring the black man to a seat at the top table', particularly in the Caribbean islands where he himself had been raised, the youngest of 21 children born to the then 67-year-old Attorney General of Trinidad, and where he, Plum, remained a hugely popular figure whenever he returned as a cricketer or administrator.

Perhaps Warner's friend Lord Hawke, the Yorkshire and England supremo of the immediately preceding era, put it best when describing his protégé's character. 'You may say that I knew him at the very peak of his humanity,' Hawke later reflected of their mutual private tour of the West Indies in early 1897. 'He was charming, intelligent, without side, and the most popular fellow in the islands.' Asked by a London newspaperman whether he would care to wire back accounts of his team's matches, Hawke had turned to his 23-year-old colleague and said: 'Plummy, you're last from school. Why don't you have a go?' Warner did, and thus began a 65-year-long cricket writing career, in which among other things he stoutly defended the gentleman and player system, and which included his founding in 1921 of the still-surviving *Cricketer* magazine – a title Warner personally edited until 1962, at which point he was succeeded by his son.

Perhaps, again like many of us, Warner had a touch of Prince Hal about him, a man who with age surrenders some of the youthful idealism that grounds him to the truth. Denis Compton once said that he had grown to 'love and trust old Plum', who came to be 'like a father to me', but that 'he wasn't exactly the sort of bloke to shake things up'. Everyone agreed that by 1945 Warner exuded a tranquil, essentially conservative view of life. Even ten years earlier, at the age of 61, he was 'above all a realist' and 'a shrewd poker player', according to one profile, who always believed – even before Churchill did – that Britain would have to fight Hitler, and that 'naturally we shall win'.

Warner's inner confidence on the point was apparent even in the dark days of December 1944, at a time when no fewer than three German armies comprising a quarter of a million men burst forth through knee-high winter snow from the mountains and forests of the Ardennes to launch what became the last great offensive on the Western Front of the war, the so-called Battle of the Bulge. With the Allies caught completely off guard and scrambling to mount a defence while Nazi loudspeakers blared out to them in between the deafening artillery salvos: 'How would you like to die for Christmas?', back home in Kensington Warner took the opportunity to send a note to his friend Sqn. Ldr. Walter Robins of Middlesex and England, who was then stationed at the Air Ministry building in Kingsway, central London.

22 December 1944

Dear Robbie,

This is to wish you and yours a very happy Christmas and every good wish for the coming year.

I hope you are going to play here next summer a lot, and I want to book you now for certain for the three 'Test Matches' which are to be on the following dates:

Saturday and Monday, 19th and 21st May 1945
Saturday, 14th July 1945, and
Monday and Tuesday, 6th and 7th August 1945

– and, of course, in any other games you find yourself able to play in.

Will you please congratulate your boy on coming out top of his class? 'Mens sana in corpore sano.'

My love to Kathleen and your son and very nice little daughter. I am hoping to see the whole Robins Commando at Lord's next year.

Mind you come to the Annual General Meeting of Middlesex, with luncheon before, on 6th February as that is the day when we are making a presentation to Jimmy.[3]

Yours ever
Plum.

It took commendable sangfroid, or perhaps merely detachment, on Warner's part to dwell like this on the fixture list of a still only dimly perceived cricket season at a time when German V-2 rockets continued to daily terrorise London, and the outcome of the Ardennes campaign – and thus of the war in the west – remained in the balance. But such was Warner's core streak of equanimity in times of trouble. Among other things, his cheery note to Robins clearly indicates that, far from being improvised at the last moment, as often reported, the eventual 1945 'Victory' matches were under active discussion at least six months earlier, and that they were then considered Tests, even if the word was invariably pinched between inverted commas, and the status was ultimately denied them. In fact, plans for some sort of resumption of organised cricket that summer were underway even earlier than that, with the publication of a report in March 1944 by an MCC committee under the former England all-rounder and Conservative politician Sir Stanley Jackson.

3 Possibly the veteran Middlesex all-rounder Jim Sims, who also played four Tests for England from 1935 to 1937.

It was imperative that there be a 'dynamic attitude to the game' in future, Jackson wrote, amidst a host of specific technical proposals he hoped would have the desired effect, although in the end the report's sole innovation to actually be adopted at county level was to allow a new ball after 55 overs. Even that modest concession to the cause of brighter cricket was at the mercy of the general shortage of commodities like leather. 'It is anticipated that in its first season the supply of balls may be insufficient for this, but possibly a used ball in better condition may be substituted.'

Cricket, then, had long been on the cards for 1945; and there was also to be a lot of it. Between early June 1944 and mid-March the following year, the MCC secretary – and Warner's notional superior – 53-year-old Colonel Rowan Rait Kerr, a decorated Great War veteran who brought a certain military snap to his office, wrote at least six times to each of his 17 subordinate county colleagues. They were to continue to make 'every effort [to] secure adequate playing facilities in anticipation of a restart', he told them in one circular; while the counties' drive for new members should be stepped up to fill the ranks of those 'incapacitated by enemy action', he noted blandly in another. There was a palpable sense in cricket's corridors of power over the winter of 1944/45, if one not always matched by the nation's war planners, that by the following spring life would have returned close enough to normal to encourage thoughts of a full fixture list.

A former Worcestershire player and RAF officer with the striking name of William Shakespeare was another of those visionaries in dark suits and county ties who would work tirelessly amidst the V-2 barrage and all the other privations that marked the last winter of the war to ensure cricket's return in the spring. A famously daredevil pilot, at 51 Shakespeare was still square-jawed and thick-haired with a habit of leaning forward when he stood, as if anticipating the future. Perhaps his real contribution to the cause lay in the sheer number of hours he was prepared to put in. While grandees like Jackson and Rait Kerr thought largely in terms of the big picture, Shakespeare was a detail man, possibly even more so than Warner: there were always jobs to be done which no one else particularly wanted, and which he was willing to take on. If there was a cricketer in military uniform whose temporary release was needed for him to play somewhere, Shakespeare was frequently the one to square the matter with the man's commanding officer. If a touring overseas team needed suitable overnight accommodation while in Brighton or Coventry or Glasgow, as often as not Shakespeare would volunteer to correspond with the desired hotel, and then be there to personally welcome the players on arrival.

Perhaps too little attention has been paid to the debt English post-war cricket owes to Shakespeare, who lived long enough to recruit an International XI to tour Pakistan early in 1971, where he was the first man in any position of influence to notice a teenaged Lahore tearaway bowler named Imran Khan, and then to invite him, at a fee of £35 a week, to play county cricket for Worcestershire. It was the start of a career that eventually saw Imran appear in 88 Tests and 175 ODIs, winning the World Cup for Pakistan in the process and in time going on to become his nation's embattled prime minister. 'I feel sure we shall survive, though both cricket and the land as a whole may be changed not necessarily for the better,' Shakespeare wrote in March 1945, impressive evidence of his insight, contrasted with wild assurances about the country fit for returning heroes that some of those in authority were then thrusting on the public.

Since the playing arrangements and the whole spirit of the matches arranged for 1945 were so completely dominated by it, it's worth again bearing in mind the harsh reality of British life that spring. Apart from the continuing rain of Heinkel and V-2 attacks that persisted through early April, there were certain other significant challenges to returning to normal daily life, let alone to the spangled palisades of cricket as men like Warner fondly remembered it. For one thing, the United Kingdom was insolvent.

The country had mobilised more completely, and for longer, than any other belligerent nation, with more than 10 million men and women either under arms or making them out of a total adult workforce of 21.1 million. Austerity was the watchword for Britain's institutions, households and political leadership as a result.

The wartime coalition government had literally gone for broke in its pursuit of victory, borrowing from the Americans and selling British overseas assets to keep money and materiel flowing; the UK lost nearly a third of its national wealth in the years 1939–45. And what the cold statistics don't properly convey on these occasions is the direct human cost, seen in one way or another, at all times, in all walks of British life, by men and women in and out of uniform, and of every political stripe.

'I find folk are grumbling more now than in the midst of war,' a 43-year-old, stoutly middle-class but progressive-minded Sheffield housewife named Edie Rutherford, married to a local timber merchant and sports fanatic, wrote in her diary. 'Then we realised the need for economy and going short, and we did it with the belief that the end of the war would see some let-up ... Instead, so far we seem to have less than ever, and as we realise how well the USA and others are, folk are getting restive. I foresee riots some not too distant day if we don't get some of the blessings of peace, instead of all disasters.'

Similarly, there were the views of Jim Griggs, a 22-year-old former infantryman invalided out of service after being wounded in the D-Day landings, contemplating life from the relative comfort of his parents' home in suburban Walsall. 'We should be grateful I suppose for small mercies – still being alive, having a bed and at least a mouthful of food on the table,' he wrote. 'But that's really all you can say. It's not thought proper to complain, but you can't beat the truth, and the fact is there's nothing much for it now except to pack up and move somewhere like Canada.'

And finally, Edie Rutherford again:

> Talking on Friday to a friend due for demob any day. He says he reckons there will be trouble in this country in the next year or so. He bases his belief on the conversation of men serving, says they won't put up with what their fathers endured last time ... Personally I welcome unrest as it shows folk are waking up and realising what they ought to have, and doing something about it.

Although Mrs Rutherford's high hopes of Britons manning the barricades – as opposed to expressing a collective irritation at the ballot box – were disappointed in 1945, it's worth remembering how a widely loved but essentially peripheral luxury like cricket might have had to struggle to reassert itself in the nation's fabric, when set amidst the events that spring. Apart from the final but painful spasms of the calamity in Europe and the continuing war in Asia, there was the fact that it was the coldest Easter throughout much of Britain in living memory. By day fog descended on central London, leaving spectacular rime deposits on streets and houses. At night sheets of ice formed on the Thames, even as Big Ben gave up the struggle and froze solid, most of its surrounding masonry blown apart by earlier Luftwaffe action and the ground beneath it weed-ravaged and hollowed out like an abandoned archaeological dig. When conditions allowed, Londoners still went down to the riverbank like their Neolithic ancestors before them to scavenge for much-needed heating materials. In Mortlake, a housewife named Pat Bell wrote in her diary: 'Old Father Thames is at least good to the people who live alongside her [*sic*] ... The tide brought in wood by the ton. When dried it lit many a fire when coal was short, as was money.'

In the normal course of affairs, there are surely few sights to compare with the annual reunion of players, officials and press on the first days of gentle practice before a new English cricket season. To believers, the start-of-term atmosphere, with its ambient smells of linseed oil and embrocation, and of freshly painted seats, is generally a time of 'awakening blue, all varnish and high hopes', to quote Harold Pinter. But that same invigorating sense of renewal wasn't entirely the case in spring 1945. At the Fenner's ground in Cambridge, where play began on the damp Tuesday morning of 24 April, there were an estimated 45 to 50 hardy souls huddled together on a row of wooden benches for the start of the annual freshmen's trial match. Later in the week, league cricket got underway at venues such as the Castleton ground in Rochdale, the Wadham Road field in Bootle and a municipal park in Formby, near Liverpool. Most of these premises were modest enough even in peacetime. The playing area at Bootle was essentially a roped-off area of a large public dog-walking park. On one side there was a wooden hut of military décor, generally foul with cigarette smoke, that served as a pavilion, and a low, jerry-built tier of benches on the other where people could sit for either 2d or 3d, depending on the importance of the game being played. The Bootle pitch similarly left much to be desired. Godfrey Evans later remarked of playing services cricket there that his main concern lay not so much in scoring runs or taking catches, but in avoiding being swallowed up by one of the 'car-sized' craters on the wicket. One new facility most grounds had in common was an updated war memorial.

It is hard to overstate the modesty of most English cricketers' playing conditions in those days. Even at the relatively affluent Fenner's, the amenities were on the spartan side, with a pervasive smell of boiling stew that wafted over from the dining tent on to the playing area and changing facilities so cramped that many players opted to don their whites behind the shelter of a nearby tree. It also rained heavily throughout that first week of the season. In fact it was so wet that William Shakespeare was left to reflect wryly 'how odd it sometimes seems' that cricket should have taken root in the English climate. 'Rain wasted a lot of time throughout the first few days,' the *Cambridge Daily News* wrote of the local freshmen's match. There were conditions of 'Biblical deluge' during the next two games on the ground, while for the following week's match between the university and a nomadic side led by Maurice Crouch, a former soldier and MCC batsman who laboured under the handicap of having been shot in 1941 not in combat, but by his girlfriend's rival suitor, the scorebook read only: 'Abandoned Due to Flood.' It was 'not exactly a classic scene of dappled sunlight and parasols', Crouch was later forced to admit in a memoir.

There was another example of the strange double life necessarily led by many of the men involved in the English cricket world of 1945, when 27-year-old Ken Cranston, a future Test all-rounder, then serving as a dental officer with the Royal Navy, was urgently called from the field in a forces game at Neston, Cheshire, on 28 April in order to return to London to examine the teeth of a trainload of British prisoners newly liberated from the Bergen-Belsen concentration camp. Cranston reported that he had been moved to tears by the sight of many of his patients. They betrayed 'terrible signs of mistreatment' and spoke of a regimen characterised by 'mass beatings by guards, individual beatings using fists, feet, clubs, rifle butts, etc ... with daily working conditions of equal cruelty, and forced rain-soaked marches in which those who couldn't keep up were shot and left in the mud'.

Even at that late stage there was still no official certainty when the war might end, and the sight of yet another returning troop train that week at Victoria station filled with hundreds of wounded and mutilated men, some without limbs or eyes, some shell-shocked, would not have conspicuously boosted morale. At a meeting in Downing Street on 15 April, by which time Hitler had only a fortnight to live, Winston Churchill told his Cabinet colleagues: 'For the purposes of planning production and allocating manpower, it [is] believed the earliest date for the end of the German conflict should be assumed to be 1st July 1945, and the latest the 31st December 1945.' Six days later, there was still no absolute conviction on the matter, although by then Churchill's mind had turned to the prospect of holding a snap general election, which itself would reflect the pervasive mood of austerity. 'There are no surplus funds,'

Churchill perhaps unnecessarily informed the Cabinet. 'The legal maximum of each candidate's expenses should be no more than a basic figure of £450, with an additional allowance of 1½d for each elector in a county constituency and 1d for each elector in a borough constituency,' he added, another sure sign that while the British might have experienced the war as a moment of national solidarity and rallying together, in peace their lives were to be more consumed by matters of making ends meet.

Merely to survive, Churchill confided to his senior Cabinet colleagues in a further meeting perhaps wisely deemed 'Ultra Classified ... Not for Public Dissemination', would mean 'containing expectations' and 'forgoing many if not all inessential or recreational comforts previously held integral to British life'.

It was largely thanks to the unstinting efforts of men like Warner and Shakespeare that cricket not only weathered the immediate crisis that summer, but actively flourished at most levels of the game. There were no rations involved when the 43-year-old pre-war West Indies great Learie Constantine went out to bat for Bootle in a pre-season tie against nearby Ormskirk, where he leant on the first ball he received with a gesture that barely seemed to qualify as a full-blown stroke, but that sent the ball skidding over the turf to the rope before any of the fielders had time to move a muscle. Constantine spent just over an hour at the crease before giving his wicket away, having scored 82 in the meantime. There were similar joys to behold 300 miles away on the south coast, where the long-time Sussex supporter Laetitia Stapleton wrote of the 'heartwarming' scene that greeted her return to the county ground at Hove, where 'the professional players were back in force, older [but] otherwise looking as if nothing had changed', even if 'the weather was dreadful. S.W. gale kept blowing bails off. V. cold, but [I] went homc happy.'

By the end of April, a full schedule of school, club, college and village cricket was also back in play. The Oxford University side advertised themselves by their wartime alias of 'The Authentics' and were led by 21-year-old Garth Wheatley, an attractive middle-order bat who went on to win a double first-class science degree and then to enjoy a brief but productive career at Surrey before being lost to the game as a physics professor. One of the sport's foremost thinkers, Harry Altham, author of the magisterial *History of Cricket* (1926), somewhat eccentrically also turned out on an ad hoc basis for the students that spring. Altham was then aged 56, and his son Richard would appear in the same Oxford team just two years later. The coming man at Cambridge was John Dewes, a compact left-hander with a wave of dark hair who had initially gone up for a term before leaving to join the navy, but later returned to complete his studies. *Wisden* called him 'the surprise of the season ... he scored six centuries, one in the opening trial, and in eleven home matches totalled 846 runs ... Both he and the Etonian freshman Hon. L.R. White played for England in the third match against the Australian Services at Lord's.' The latter, known more formally as the 5th Baron Annaly, was just 18 when called upon to represent his country, sharing a fourth-wicket partnership at Lord's of 55 with Len Hutton (whom he addressed by his surname), but in the measured words of his eventual *Wisden* obituary 'had no further ambition to pursue a first-class career, preferring to take his cricket for such clubs as MCC, the Ramblers and I Zingari'.

Paul Brooks was at one time meant to have gone up to university from the City of London School, and in the normal course of events would have played alongside Wheatley and Altham at Oxford that first post-war summer. Born in May 1921, Brook was a brisk left-arm seamer who had joined the Lord's ground staff in his 1938 summer holidays and became a teenaged celebrity by clean-bowling Don Bradman at practice one morning in the nets. Such was Bradman's stature that season, when he finished the Test series against England with a batting average of 108, that the story made headlines on the back page of almost every newspaper across Britain. Brooks was thought to have a golden future in the game, but instead of that he volunteered immediately on the outbreak of war for the national fire service. Following that, he took a commission with the Coldstream Guards. Brooks was shot in the spine by a sniper during the climactic fighting in Italy in April 1945 and died of his injuries in a London hospital nine months later, still aged just 24.

Services cricket also resumed that spring, or perhaps more accurately never really stopped in the first place. The RAF, with players of the calibre of Bill Edrich, Les Ames, Bob Wyatt and 34-year-old 'Young' George Cox (so named to distinguish him from his sporting father), as well as a brace of future Test match umpires in Syd Buller and Arthur Jepson, swept all before them. The navy also boasted a strong side, with men like Ken Cranston, John Dewes and a 21-year-old, recently discharged Royal Marine-turned-schoolmaster with crinkly hair and an excitable but essentially correct bowling action, named Trevor Bailey, in its ranks. Bailey was not a big man, but he projected a certain wiry physicality. In those days he was widely considered something of a thruster with the bat, which might have come as a surprise to those who later knew him as one of those peculiarly English, back-to-the-wall grafting types who tend to rate more highly with the connoisseur than the average fee-paying spectator, a player who once raised the touring Australians' hackles by occupying the crease all day for a languid 71 at Lord's, before going on to bowl wide of the leg stump for hours on end to the same opponents at Headingley, driving both the Aussies and at least some of the crowd half mad in the process. There is a photograph of a Naval Officers versus Women's Service (or Wrens) fixture played at Oldham that spring of 1945, both sexes attired for the occasion in bell-bottomed trousers and white, short-sleeved shirts, appearing cheerful and relaxed while two crew-cut men in dark overalls with brooms lurk behind them. They were German prisoners of war being held at the nearby Glen Mill estate in Cheshire, a stately home with an attached cotton-processing factory requisitioned as a detention camp. The men had been pressed into service as ground staff.

* * *

There must have been moments in the spring of 1945 when Pelham Warner and the other authority figures at Lord's wondered whether they could actually bring off an enterprise with as many moving parts to it as arranging a series of cricket matches between two international representative teams at a time when both their host nations were still involved in a world war. Had he known what lay ahead, perhaps Warner might have opted for the quiet life instead. But by late April of that year the whole crazy scheme had a certain unstoppable momentum to it, and Warner himself had remarked in the pages of the *Cricketer* that the proposal for some sort of top-flight fixture or fixtures had been put to him and his colleagues the previous winter, and on the whole seemed to them 'sound'. He was not a man to lightly renege on a project to which he had given his public blessing.

Among the many other challenges facing the organisers of the 1945 series was the significant matter of securing the services of the players under consideration. Fresh from confinement in a series of Italian and German POW camps, Bill Bowes, now aged 36, understandably chose not to chance his arm by playing again in the immediate future, and delayed his full comeback until a services match in June, where, bowling off a shortened run, he took 1-64 off nine overs and promptly left the field to be physically ill in the pavilion. His fellow inmate Freddie Brown waited until after his wedding in early July to appear for an Army XI against the RAAF at Lord's, top-scoring with 17 out of a total of 80 all out. There were others, too, with the competing demands of families, or full-time jobs, to consider, which again raises the matter of the lengthy George Pope correspondence which so exercised both Warner and the best minds at Lord's through much of the early part of the 1945 season.

Its subtext is really that of a clash of two cultures, with a generally benign but authoritarian officer class for which discipline, unquestioning obedience to orders and conformity were paramount on one side, and a gruff, lateral-thinking working man with a family to feed on the other.

Pelham Warner wrote from Lord's on 30 April:

> Dear Pope,
> Will you play for England against Australia on the 19th and 21st May here? Play begins at 11.30am on both days, and stumps are drawn at 6.30pm on the first day and 6.30pm, or 7 o'clock if there is a chance of a finish, on the second day.
>
> M.C.C. will pay your railway fares, cabs, and reasonable accommodation in London. In regard to the last, will you make your own arrangements?
>
> Would you kindly let me have a reply as soon as possible? I am hoping very much you will be able to play.
>
> Sincerely,
> Deputy Secretary.

In those days, if you wanted to correspond with someone about a matter such as their availability to play cricket for England, you did so by writing them a letter, putting it in an envelope, affixing a stamp, taking it to a nearby pillar box and then awaiting developments. The nearest thing to today's text or email was to send an expensive telegram, and even that would normally have to be dictated over the phone, transcribed by a post office clerk and then borne to its final destination as often as not by a boy riding a bicycle. Having devoted much of his own playing career to 'eliminat[ing] so far as possible any and all risk from the art of batting', Warner was now confronted by the uncertainties that dogged the whole process of organising the first post-war England team to represent their country in a Test series. It's worth remembering, too, that he had little by way of support in his small upstairs room at Lord's, just a part-time typist and the services of Lt. Col. Hugh Henson, a genial Malvern old boy and occasional west country cricketer recently appointed as the

MCC assistant deputy secretary, of whom it was said, quite possibly unfairly, that he spent much of his time that summer batting for the Gloucestershire Gypsies, attending garden parties and recovering from hangovers. In any event, Warner shouldered much of the work himself, often carrying away a briefcase full of papers to read back at his flat each night, taking calls there on his 'private' but still widely circulated home number of Kensington 8335, and writing voluminous notes in spidery longhand to be deciphered at Lord's the following morning.

'I thank you kindly for your letter of the 30th instant,' Pope replied, courteously enough, on the stationery of his other commercial enterprise – the Cuttholme Woodturning Company of Chesterfield – four days later. 'But I regret to inform you that I am advised most strongly by my medical man not to accept the invitation, owing to my recently injured jaw and weak state of health … I am very sorry to have to write in this way,' Pope continued, 'but I am sure that you will appreciate my position. I would not like it said that I let the side down by being foolish in not accepting the doctor's advice.'

This was all eminently fair on Pope's part, and Warner in turn wrote back sympathetically: 'I do hope you will be able to play later in the summer, and if so will you kindly let me know?' But perhaps something in his prior experience of dealing with the richly gifted but occasionally truculent Pope suggested itself to Warner, because across his reply he scribbled the one word: 'Money?' There's no doubt that the Derbyshire player was genuinely hurt, just as he said, although curiously enough he was back on the field as a paid professional for Colne in their Lancashire League tie away to Ramsbottom just three days after informing his own county secretary that he was *hors de combat* with a 'completely wired jaw … and am not able to eat solid food – there is no chance of [any] return for now'. It wasn't as easy in those days to hear the scores from elsewhere in the country as it is now, so neither Warner nor the Derbyshire secretary may have immediately known that in the match at Ramsbottom Pope somehow managed to take 5-16 off 12 overs, which represented by a distance the best bowling figures of his league career to date.

As we've seen, there was also some question as to who might captain England that summer. Walter Hammond had been the man in charge for the side's last Test fixture before the war, a draw in August 1939 against the West Indies at the Oval. Hammond himself was clearly the best batsman England had produced since the Jack Hobbs era of 20 years earlier. Yet doubts about his fitness to 'continue to assume the high honour of the England Test Match captaincy', as *The Times* put it, remained. He was perhaps lucky in that respect to enjoy Pelham Warner's unstinting support and friendship. In that elaborately formal age, when even routine business letters tended to open with phrases such as 'Sir, I have the honour to state that consideration has been given to the matter of your application for overdraft facilities at this institution …' and were topped-and-tailed either by the use of precise titles, or merely by surnames, the correspondence between Warner and Hammond was generally of the 'Dear Wally' and 'Yours ever, Plum' variety.

Like Warner, Hammond had spent his early years overseas. His father, a corporal with the Royal Artillery who seems to have been of the opinion that children should be brought up in mild fear of their parents, was posted successively to Hong Kong and Malta. The family returned to England just before the First World War, and Walter, an only child, was sent to boarding school. His father was killed fighting in France in 1918, and his mother seems to have been more concerned with her social status than in the daily welfare of her young son. She handed him over to tutors during the school holidays, starved him of love and on the occasions they did meet beat him regularly. It's surely not stretching psychology too far to conclude that this upbringing turned Hammond into something of a loner and a bully, 'a dreadful little shit' as he admitted years later to his much younger Gloucestershire county colleague Tom Graveney, none of which should in the least detract from a proper acknowledgement of Hammond's obvious skills as a magnificent all-round cricketer.

After 17 years as a professional player, Hammond turned amateur in 1938, which allowed him the curious distinction of leading out the Gentlemen against the Players at Lord's, having done the honours for the Players in an earlier fixture. He counted himself a close friend and in some ways almost a son to Pelham Warner, who clearly believed he had the right note of authority and essentially pragmatic approach to lead England. But even someone as well versed in the nuances of the British class system as Hammond could perhaps mistake widespread respect for his undoubted technical skills for broader social acceptance. Cricket has a way of finding the truth about people, and the evidence suggests that although the incumbent England skipper might look, behave and sound not unlike a proper gentleman, that did not necessarily mean that he would be universally treated as one. Walter Robins, a man whose own personal charm came with a sensitive on-off switch, once referred to him as 'a five-foot-ten scowl', while the Cambridge-educated Basil Allen, Hammond's predecessor as Gloucestershire's captain, was on ground well beyond this when he spoke of his dislike of a 'moody bugger' who took 'no interest in other people's lives unless they happened to be pretty girls'.

The author David Foot quotes an exchange of views between Allen and Pelham Warner during the last pre-war Gentlemen v Players match at Lord's:

'Basil, that Wally Hammond of yours really is a wonderful chap, isn't he?'

'If you want my honest opinion, Plum, I think he's an absolute shit.'

Nonetheless, Hammond would return to lead England when international cricket resumed in May 1945. He was then nearly 42, somewhere between muscular and heavyset, a chain smoker and a martyr to lumbago, with a love life that attracted a certain amount of what passed for tabloid scrutiny in those more reticent times. It should also be noted that Hammond played a total of six matches deemed first-class in 1945, scoring 592 runs in them at an average of 59. It says something for his reputation over the years that some observers gave the opinion that the figures were evidence of his waning powers with the bat. Tom Graveney once told me that 'Wally eventually slowed down a bit, like the rest of us, but if you're talking about having had every shot in the book, and the power to bring them off, I don't doubt that he was by far the greatest of his generation, not excluding Bradman.'

Since even a big name like Hammond would have earned only around £800 (£14,000 today) from playing cricket in his latter days as a professional, it's not surprising that many of his England contemporaries sought to supplement their earnings in any way they could. Hammond himself took a pre-war position at Henlys, the country's biggest distributor of Austin cars, based at their Bristol headquarters, for the then fabulous sum of £1,500 (£27,000) pa. The England skipper had a natural affinity for cars, and frequently used them as an analogy in his pep talks in the dressing room, as in, 'They've got no petrol left in their tank' or 'Let's put our bloody foot down and finish this, shall we?' Displaying a flair for public relations that was rare at the time, Henlys even installed a cardboard cut-out of their celebrity frontman to greet visitors at their city-centre showroom, and green baize was laid on the floor instead of the traditional carpet. Hammond's job was never fully defined in any formal sense, but it essentially called on him to shake hands with potential buyers and take specially favoured customers out to lunch on the firm. One colleague at the dealership remarked of his role there: 'He was never in any sense a grafter. He'd never have landed a sale by sheer persistence. The romantic view was that a deal could be concluded over a good meal and a couple of gins across the road. And because he was Wally Hammond, it sometimes was.'

If only to make ends meet, the professional arrangements of several of Hammond's senior Test colleagues perhaps defied the ideal MCC orthodoxy of the day. There were famous cricketers, whom tens of thousands of spectators paid to admire during the summer months, who variously served in the off-season as manual labourers, valets, tutors, lavatory attendants, shop assistants, local government clerks, bank tellers, municipal gardeners, and, in the young Godfrey Evans's case, a light-heavyweight boxer working the unlicensed Herne Bay Saturday night fight circuit. Many individual cricketers and for that matter cricket clubs turned to wealthy patrons to supplement their incomes. Nottinghamshire, for one, were generously subsidised throughout the war years (or at least up until his death in late 1944) by Sir Julien Cahn, an eccentric Welsh businessman born in 1882 of German-Jewish stock, who made a fortune before the war in the hire-purchase furniture trade. Dark-eyed, with a bushy moustache and bulbous W.C. Fields nose, it was said that Cahn 'lived for cricket and sex' in so far as he made a distinction between the two. One half-admiring guest later wrote that 'the little chap went about in his frock coat and spats like a slightly overdone version of an English gentleman. Correctness in dress was for him almost a religion.'

In time, Cahn installed his own full-scale pitch on the grounds of his stately home at Stanford Hall near Lutterworth in Leicestershire (another county he helped bankroll), where he hosted regular Sunday afternoon matches during the summer months. He was the John Paul Getty Jr of his day. Those lucky enough to come into Cahn's orbit were showered with cash and other perks. Not surprisingly, there was often keen competition among England's top players to catch his eye. Following stumps at Stanford Hall, the players would each be handed an envelope stuffed with crisp £10 notes and then entertained to a lavish dinner followed by a performance in their host's private theatre, complete with a Wurlitzer organ that went up and down on a hydraulic platform in front of the stage. These were far from the only attractions on offer for those who fairly queued up for an invitation to play at Lutterworth to enhance their meagre Test or county wages. Vic Jackson, a New South Wales all-rounder who for some years made his home in England, long remembered a fixture at which, Lady Cahn not being present, Sir Julien was attended by a young nurse who appeared to have been sewn into a flesh-coloured costume that Jackson noted appreciatively 'only accentuated her natural contours'. After dinner that night there was mixed bathing for those who wanted it in the heated outdoor pool, which they shared with Cahn's pair of trained seals, while others preferred to make the better acquaintance of several more nurses who appeared on the scene.

Cahn himself generally turned out to bat in the middle order for his own XI, equipped for the occasion with a pair of inflatable rubber pads which his butler pumped up for him before he left the pavilion. Deliveries were said to 'ping off them like a tennis ball thrown against a stone wall'. The Cambridge and Minor Counties all-rounder Tom MacDonald remembered of the protracted dinner and games that followed one midsummer wartime match at Stanford Hall: 'Everyone dressed up. Cahn, rather oddly, marched up and down in a belted trench coat, jerking his right arm aloft, possibly an allusion to certain continental dignitaries. One big Irish lad who shall remain nameless wiggled around in a tight black shift and a ratty silver-fox fur. He looked like Marlene Dietrich.'

* * *

Walter Hammond may have been unique as a cricketer, but in at least one sense he was also typical of the sort of split personality many English sportsmen, and others, developed during the war years. On the surface, he remained serious, businesslike and a bit remote, dedicated equally to putting his young RAF charges through their paces as to drilling his county and Test colleagues into a well-disciplined fighting unit. This was the dour, unsentimental 'Sqn. Ldr. Hammond', respected and often a little feared by his subordinates. Wars are by definition times of intense nervous strain, and the air of tension that sometimes seemed to follow Hammond about like a dark cloud was one many other Britons, both in and out of uniform, would have recognised as a pervasive part of life.

But set against this there was Hammond's other side, the more convivial, beer-swilling 'Uncle Wally' he revealed to friends and patrons like Julien Cahn and the better-heeled customers at the Austin car dealership – as well as to the young women with whom he could, and did, let himself go in a carefree display of emotion, an uninhibited effusion of irresponsibility, happiness and even of love. Similarly, the war years as a whole undoubtedly produced episodes of high exhilaration, and moments of humour, if only as part of one of those unconscious defence mechanisms that help people cope.

We live in an age when there are ever fewer witnesses to the realities of sporting life – or any other sort of life – in 1945, and are left with caricatures of the men and women involved as a result: a minority of toffs with cut-glass accents who lorded it over the cricket world much as if it were their own personal fiefdom; just below them a few privileged amateurs recruited to lead the various teams based more on their social status than any particular gift, or even feeling, for the game; and further down still the large number of 'useful grunts', as Godfrey Evans called them, who actually did most of the work on the field.

The spectre of the British class system certainly stalked cricket in 1945, but perhaps it wasn't always strictly a case of a few cruel and effete snobs quaffing pink gin and oppressing the proletariat. Men like Julien Cahn and Walter Hammond had many sides to their characters. At times, Hammond, the old-school disciplinarian, displayed a love of mischief of the sort readily available after hours at Stanford Hall. Cahn, the bohemian comic seemingly plucked direct from the stage of the Edwardian music-hall, was also the self-denying patriot who eventually turned his country seat over for use as a rehabilitation centre for wounded soldiers, the same role it performs today. The 32-year-old soldier and former coffee trader Brian Johnston was another of those to embody this duality of high purpose and low entertainment so prominent in war. The seemingly charmed life of 'Johnners', the debonair Old Etonian whose latter-day cricket commentary famously dwelt on matters such as the number and variety of cakes to be found in the box, came to an abrupt halt that spring of 1945 when his unit of the Grenadier Guards took part in the bloody final push into Germany. Along the way, Major Johnston was one of those to personally liberate a concentration camp at Zeven, located on the banks of the Oste river between Bremen and Hamburg. War-hardened British squaddies had been 'all-too literally ill at the sight', Johnston later reported. The essential polarity of his approach to life surfaced again just five days later, when he wrote an urgent letter home to his mother: 'Could you send a parcel sometime? Containing: Wicket-keeping gloves, three cricket shirts, three pairs white socks, cravat … etc.'

Although Pelham Warner often struggled to locate 11 suitable candidates to put into the field to represent England that summer, and even then never quite resolved the side's glaring shortage of a pair of truly fast bowlers, within only a few years he and his successors in office would come to be almost spoilt for choice in that and other areas of the game. Like a stagnant pond, motionless to the naked eye, English youth cricket was teeming with furious activity that first post-war season. In the small mining town of Maltby, near Rotherham, a 14-year-old school leaver then answering to Frederick Trueman was already terrorising local club batsmen twice his age, while his fellow Yorkshireman Jim Laker, after being, as the jargon of the day had it, buggered about by the army, eventually landed a desk job at the War Office in Whitehall and decided to join the staff at Surrey as a result. On his second day at the Oval, Laker would make the acquaintance of a notably self-confident young colt named Tony Lock, his 'spin twin' for the next 13 years.

The somewhat plump but precociously gifted 12-year-old Colin Cowdrey was meanwhile honing his skills at Alf Gover's cricket school in Wandsworth, and as it turned out was only five years away from the start of a first-class career that saw him become the first player to win 100 Test caps for his country, scoring over 42,000 runs along the way. A slightly older boy named Peter May was already setting records at Charterhouse school near Godalming, whose magazine for June 1945 notes: 'There are high hopes abroad for this prodigy who appears to the obvious appreciation of the multitudes, and for whom great things may lie ahead.' For his part, 18-year-old 2nd Lt. Tom Graveney, recently posted to Egypt, was, he later confessed, 'doing bugger all for the army' in its mopping-up operations against the Axis powers, but 'having the time of my life playing nonstop cricket around Cairo', where he also came to disabuse himself of any hopes of becoming a true all-rounder. 'I dropped bowling because it was too bloody hot overseas. For sheer slog, running in twenty or thirty yards every couple of minutes in that climate couldn't be beaten. As far as I was concerned, the Other Ranks could do the bowling.'

Back in England that summer, a cricket-mad ten-year-old was being 'chafed' – or bullied, as we might call it today – for the offence of having been born in Italy, a stigma he countered by not only breaking batting records at his Beaconsfield prep school but by proving himself equally adept at rackets, golf, tennis, rugby and just about every other activity involving a moving ball. The young all-rounder grew up to become the successful insurance broker, qualified pilot, male model, author, broadcaster, public relations tycoon, greyhound owner, would-be Tory MP and future England Test captain, Ted Dexter.

* * *

'The ship is without a rudder,' the Australian prime minister 'Honest John' Curtin observed sadly, as he followed his nation's attempts to muster a full-strength representative cricket side to play England in 1945. Both a sports lover and a confirmed anglophile, Curtin had been in the pavilion at Lord's in late May 1944 to watch a hurriedly assembled XI of his country's airmen play The Rest under Walter Hammond, a game 'the colonials', as *The Times* called them, thanks largely to a century by their opening bat Jim Workman, won by one wicket. 'No two teams could have risen to the occasion more nobly,' the paper added. Curtin himself, who had overcome a vision disorder to play grade cricket in and around his home town of Melbourne, remarked at a reception at London's Café Royal that week: 'Lord's is to Australia what it is to this country,' adding, 'Our common glorious sport is the tie that binds ... Australia is a British land and seven million Australians are seven million Britishers,' a sentiment that 'raised the roof of the old building [in a] thunder of applause that for a time made the unpleasantness and sacrifice of war seem far distant.'

But just a year later, the available pool of Australian cricket talent, while it included Keith Miller and several other RAAF airmen, was a far cry from the muscular, unified force Curtin had hoped to see put in the field. Largely drawn from the hard-pressed ranks of the recently freed POWs and other recuperating combat veterans billeted in the seafront Cumberland Hotel in Eastbourne, it indeed lacked its 'rudder', the man Curtin praised as the 'modern titan' who rather paradoxically believed that cricket was a matter of 'independence of effort – every man for himself – but all in it together for the team'. The titan in question, Don Bradman, was 36 that spring, and as we've seen in neither good physical nor financial health. He had commented of the mounting losses among the comrades with whom he had played pre-war cricket, 'It seems so unfair, somehow' – an expression of that phenomenon commonplace among those who came through the conflict relatively unscathed: survivors' guilt.

On 2 June 1945, the same day on which the RAAF side under the heavyset New South Wales seamer Mick Roper took on Cyril Washbrook's RAF at the Wagon Works ground in Gloucester, Bradman was 10,000 miles away dealing with the fallout from the crash of the stockbroking firm he co-directed with his partner Harry Hodgetts. The subsequent investigation led to a five-year prison term for Hodgetts and came as an obvious blow to Bradman's own reputation for probity, which arguably he never quite recovered. As a result, Australia's pre-eminent sporting hero would have to start his business again from scratch. To his credit, Bradman worked long hours in an attempt to recover both his clients' losses, and perhaps more importantly the wider public's trust, but clearly a long uphill battle lay ahead. It was increasingly obvious that he would not be playing any competitive cricket, overseas or anywhere else, that summer of 1945.

In Bradman's absence, the Australian team in England would be led by 31-year-old Lindsay Hassett of Victoria. A cartoonist's delight with his prominent nose and ears, jockey-like stature and Buster Keaton face (with a matching talent for deadpan comedy), he was also an accomplished batsman and a warrior who had distinguished himself fighting with the Australian Imperial Force in the Pacific. Hassett by then had played four matches for his country, with a top score of 56 against England at Lord's in June 1938, finishing with an eventual Test batting average of nearly 47 and one of 58 in first-class cricket as a whole. He was ferociously competitive and, as such people often are, quite insecure, a fact he hid behind his pronounced gift for puckish humour. Other than his liking of a drink, Hassett was also moderate in his habits, highly organised, self-disciplined and modest. When approached, he readily agreed to lead his fellow servicemen on what became a year-long tour of first Britain and then the Indian subcontinent for a personal fee of Aus15s (about £8 in our money) for each day in the field.

So perhaps the Australian cricketers had a rudder after all, even if they still had their issues elsewhere in the ship. As we've seen, at least two members of their side had only recently returned from long-term captivity. The then 25-year-old Flt. Lt. Keith Carmody of New South Wales had been flying a Bristol Beaufighter while serving with the RAAF's 455 Squadron on a reconnaissance mission in June 1944 when he was shot down over the coast of Holland. That was the last any of Carmody's comrades had heard of him until ten months later, when the news came through that against the odds he had survived not only the crash but an operation carried out without anaesthetic in a German field hospital and a subsequent stretch at the Stalag Luft III camp, later of *The Great Escape* fame, in Lower Silesia. On release, Carmody spoke feelingly about the misery and self-pity that had sometimes threatened to engulf him while in custody, but also of his determination to live life to the full, not least by playing cricket, now he was free again.

Carmody's brother-in-arms, 34-year-old Warrant Officer Graham Williams, had made his debut as a seamer for South Australia as far back as the 1932/33 Australian season, playing for his state against Douglas Jardine's notorious 'bodyline' team in a match at Adelaide where he took five wickets. Williams was a large-boned man with piercing dark eyes, receding hair and slightly blubbery lips. As he demonstrated on his release after four years' imprisonment, he was also impressively patient, even-tempered and unflappable. 'Here I am. Never felt better', he announced in a telegram sent home to his parents in Adelaide on 20 April. Williams's father Spen said that the cable was the first intimation he had had that his son was still alive, let alone at liberty again. 'I imagine he will be in England resting for a time but knowing him keen to knock up a game of cricket,' Mr Williams added. That all proved true enough, even if it was to downplay the matter of his son's overall state of health after his years of confinement in what the *South Australian News* called delicately the 'rather cramped' conditions of three successive German POW camps. The inmates in these had apparently witnessed 'regrettable lapses amongst the guards, [which] had included instances of beatings and general cruelty that seemed to belong to some infernal, earlier time' – and certainly one far removed from the arcadian world of an English summer day's cricket.

There were several other members of the Australian team-in-waiting for whom the war had been a matter not just of tedium and discomfort, and separation from loved ones, but of real physical peril. Reg Ellis, the 27-year-old South Australian left-arm spinner, had flown 12 wartime sorties over occupied Europe at the controls of an Avro Lancaster, twice landing wheels up after being hit by ground fire. While stationed in England he had struck up a particular rapport with Keith Miller. It was in some ways an unlikely friendship. The soft-spoken Ellis was a man of moderate habits who as a rule liked to be tucked up in bed early with a good book. But he occasionally overcame these defects in order to enjoy a night out with his fellow RAAF pilot in the west end of London. As always with Miller, there were both exhilarating and challenging aspects involved. 'Keith was one of those guys who could stay up until dawn, swallow a cup of tea and a couple of aspirin, and then walk out to play cricket in front of 20,000 people,' Ellis remembered. 'I preferred the quiet life.' Even so, he was impressed by the sheer gusto of the man he called a human typhoon, and particularly by his easy-come, easy-go approach to money. 'I saw him drop £250 at the races one afternoon, then scoop every penny back that night playing roulette, and you could never tell from his expression the difference between the two. Keith just laughed his way through the wins, and kept smiling during the losses.'

Their Services' 27-year-old teammate Ross Stanford, of South Australia, actually saw his time as an RAAF flight lieutenant flying a total of 47 low-level raids, latterly with the 617 'Dambuster' squadron - winning the DFC along the way – as a positive asset to his cricket career. 'If it hadn't been for the war, I would never have been in England,' he later rationalised of his experience in 1945. 'I would never have played on those famous English grounds, and never have met blokes like Wally Hammond, Len Hutton, Cyril Washbrook and quite a few others.' With those same factors in mind, 29-year-old Stan Sismey, a wicketkeeper-batsman from New South Wales, rarely if ever spoke of his experience of co-piloting an RAAF flying boat when in 1942 it had been attacked by fighters of the Vichy French Air Force and forced down into the Mediterranean, where he was rescued unconscious after eight hours in the sea. Instead, he preferred to dwell on the 'absolute joy and privilege' of playing cricket in England during his long convalescence. Despite carrying an estimated two pounds of assorted shrapnel in his back as a result of the enemy action, Sismey proved not only agile behind the stumps but, as a squadron leader, also acted as the nominal commanding officer of the Australian Services, while allowing Hassett to lead the side in the field. Such distinctions may seem quaint to us today, but to a tight-knit group like the Australians, they were held in almost spiritual reverence, the emblems of a shared ordeal and sacrifice. Like their English counterparts, the players often referred to each other both on and off the field by their military title, although as a sign of special friendship these could be substituted for the use not of first names but of matey abbreviations or nicknames – 'Nugget', 'Tiny', 'Peppy', though Hassett was always 'Skipper' – a natural deference to rank that might be hard to replicate in these egalitarian times.

Australian Test cricket had also lost one of its finest in June 1942, when Pilot Officer Ross Gregory of Victoria died while on air operations near the town of Gaffargaon in present-day Bangladesh. A diminutive but assertive character, Gregory brought a similar directness to his batting. Everything that could be hit, he hit hard and straight. In 1936/37 he had played two Tests against England, scoring 23 and a run-out 50 in the first, and 80 in his only innings in the second, against a visiting side that included both Ken Farnes and Hedley Verity in its bowling attack. Early in 1942, Gregory had written to his family that in the event of his loss they should 'take a certain amount of comfort from the knowledge that I went down doing my duty'. He was 26 at the time of his death.

Although 'not a particularly religious cove', before taking the field each day Lindsay Hassett led his Australian teammates in prayer, 'thanking the Almighty for our players who had made a safe return', and commending to Him the names of those, like Gregory, who hadn't. Stan Sismey later remembered that everyone had been encouraged to contribute a brief word of personal experience, although when the time came some of the team, like Keith Miller, 'seemed content to observe the moment in silence, rather than seize the chance to participate'. It is not thought that Walter Hammond instituted a similar practice in the England dressing room, although he did sometimes ask his teammates to reflect on such weighty thoughts as 'He who conquers self is the greatest victor,' or the line from Galatians, 'But let each one prove his own work, and then shall he have rejoicing in himself alone, and not in another.' Quite what he meant by these aphorisms was one of the enduring mysteries of the England camp. 'Wally was always a deep bugger,' Bill Edrich observed many years later.

At other times, upstairs in the amateurs' dressing room, Hammond adopted his habitual pose with one thumb hooked in his plum-coloured waistcoat pocket, and explained how the England side he inherited might be only modestly gifted, but that the Aussies were 'scobs', or dross, at best, with 'little Lindsay' their only player of recognised class. Perhaps it was his way of motivating both himself and his men, reminding them that they had a solemn duty to restore some measure of the natural order of things by trouncing their callow if plucky colonial opponents.

It was true that, on paper at least, Hammond's team held the advantage. The visitors did not immediately inspire confidence, consisting as they did of a mixed bag of untried club cricketers and returning POWs who could be seen practising at the Saffrons in a mismatched variety of army khaki uniforms and black boots, although, unlike their modern counterparts, they were at least unlikely to feel jaded almost before the season began thanks to the demands of a non-stop touring schedule. There was no Bradman; and men like Ray Lindwall and the teenaged Neil Harvey were still a year or two away from taking their place in the side fittingly known as The Invincibles. But set against that, Keith Miller always thought that same lack of experience might have been to the visitors' advantage. None of Bradman's innate conservatism appeared to have rubbed off on Hassett, and the truth was that 'with absolutely nothing to lose, we could afford to go out and swing the bat'. The tourists by definition also spent more time in each other's company than the home team and, as often happens, proved to be the more cohesive unit of the two. 'I told the buggers that whatever else happened they were there to play together as a team,' Hassett remarked, adding the unarguable truth that, 'Being a great genius means nothing unless you're doing it in the service of the side. You don't get 30,000 people watching some prima donna hitting the ball beautifully in the nets. They want to see him do it in the context of the match.'

On 28 April 1945, a side billed as Australian Imperial Forces (AIF) opened their tour with a one-day game at Eastbourne against nearby Bexhill. All the evidence suggests it was a somewhat ramshackle affair. Hassett led the visitors, as they were officially listed, even though they were playing on their de facto home ground, which besides him included four other men with state experience, but as yet no Miller, Sismey, Stanford, Williams or Ellis. For their part, none of the Bexhill XI would go on to trouble the first-class cricket world. The sun had actually appeared from time to time earlier that week, and on the Saturday morning of the 28th, with an overflow crowd of 4,000 on hand, the Saffrons had been lovingly prepared for the occasion by a team of volunteers who had been hard at work erecting a huge marquee at the sea end, with plates of brightly coloured cakes and jugs of lemonade laid out on two long trestle tables said to have been groaning under the strain. There was also a well-stocked beer tent, and a variety of patriotic flags and bunting flapping from the front of the hurriedly erected wooden stand at the Larkins Road side. Two groundsmen and a boy had meticulously rolled the pitch, which on the face of it looked good for thousands of runs.

Unfortunately, it didn't just rain for most of the day. Cricketers and spectators alike had a mini pop-up tropical storm to deal with, and the same crew of volunteers had to hurriedly tear down the marquee again as it strained at its moorings and remove its contents as best they could to the relative safety of the ground's timbered pavilion. 'For the opening match of the season wintry conditions prevailed,' *Wisden* was left to record. 'Besides two falls of snow, lightning, heavy thunder, hail and sleet all held up the play, which was reduced to three hours.' Batting first, the AIF scored 165/3 in 36 overs, and Bexhill then subsided to 39/9 before providentially for them the heavens opened again for the day's climactic downpour, which concluded proceedings as a draw. It had not snowed like that, they said, during 50 years of local Sussex club or county cricket.

The weather aside, it was a poignant scene. Representative cricket was back. But few of those braving the storm at the Saffrons had ever experienced the game quite like this – some of the visitors' team looked painfully frail, most moved sluggishly in the field, and all of them were chilled to the bone thanks to a delay in receiving their issue of sweaters. Hassett looked around at his side and saw 'eleven pale and tired-looking men trying their best to be cheerful for the crowd's sake'. It was austerity cricket played in mid-winter conditions that few of the Australians could have encountered before. Yet it was also now that Hassett wrote of his pride in witnessing men 'doing their utmost to rise above their circumstances in the interests of team spirit and, more than that, of cricket as an ideal of peace'. The Australian captain knew that the actual result on the field was only one part of a bigger mission, to 'help bring a sense of normal life back to a people who so desperately craved it'.

Meanwhile, Pelham Warner and his colleagues at Lord's had continued in their efforts to arrange a series of international sporting fixtures with none of the benefits of our modern communications technology at their disposal. After a month-long exchange of letters on the subject with Stewart 'Billy' Griffith at his officers' mess at RAF Keevil in Wiltshire, Warner wrote on 23 April:

> Dear Billy,
> Thank you for your most recent note. I must apologise most sincerely to you as I have made a mistake. The match I want you to play in is not the one on 30th June, South of

> England v. RAAF, but on Saturday, 14th July for England v. Australia. I do hope you will be able to manage this 'Test Match' as I think it should be a very good game.
>
> I am most awfully sorry I made the mistake, but I am very busy indeed getting up various teams and I find that occasionally I do slip up; unfortunately you were a victim of one of my errors.
>
> Yours sincerely,
>
> Plum.

As seen by the inverted commas, there was still some question of whether or not the matches with Australia would indeed be designated as official Tests. Elsewhere in Warner's correspondence that spring, he suggested that the games might go by the collective name of a 'Representative' or 'Allied' or 'Dominion' series. At that stage, no one in authority presumed to use the word 'Victory' Tests. To have done so might have seemed to tempt fate at a time when Hitler was still alive if not well, directing phantom armies from his bunker 30 feet below the garden of the Reich Chancellery in Berlin, and Allied troops were locked in hand-to-hand combat with Japanese forces 6,000 miles away on the island of Okinawa. Although 'the broad lines of success were plain to see in Europe, it [was] still far too soon to conclude more than that', Warner wrote that same St George's Day. So, when the deputy secretary of MCC cabled his opposite number on the Australian board of control in Melbourne later that week, he did so only to express his relief that, at long last, 'proper cricket' was back.

4.
A Match for the Ages

THE 158th annual general meeting of MCC took place at Lord's on 2 May 1945, the day on which the Soviet Union announced the fall of Berlin, and the remaining Axis troops in Italy gave up the fight. For more than a year and a half, Italy had been ruled over by two puppet regimes, the king – or 'Lieutenant General of the Realm', as he came to style himself – in the south, the Germans with Mussolini's fitful help in the north. Mussolini himself had been summarily executed by pro-Communist partisans on 28 April, his body and that of his mistress hung from their heels for the benefit of an enraged mob in central Milan. Hitler followed just two days later, pausing only to dictate a familiar spew of anti-Semitism as his last Will and Testament, and to make an honest woman of his own long-standing mistress, conforming to his essential petty bourgeois sensibility to the end.

None of these quite significant events troubled the proceedings at Lord's, whose minutes noted only: 'The President proposed and the Treasurer seconded the adoption of the report and accounts, which were passed without dissension. In his address to one of the most largely attended meetings of the war, the President[4] complimented the staff, both inside and out, upon the way in which they had carried on in a rather difficult time ... Canon F.H.

---

4 Eighty-three-year-old Stanley Christopherson, who had appeared alongside W.G. Grace in a single Test for England, against Australia at Lord's in July 1884. Christopherson and his nine brothers all played competitive cricket in Kent, for several years operating as a team on Blackheath with their father making up the eleventh member.

Gillingham[5] proposed a vote of thanks for the efficiency with which the authorities at Lord's contrived to produce interesting cricket for the duration. He praised the amateurs and professionals who took part for giving up a great deal of time to play and for overcoming certain travelling difficulties to do so.'

It would be hard to beat the MCC minutes as an example of old-fashioned British grace under pressure – for keeping calm and carrying on – or, for that matter, the club's diligence in hastening to preserve the essential status quo of pre-war English cricket. Despite all the talk from Sir Stanley Jackson's committee, there would be no vulgar, football-like knockout competition in 1945; nor in future would there be two- as opposed to three-day county matches, or first-class cricket on a Sunday, nor any adjustment either to the northern leagues or to the game's hallowed class divide. At the end of the proceedings on 2 May, Col. Rait Kerr, the club secretary, noted merely:

> The meeting was deemed special, and certain alterations of a purely administrative nature were made in the existing rules of the MCC. The Committee were given discretion to elect, as special cases, a certain number of candidates who had been entered and subsequently became incapacitated by enemy action from qualifying in the ordinary way as playing members. A resolution to this same effect was passed and put into operation in 1919 at the end of the last war.

5 Rev. Frank Gillingham (1875–1953) played 210 first-class matches as an amateur for Essex. As well as being appointed chaplain to King George V, he would go on to become the BBC's first ball-by-ball radio commentator, in a match his county played against the touring New Zealanders at Leyton in May 1927. According to his Essex colleague T.N. Pearce, Gillingham got the job because he was 'a terrific preacher' who was 'as comfortable in a packed cathedral as in the meanest shack provided for the press in those days'. Instead of talking exclusively about the cricket, the reverend's inaugural broadcast 'dwelled upon matters such as the number and species of passing birds, and the variety of interesting hats to be seen in the ladies' stand', surely a harbinger of today's commentary. It's said that Gillingham continued to provide occasional match reports until he infuriated Lord Reith, the BBC's overlord and a stickler for a complete absence of anything commercial, when he once filled in time during a rain delay at the Oval by reading out the slogans of the advertising boards around the ground.

After that it remained only to consider the matters of MCC's 'existing policy to insure the pavilion and other parts against hostile intent', to finalise arrangements for a Grand Spring Dinner to be held on the premises of the Reform Club, as well as to conclude the draw for the annual real tennis tournament, and finally to consider the matter of expanding the facilities of the Lord's bakery, among other housekeeping items. Taken as a whole, this was probably not at all life in England as the late German Führer must have imagined it.

Cambridge University at least got on the field at Fenner's for a few damp hours that week to play a series of single-innings games with relatively unprepossessing sides ranging from The Trundlers to a local borough police XI. They had better luck there than at Lord's, where rain washed out a charity match scheduled for 5 May, while at Uxbridge the RAF similarly abandoned any thoughts of playing the British Empire XI, with the *Daily Herald* reporting on the 'Dickensian gloom' of a waterlogged field, 'haunted by a few dispirited-looking souls huddled together for warmth' under the tree at the Golf Course end. More than 12 inches of rain fell that week in south-east England, nearly a third of the normal total for a year.

The unreal atmosphere that spring included extraordinary scenes in central London, where the *Daily Express* mounted an exhibition of photographs of recently liberated concentration camps in an improvised gallery set up under a sign saying 'Seeing Is Believing' in a corner of Trafalgar Square. Despite the weather, British men and women queued up each day in the tens of thousands to look in stunned silence at the images of emaciated survivors staring back at them, their eyes sunk so deep they looked blind, and at the unimaginable horrors of the gas chambers. Visitors to the exhibition were interviewed on their way out. 'After seeing this I feel we should shoot every last German,' one well-heeled woman remarked. Another spoke of her 'bodily revulsion' at the sight. 'I don't think we could ever be hard enough on the Nazis. Primitive savages would not behave as they did.'

* * *

A less exclusive body, but perhaps one of even greater stature, than MCC met at Downing Street that week. For the first time in a decade, the British Cabinet again considered the matter of holding a general election. As we've seen, much of the early discussion centred more on the fine detail of the costs than on the great philosophical issues that divided the parties. In the home secretary Herbert Morrison's nuanced phrase: 'After carefully considering the views put to me, I am personally not convinced that the 25 per cent increase in prospective members' campaign expenses previously suggested would not be justified in present circumstances for the next General Election, and subsequent by-elections up to any future General Election, [but] it is clear that any such adjustment might be met with not insignificant opposition from certain quarters of the House.'

Loosely translated, this meant that parliamentary candidates should be allowed to spend a bit more on their campaigns, but there were limits. After Morrison had finished his oration, the members of the Cabinet began slapping their palms on the table in rhythm. Apparently they were saluting the voice of reason. In May 1945, there was the side of government that dealt with the great issues of settling the European peace, and then there was the necessary triviality and tedium of worrying about finding the money to keep the nation's lights on. Later that week, the Cabinet, much like Stanley Jackson's MCC committee before it, discussed possible reforms to the existing electoral procedures. The results were similarly non-conclusive.

'The War Cabinet … now had before it, in addition to W.P. (45) 215, the Memorandum by the Home Secretary reporting the results of his consultations; and the Memorandum by the Secretary of State for Scotland on defects in the electoral register. These were discussed, before the Cabinet turned to a preliminary examination of the proposals in Sections I (c)(i) to (iv) of W.P. (45) 215 and W.P. (45) 278 [in] regard to actual voting arrangements, and the distribution of appropriate application forms under the scheme of postal voting for the Forces. No decisions were reached.'

While the vast and often mysterious workings of the central government, as inscrutable in their way as those of any oriental sultanate, continued to debate the particulars of the 1945 general election, the Australian cricketers at least managed to get on the park for a one-day match against the Public School Wanderers at Dulwich. The word 'school' seems to have been broadly applied in this case, because the home side included players such as 25-year-old David Knight, late of Cambridge University, and the Aussies' own leg-spinner Jack Pettiford, a veteran of Sydney club cricket between the wars, as well as two senior citizens who had been hurriedly pressed into service to make up the numbers from the adjacent Crown Green bowls club tournament. The visitors won by ten wickets.

Lindsay Hassett's team faced more serious opposition later that week in the course of a single-innings game against the British Empire side at Lord's. The Empire were all out for 118, thanks largely to a return of 8-21 by Reg Ellis, the South Australian left-armer who had been at the controls of an RAAF Avro Lancaster dodging enemy flak just a fortnight earlier. Back in the players' dining room, he found it mildly amusing when his lunchtime bowl of vegetable soup with dark, crusty bread was served to him by a German prisoner of war. Ellis's fellow pilot Keith Miller hit an even-time 50, in an innings full of shots that stirred memories of Gilbert Jessop or Albert Trott among the more seasoned spectators, then airily clipped a straight ball from the leg-spinner Bertie Clarke of Northants and the West Indies down long leg's throat.

Clarke wasn't far behind Miller himself as one of the game's characters. Born in 1918 in Barbados, he had settled in England in order to study at Guy's Hospital, and eventually to practise as a rural Northamptonshire GP. Clarke was a widely respected member of the community, exuding an enjoyment of life and an unshakeable optimism that communicated itself to his patients, but problems lay ahead. *The Times* reported that after the war he had been 'forced to accept the hospitality of the Crown for three years' due to his illegal termination of a pregnancy. Putting this setback behind him, Clarke went on to win the OBE for services to charity, and was still playing competitive league cricket well into his sixties, finishing his career with an appearance for the Old World XI against Old England at the Oval in September 1983.

The Australians won their match against the Empire by six wickets, to complete what Pelham Warner called a 'sun-blessed occasion adorned by Flying Officer Miller, with many strokes previously considered foreign to the batting manual', and of which *Wisden* more prosaically said: 'On a glorious summer day 12,250 paid at the gates, the proceeds going to charity.'

In the midst of this great events were being glimpsed in miniature, almost as if people were looking through the pinhole of a souvenir scenic charm depicting some tremendous national gala. Late on the Monday evening of 7 May, Miller was on a crowded train travelling between London's Liverpool Street station and the rural halt of Massingham, when 'I looked out past a row of houses by the track and saw these streams of lavatory paper come cascading down from people's windows. Unusual, to say the least … When I got back to base the guard on duty signed me in and did all the paperwork, and after that I opened the door to walk over to the mess. And it was only when I was on my way out that the guy looked at me steadily for a moment and allowed himself a half smile. "You haven't heard, have you, mate?" he asked. "Heard what?" "It's all over, son," he said. The jerries had finally surrendered. And that's how I found out we'd won the bloody war, not from some big speech at Buckingham Palace but by seeing toilet rolls flying out of windows in the Norfolk countryside, and some bloke muttering a few words to me out of the corner of his mouth in his little wooden guardhouse.'

The following day, the 8th, not only did Miller manage to subvert his commanding officer's standing orders about teetotal regulations, but 'personally organised a shuttle service to extract suitable supplies from a wine merchant I knew in King's Lynn'. A hundred miles away in London there was a solemn thanksgiving service that morning in St Paul's, followed by a series of more ad hoc celebrations that lasted far into the warm spring night both in the city's streets and pubs. As a snapshot of the occasion, on one level there was the 45-year-old actor, singer, writer and acknowledged master of quilted theatrical farce Noël Coward, who reflected in his diary: 'A wonderful day from every point of view. Went wandering through the crowds in the hot sunshine. Everyone was good-humoured and cheerful. In the afternoon, Winston made a magnificent speech, simple and without boastfulness, but full of deep pride … I suppose this is the greatest day in our history.' In contrast, there was the experience of the teenaged Harold Pinter, whose own line of cryptically mysterious drama imbued with hidden menace would in time come to eclipse the Coward school of neatly turned drawing-room wordplay. Pinter (then, and later, a serious cricket buff) once told me that he had become 'possibly overexcited' by the collective euphoria of the crowds pressing against the front railings of Buckingham Palace for a glimpse of the royal family, and in his emotion had pinched the 'very inviting' bottom of the young woman standing in front of him. 'At that her soldier boyfriend turned around and knocked me out cold,' the future Nobel Laureate recalled.

One way or another, it was a heady moment in Britain's island story. Traditionally minded historians view the events of 8 May 1945 as a glorious moment of vindication for the values of individual liberty, freedom of speech and the sovereignty of nations. Revisionists argue that the celebrations echoing out over both the capital and much of the rest of the country were merely the expression of a last communal hurrah before the fears that Britain was falling ever further behind other countries, if not into perpetual decline in absolute terms, that became a consensus in the years ahead.

Leaving aside any notions of geopolitics, or of Britain's recurring cycle of reform and regression, there was a more immediate result of the collapse of the Third Reich in terms of its practical implications for the nation's way of life. As Norman Preston reported in *Wisden*:

> When VE Day came on May 8, the existing [fixture] arrangements grew like a snowball. The three games at Lord's between England and Australia were extended to three days each, and the British Inter-Services Committee staged two more representative matches in the provinces at Sheffield and Manchester. At no time [*sic*] was there any suggestion that the games should count in the regular Test series, and no doubt this decision went a long way towards making the cricket so agreeable. In fact, all five games were contested by each side in a spirit of friendship and goodwill, which I, among many, would like to see continued when the real Tests come round again.

William Shakespeare, in his role as secretary of the Services (War Emergency) Cricket Council, wrote to Pelham Warner from his RAF station in Cambridgeshire on VE Day itself, for once provoking a note of mild rebuke in reply.

> Dear Sir Pelham:
> I understand that with the return of repatriated prisoners of war the New Zealand Army and Air Force will have a reasonably strong side, and in the interests of Commonwealth relations I feel that we should stage an RAF v N.Z. Forces XI match during the season.
>
> With respect to the names of the side for the 'Test Match' with Australia at Sheffield, I think we might have our first selection meeting on June 9th when we visit Lord's for the match against British Empire XI. We could pick the captain then, and arrange to hold a further meeting or meetings for the final selection of the side early the following week … If you think that the 9th is a bit late, or

> you have any other views on the matter, perhaps you would let me know ...

Warner did let him know. In a letter by return post touching not so much on the England players' technical merits but on their record of service over the previous five years, he wrote:

> Dear Shakespeare,
> I will mention the question of a match between the R.A.F. and New Zealand Forces to some of the Committee here and will let you know within a few days, I hope.
>
> With regard to the names for the match at Sheffield, I really would rather not be personally on the selection panel. I am very busy here and further I think that it would be best if a civilian did not come into it. I can tell you this, however, that I enquired of the Derbyshire secretary about Pope, Copson, etc., and he wrote and told me that Pope had been first in the Home Guard and then in the Army; he was invalided out with an accident to his knee while he was doing a course and is now working with some firm. Copson has been in munitions since the beginning of war. [The all-rounder Stan] Worthington served abroad, Gibraltar and other places. I merely give this to you for your information.
>
> I hope you are flourishing, and shall be looking forward to seeing you at Lord's on June 9th. But again, please do not urge me to be on that selection committee.
>
> Yours truly,
> P. F. Warner.

Warner didn't exaggerate when he emphasised to Shakespeare how stretched he was just then. By the middle of May 1945, MCC's septuagenarian deputy secretary spent much of his time corresponding with the officials of the 17 English and Welsh first-class counties, as well as the commanding officers of various far-flung military units around Britain and overseas to enquire into the availability of their personnel to play cricket. Then there were the questions, which also occupied Shakespeare himself, of the teams' overnight accommodations, transportation and living expenses to be considered, advertising notices to be sent out, day staff to be briefed, pitches to be properly prepared and facilities on the grounds themselves to be upgraded.

At Lord's, many of the internal fixtures and fittings had gone into storage in September 1939, leaving the already harried Warner and his small staff to scour London for accessories such as 'shaving mirrors, wash-bowls, adequate cutlery, etc'. Perhaps it's no wonder that he declined Shakespeare's invitation to join him on the selection committee for the Sheffield match, or that he confided that month to Billy Griffith, 'I increasingly find myself working as a sort of glorified housemaid, or, on second thoughts, not even a particularly glorified one. Most domestic staff would have the edge on me in terms of gratitude.' There was the side of cricket administration that involved highly qualified and self-sacrificing individuals going about their business to the best of their abilities, and then there was the triviality and bureaucratic wasteland that characterised so much of their actual daily routine, where people talked about restoring a vital and much-cherished national institution after the dislocation of a global war, but actually spent their time worrying about matters like catering arrangements and train timetables, or the nuances of a 'Test', as opposed to a mere 'representative' cricket match.

By the second week in May, Warner was faced with the prospect of finalising arrangements for the first of the season's international fixtures scheduled to start in just over a week's time. Even as the VE Day confetti was being swept up from the streets of London, he still didn't know the names of the players in the England team, nor for that matter how long the match itself might last. He wrote to Billy Griffith again on 10 May:

> Dear Billy,
> It is now possible that the game, England v Australia, fixed for 19th and 21st of this month will be extended to 3 days, i.e. 19th and 21st and 22nd May. I had originally asked Evans to keep wicket but now he writes to say that there is some doubt of his being able to get leave, but will let me know on Monday next.
>
> I wonder if you would be very kind and hold yourself available to play for England on these days if Evans cannot manage it? I hope you won't mind this request. Can you reply by telegram here, just saying 'available if wanted' and I will let you know definitely on Monday or Tuesday next week at latest?
>
> Yours ever,
> Plum.

Griffith did make himself available as Warner asked, and in the event played in all five of the summer's international matches. After his sobering experience with the downed Luftwaffe pilot in Ossett, Godfrey Evans had spent most of the following four years being 'arsed about' by the army, he later remarked, migrating between a series of training camps in the north of England and Scotland until the actual eve of victory in Europe. At that point in the war's fortunes he learnt that he was being posted overseas for the first time as part of the 255 Car Company, RASC, initially based at Versailles and subsequently at Herx, near Frankfurt. After an exchange of telegrams with Pelham Warner – 'Regret required [to] drive army postal delivery van around Paris area' – to which Warner graciously replied, 'Your day to represent England will most certainly come soon', the matter was left there. Much to Evans's chagrin, he then did 'literally fuck all' in the summer of 1945, except to 'drink a lot of cheap French wine and deliver the squaddies' mail to them'. The lack of available 'crumpet' did little to improve the young wicketkeeper's morale, and 50 years later he could still remember his sense of frustration at being 'stuck behind the wheel of a jeep, instead of doing something useful for my country at Lord's'.

Warner saw the job of staging a series of top-level international matches only days after Germany's defeat as a double challenge. 'We're really answering to two audiences,' he told his friend Griffith. 'We're doing it for the traditional cricket man, but we're also doing it for a wider cause, too, at the same time.' By that Warner seems to have meant that even then he could appreciate that cricket was an important piece of a bigger jigsaw, at once a tangible and a symbolic sign that something resembling normal life might be returning. Even now, he wanted a fresh coat of paint applied to some of the stands at Lord's, 'as we are on parade to the world next week'. An outside firm was hurriedly called in, and they told him that they could do as he wished, but that paint was in short supply and cost a great deal of money. Warner asked how much, and the foreman involved came out with 'a hair-raising figure. I had to haggle, and we reached an agreement.'

Unfortunately, it was also another of those weeks that had made William Shakespeare wonder how the English could ever have come up with a summer sport with a minimum requirement of at least halfway dry weather. VE Day itself had been bright and dry, but conditions soon deteriorated. It rained torrentially at Northampton on 12 May, where the county side took on one representing the RAF. Squelching out to bat when play finally got underway after lunch, Bill Edrich made up for lost time by hitting 28 in three overs at the crease, and his 26-year-old teammate Percy MacKenzie added an unbeaten 103 at a relatively sedate run-a-minute. MacKenzie had played 22 pre-war matches as a young all-rounder for Hampshire, but perhaps his real distinction whilst in the RAF's distinctive khaki flight uniform had come when he was successively awarded the DFC and DSO for his service as a Lancaster bomber pilot, 'navigating through almost impenetrable ground-fire', according to the citation in the *London Gazette*. MacKenzie later described his system for dealing with such inhospitable behaviour. He explained that he and his fellow crew members simply 'ignored the existence of the nuisance from below', instead pushing forward as if it didn't exist. According to a later account in the *Gazette*:

> Since being awarded the DFC, Acting Flight Lieutenant MacKenzie has participated in numerous successful sorties. One night in January 1943 he piloted an aircraft detailed to attack Berlin. Whilst crossing the coast on his homeward flight his aircraft was subjected to heavy and accurate ground fire. Two of his machine's engines were damaged and rendered unserviceable. Height was lost but, although faced with a 300-mile passage over the sea, Flt. Lt. MacKenzie continued his onward journey. When halfway across the water a third engine became overheated. The plane was now down to 600 feet and the situation appeared hopeless, but MacKenzie, displaying grim determination, flew on at this height and eventually reached these shores, where he landed safely. By his high courage and superb skill, this officer was undoubtedly responsible for the safe return of his aircraft and its crew.

Although MacKenzie survived the war, he was one of the generation of cricketers who lost six of their most productive years in the game. He officially retired in September 1945, left the RAF soon afterwards and went on to a civilian career with British Caledonian, dying at home in Sussex on New Year's Day 1989 at the age of 70.

Meanwhile, the game at Northampton that monsoon-like day in May 1945 was abandoned as a draw. In the pavilion, the home team's opener Dennis Brookes saw Bill Edrich 'calmly having a post-match drink of dynamite-strength German schnapps, amusing us by lighting his exhaled breath on fire with a match'. It was a somewhat less animated scene out on the field, where the pitch was a mud-bath, the roofs of the nearby houses were steaming, the stands were waterlogged, and the few spectators remaining at the close as inert as waxworks. 'But at least the local pub was friendly,' said Brookes, who remembered the place as a timbered old inn frozen in an apparent time-warp, 'with Civil War relics on the walls, a roaring fire in the hearth, and no sign of any rationing behind the bar for the cricketers'. Edrich himself must have joined them there, because he could still warmly recall the scene 40 years later. 'I woke up in a friend's bathtub in Neasden,' he noted.

Amidst the downpours, the Australians had continued their rapid if somewhat fitful evolution from a servicemen's convalescent group into something approaching a full-scale cricket Test team. Billed as the RAAF, they had comfortably beaten the British Empire XI at Lord's, even if some of their individual batsmen's innings owed a debt to the Empire fielding, with no fewer than seven dropped catches in the afternoon session. British self-effacement could hardly go any further than this. On a purely technical level, the visitors appeared to some critics to be a somewhat lopsided outfit. The middle-order batting looked solid enough and there were three quality all-rounders in Pepper, Cristofani and Pettiford (all leg-spinners), as well as the force of nature that was Keith Miller. Set against this, there was no very obvious candidate to open the innings with the moustachioed Dick Whitington, a 32-year-old recent veteran of the desert campaign, and, Miller aside, even less by way of a pace attack worthy of the name, meaning that there were sometimes five spinners in the side.

In fact, it seemed that the Australian team consisted of little more than a few hopelessly ill-prepared individuals united by a cause. Whatever the merits of the summer's Tests (as we'll continue to call them) as entertainment – and in the end nearly half a million men, women and children paid to watch some or all of the 15 days' play – the tourists clearly did far better in terms of results than anyone could have expected of them. The advance betting was that they would be lucky to draw a couple of the games and more than likely lose the rest. In the event, this was not quite what happened, and Hassett's men proved tough to beat. Perhaps it was down to the fact that several of the players had already served alongside one another in the unique intimacy of military life. Or perhaps they simply rose to the occasion. Jack Pettiford remembered: 'Hassett told us we should give it everything we had, remembering the people back home who had suffered through the war and badly needed the pick-me-up we could give them, and his order was carried out.'

The newly liberated POW Graham Williams made his comeback for Australia in the same Empire match at Lord's, where, sustained by a glucose drink brought out to him every few minutes, he scored a significantly above-average 51 not out. Applauded all the way to the crease, Williams would have been relatively easy to spot even in the absence of a functioning public address system, because he was so painfully thin. This had prompted his ironic team nickname of 'Muscles', which he accepted with good grace and stayed with him for the rest of the tour. It may seem insensitive from our modern perspective, but there's no doubt of the genuine regard in which Williams's teammates held him. Keith Miller, on one level the personification of rugged Australian values, sometimes displayed a surprisingly emotional side. I once asked him how it had felt to go practically overnight from piloting a napalm-laden aircraft over enemy territory to playing cricket in springtime England. Miller said:

> Well, you can imagine. Those days weren't real, were they? They were different. They felt different. But at least you were still alive, and you were playing cricket, and it all suddenly came flooding back to you as I imagine performing in an orchestra does to a top musician. It was only when Graham Williams came out to bat that day so soon after leaving the POW camp that I began to lose it a bit. It was really a miracle, you know. Williams wasn't meant to be there. He'd been sent to that camp to die.

* * *

All this was a prelude to the first three-day Test (so rendered by most of the press) beginning at Lord's on Saturday 19 May. It was the first game played on an English ground to be designated first-class since September 1939, and it came at a time when Hitler's chosen successor as head of state, Grand Admiral Dönitz, still ruled over a rump Nazi regime based at Flensburg in northern Germany. It was only later that the term 'victory' would come to be applied to the summer's cricket.

Lord's itself was in surprisingly good repair. There was a grey barrage balloon moored over the Nursery Ground, and one or two of the facilities elsewhere might have fallen foul of today's Health and Safety Act provisions, while at the lunch and tea intervals a one-armed man dressed in brown overalls patrolled the boundary rope, shouting out an appeal through an old-fashioned tin megaphone nearly as large as he was for funds to benefit both the Red Cross and Australian service charities. But in general things looked as cheerful as they reasonably could on a blustery, cloud-strewn morning.

Looking down from the top of the tiered grandstand, as though in the dress circle of a vast theatre, the field itself was a vivid emerald green with one or two biscuit-coloured patches on either side of the covers, with banks of once-white, now utilitarian grey, benches, the pavilion itself flag-strewn and decked out with hanging baskets splashed in red and yellow, and a pleasantly leafy backdrop overall. The public were admitted at 10am for the 11.30 start. The first man in line at the Grace Gate was a retired south London surveyor, who in those more demure times gave his name only as Mr King, and who told the *Evening Standard* that it was 'just like the old days when there was a large crowd early in the day, and when I frequently waited from 6 in the morning'. There were 23,000 spectators present on Saturday, each of whom paid their shilling (5p, or roughly 75p today) admission, many of them following the pre-match advice to bring their own refreshments with them 'as Lord's and MCC cannot guarantee comestibles will be available in sufficient quantity'. There was a 'certain degree of satirical comment about the weather', the *Standard* noted. But the crowds who clicked through the ancient turnstiles at the rate of about one a minute were 'cheerful and buoyant ... heartily representative of the spirit that had sustained cricket even in its darkest wartime hours'. In that same context, the next spring's *Wisden* noted drily:

> Until the flying-bombs arrived in London in the middle of June, there was every indication that the 1944 cricket season at Lord's would break all wartime records in the matter of crowds and gate receipts. As it was, 167,429 people paid for admission, against 232,390 in 1943. Bad weather accounted partly for this reduction, and the flying-bomb menace caused some fixtures to be put off.

Rising above this inconvenience of the V-1 rockets, notices erected at Lord's that summer advised merely: 'In the event of a raid, good cover from shrapnel and splinters should be obtained under the concrete stands. Public shelters will be found outside in St John's Wood Church, Wellington Road and Circus Road', although spectators were urged not to 'loiter unduly' in the street, and would be informed 'the moment a resumption of play becomes practicable'.

Again, it seems likely that this was not exactly life in war-torn Britain as Hitler might have imagined it.

The visiting players – now known collectively not as a Services side, but merely as Australia – arrived early on the 19th, already wearing their distinctive navy-blue blazers with the emblem of a yellow rising sun over a white eagle with a green leaf spray embroidered on the breast pocket. As well as Hassett and Miller, they had men like the middle-order bat Ross Stanford, the former bomber pilot who had since gone on to serve as the baggage and sports officer for the returning POWs in their camp at Eastbourne; the aptly named Jim Workman, known for his gritty application at the crease rather than any swashbuckling tendencies, at the top of the order; and the 16-stone all-rounder 'Big Cec' Pepper, whose enjoyment of a drink, and occasional flashes of fiery temper, also emphasised the aptness of his surname. In 1945 the sight of Pepper walking into a pub was a bit like that of Cary Grant walking into a tailor's shop, or Winston Churchill into a cigar outlet. He was happy to be there, and on the whole they were glad to accommodate him. Pepper played in all five of the Victory matches, but in the end never represented his country in an official Test. His omission may have owed something to an incident in December 1945 at Adelaide, when, in one account, 'discipline and duty deteriorated rapidly'. Pepper had been bowling for a Services team against a South Australia side that included no less a figure than Don Bradman, making only his second first-class appearance in five years, in its ranks. Frustrated towards the end of the match in a prolonged lbw shout against the local hero, Pepper had proceeded to 'ponder the official's response', in the measured words of the Adelaide *Advertiser*, before going on to 'enquire into its soundness'.

This was a notable paraphrase on the paper's part. What Pepper actually said to the uncooperative umpire was 'What do you have to do to get the little bastard out?', before adding, 'You're both fucking cheats.' As Bradman was then not only the world's pre-eminent batsman, but also a voting member of the Australian board of control, this was not, perhaps, a conspicuously shrewd career move on the bowler's part. Pepper eventually settled in the north of England, played league cricket in Lancashire, and made a small fortune in the food-packaging business that allowed him to buy homes in Blackpool and the south of Spain. His obituary notice in *Wisden* in 1993 quoted the correspondent of the *Manchester Evening News* who said he could 'not imagine any match involving Pepper pursuing a peaceful course' but adding that usually 'there was more humour than anger'.

One or two of the cricket press went up the pavilion stairs to the sanctuary of the Australian dressing room just before the toss, which Hassett lost. The opener Dick Whitington assured the journalists that he 'liked the extra bit of time English wickets give, compared to the fast strips back home', although there was always a possibility, he conceded, that he and his colleagues 'might make utter fools of ourselves'. He was suffering from hay fever. Pepper, for his part, was not so much sitting in an armchair as lolling in it full length, legs crossed, cigar in mouth. Miller also appeared 'almost beatifically relaxed, engrossed in his morning paper', while the faces of the others were 'like stunned mullets.' A few minutes later, the Australians walked out into the field, throwing the ball hard at each other as they went, tall and further broadened by their new supply of sweaters, with no visible signs of nerves. A north wind played across the ground as 29-year-old Captain Bert Cheetham, late of El Alamein, once and future right-arm seamer for New South Wales, bowled the first ball of the match to Len Hutton. Hutton raised his bat disdainfully as it sailed far down the leg side. On the face of it, the Yorkshireman looked good for another century to follow the one he had scored in his last first-class appearance, against Sussex at Hove in the week that war had broken out nearly six years earlier. But an over later Hutton came down the track to have a go at Graham Williams, the ball took the edge and he was caught behind for just a single. 'There was unrestrained glee among the Australians in the crowd,' *The Times* noted.

Watching from the England balcony, Walter Hammond was less pleased by these developments. Everyone, including Hammond himself, agreed that he had been Bradman's only serious rival as the world's foremost Test batsman of the inter-war years. But the England captain would turn 42 the following month, and the old magic came more fitfully than it had before. At any moment Hammond might still dismissively whisk away a devastatingly fast delivery from a bowler like Miller that lesser men would have been content to block. But his footwork against spin was now increasingly suspect, and he was naturally averse to the quick single. Over and above that, Hammond was only a partial success as a team captain. Never particularly well cast as one of life's back-slappers, 'Wally basically believed in letting you get on with it, rather than offering you the benefit of his support or wisdom,' his Test colleague Paul Gibb later remembered. 'I think "reticent" would be the word now, but at the time we just thought him a gloomy sort of bugger.'

Gibb wasn't the only teammate to note the discrepancy between Hammond's all-but peerless batting skills and his only modest talent for man-management. George Pope, the mercurial Derbyshire all-rounder who played in three of the summer's Tests, was also withering in his criticism. 'He should have been there to dispense advice and steady the younger men's nerves,' Pope reflected. Instead, as the summer progressed the England captain was consumed by the perennial need to make money, which was understandable but hardly the way to go about the minute-by-minute business of leading a team in a series of tight matches. At Lord's, the Kent and England spinner, and returning army veteran, Doug Wright heard 'the skipper talk[ing] to Sir Pelham Warner just before the start, and the gist of it was that Wally wanted to know whether, if he moved out of the team hotel into a friend's house, would MCC reimburse him for the savings in cash? That was his top priority while the rest of us were shitting bricks with nerves thinking about facing Miller and the other Aussies.'

Those who witnessed one of Hammond's occasional but colourful flashes of temper at around this time would long speak of the scene in hushed tones, like old salts recalling a historic hurricane. Sometimes the outburst at least bore positive fruit, such as the occasion when an opposition player rashly remarked that it was 'typical of Wally to sit on his arse and sulk' one day when the England captain had complained of one of his recurrent outbreaks of lumbago. Hearing of this, Hammond had soon appeared in the middle to score an explosive innings of 302, with 35 fours and two sixes, one of them a shot that cleared the ground and broke a window of the nearby municipal power station, a carry of some 130 yards. *Wisden* gives a specific date for the onslaught, but it also continues to exist in a sort of cricketing limbo, time-free and always able to draw a sigh from the hundreds who witnessed it and the many thousands who heard about it later.

But at other times, Hammond's generally low opinion of humanity took the less productive form of mere petulance. At the end of the 1945 series, Australia's captain Lindsay Hassett would express the hope that in future all England–Australia matches would be played in the same 'wonderfully convivial' atmosphere. Within an hour of the start of the first full post-war Ashes Test, at Brisbane in November 1946, that particular wish had gone out the window. With his score on 28, the returning Don Bradman faced a full-length ball from Bill Voce, the Nottinghamshire left-armer, that he managed only to steer to Lancashire's Jack Ikin, who was standing at second slip. Ikin caught the ball without undue difficulty. The Englishmen were thus surprised, to use the mildest word possible, to then see Bradman continuing to stand his ground, 'idly looking away over the square leg boundary', as Hammond put it, while the umpire at the bowler's end slowly shook his head, apparently in the belief that the catch claimed by Ikin had been a bump ball. At the end of the over, the England captain walked up to briefly confer with his opposite number, who was by now busily tapping the pitch with his bat, ready to resume what became a marathon knock of 187 in a partnership of 276 with Hassett, a key component in the eventual crushing Australian victory by an innings.

Could this be the moment for some dry but essentially good-natured exchange, one veteran Test captain to another, or even a sardonic comment on Hammond's part on the occasional vicissitudes of the sport both men had so adorned over the course of so many years?

Not exactly. 'You fucking cheat,' the England skipper informed his distinguished Australian counterpart.

Hammond scored 29 out of an England first innings of 267 at Lord's, Cheetham taking 3-49 and Miller, marking his run-up with an at best cursory swipe of his boot, thrifty figures of 1-11 in nine overs of mixed seam and raw pace, a bowler who without change of action or angle of delivery could suddenly switch from a ball of relative innocuousness to one that sent his fellow airman Bill Edrich's bails whistling towards fine leg. Curiously, Miller had never really been considered a bowler in his dozen or so first-class matches before the war, and it was almost as if he was now making it up as he went along. The Australians went in before tea, and scored 82/2 by the close.

No one then played organised cricket on a Sunday, so the drinkers among the two sides made for the saloon bar of the nearby Crown pub, later rechristened as Crocker's Folly, secure in the knowledge that they could sleep it off in the morning. Robertson, Edrich and Wright were there for the home team, and Hassett, Stanford, Pepper and Miller represented the visitors. There was little sign of the sort we might expect today that these were top international sportsmen with an entourage of managers and agents. But perhaps some of them were really leading a double life. On the surface, Miller remained charming and jovial, quick to stand friends or admirers a round, to tell a dirty joke, and above all to appreciate a pretty face. This was the golden boy, or 'Nugget', known to most of his fellow cricketers and the public. Miller only revealed his other side, the mentally scarred combat veteran, to those who had shared his experience, a few trusted colleagues and his family back home. To them, he was often serious and reflective, sentimental almost to the point of being maudlin, and never far removed from the war, a man who later named his first child William after an RAAF comrade who had been lost over France in 1944.

Meanwhile, Hassett wrote – or at least put his name to – a review of the first day's play that appeared overnight in the *Melbourne Argus*:

> By the time we had dismissed the formidable English batting side today, we had every reason to be satisfied. It was a curious day's play on a wicket which was all in favour of the batsman and never took spin – which our attack largely relies on. Williams did us a great service

> by so quickly dismissing Hutton. Cheetham, Price and Ellis also had their moments, but Cecil Pepper [Hassett's companion at the bar that night] never found his true form. Miller, though, is approaching the stage when he will be considered an all-rounder.

This was an accurate prognosis. On the second day, which was the Whitsun holiday, 28,000 people saw Miller score 105 in a masterclass of controlled aggression, in a fraction over three hours at the crease. What was perhaps most attractive about the innings was the fact that the batsman himself remained so obviously and enjoyably fallible throughout. There was none of Bradman's sense of industrialised efficiency about it. For Miller, making contact with the ball was often as seemingly elusive as scientists seeking to determine if there was life elsewhere in the solar system. At other times, he cut and drove and hooked bowlers right and left, playing like a singularly uninhibited father toying with the opposition in a prep school match. Towards the end, *The Times* correspondent was left to wonder whether 'Lord's [was] quite big enough a ground for such terrific hitting, as one Miller six crashed into the top-tier seats between the towers of the pavilion, and another one with even greater carry struck a chimney pot just above the radio broadcasters' eyrie.'

But all these fireworks were merely a prelude to the moment during the afternoon session when, at the fall of the seventh wicket, Graham Williams came out to join Miller at the crease. Tall, wavy-haired and full-faced, but otherwise almost concave from his four years as a guest of the Reich, Williams modestly raised his bat to the ensuing applause, which proved even more spirited and protracted than at the previous week's British Empire match on the ground. Miller later said of the ovation that it was the 'most touching thing I ever saw or heard, almost orchestral in its feeling'. In time, the noise rose to a 'great swelling crescendo, but it was not the sort of clapping and cheering that greets a hundred. This was different. Everyone stood up. They all knew about Graham's ordeal. He was a big fellow, but he was gaunt from his experience, and he just walked round for a while as if in a trance.'

Following that Williams scored 53, including 11 fours, off 56 balls faced, which proved to be the second-highest innings of his interrupted 14-year-long first-class career. The batsman later remarked that he had felt compelled to score the majority of his runs in boundaries, as 'I couldn't be confident I could race up and down the wicket without the risk of collapse.' All out for 455, Australia, on whom the weather gods seemed to have smiled more often than not that series, would bowl to England on a third day pitch described by *Wisden* as 'difficult, the turf drying after more overnight rain', and which Hammond, with his gift for the motoring metaphor, compared more bluntly to 'driving down a road filled with potholes in an old banger, towards a destination that might as well have been Timbuctoo for all our hopes of making it'.

There was another crowded house on Tuesday for the climax of a match throughout which, despite frequent fluctuations, Australia had called the tune. Pepper was soon on from the Nursery End, with three successive full-throated shouts for lbw, all of which the umpire declined, before letting Hutton have a fast googly that kept low and ripped back to flatten his middle stump. '*That* was close,' the bowler observed. Perhaps Pepper had read his captain's earlier remarks about him in the press, because he bowled beautifully now, to a ring of three men close in on the leg side, their hands outstretched as if expecting the batsman to swoon at any moment. Jack Robertson of Middlesex, playing on his native heath, showed how it was done with an innings of 84, including two sixes and five fours, before Stan Sismey, standing back, caught him off the first delivery by Cheetham, coming on with the new ball: England 218/5. A lesser technical craftsman than Robertson, but on his day fully his equal as a red-blooded destroyer of bowlers, Edrich made a typically robust fifty, including a lofted drive hit so high that the batsmen had time to cross twice before the ball finally fell into the hands of long leg, who grassed it. After that, the last four England wickets went down for only eight runs, leaving a grand total of 294.

The Australians went back in at 5.50pm, needing to score 107 in a maximum of 70 minutes. More rain was rumoured to be approaching, but the light, though deteriorating, was playable, and much to their credit Hammond's team, to quote *Wisden*, 'deserved praise for their splendid sportsmanship in doing their part in the speediest manner, changing positions quickly and without a suggestion of delay', getting through their overs at the rate of 20 an hour. The crowd, with admirable even-handedness, did their part by promptly throwing back the ball whenever it crossed the boundary.

In the end, it all went down to the wire in a finish that combined the devastating tension of a tight Twenty20 and the grapple of a hard-fought ODI, yet one stretched out to last the better part of a week, with some fickle weather and a pervasive sense of joy at the return of such top-level sport thrown in. It was the sort of frantic climax generally shunned outside of the most extravagant *Boy's Own* fiction, but, as any true lover of the game knows, not uncommon in long-form cricket. Australia soon lost Whitington and Miller, the latter when setting off for a suicidal run that suggested the batsman might be late for an appointment with his bookmaker, but then Hassett and Pepper came together, the former discreet but adhesive, the latter dealing in cuts and slashes and thick edges in a brief but statistically vital stand of 52.

The climax could almost have been scripted. With the clock at 6.59pm, Alf Gover of Surrey, his right knee still heavily strapped from a wartime injury sustained while serving as a sergeant-major with the Army Physical Training Corps, came in to bowl the final over. Australia needed four to tie, five to win, with Pepper and the 28-year-old Charlie Price, of New South Wales seconds, at the crease. Price was a purveyor of useful left-arm spin bowling but unregarded batting. The first ball of Gover's over shaved his off stump, and to the second the batsman played what may have been a purely reflexive jab as much as a recognisable stroke, to fend the ball away from in front of his face to run a quick single. Pepper lofted the next delivery high over midwicket, where a sprinting Doug Wright just failed to catch it, and then fumbled the pick-up, for two. Three balls left, two to win. Not only was it the occasion of a rousing team effort, but it would also come down to one of famous individual performances.

Gover's walk back to his mark before the next delivery was noticeably more pensive, and at the end of it he paused to stare steadily down the wicket at Pepper, then turned and took several more steps, walking at a serpentine angle in the general direction of the long-off boundary before revving up from somewhere behind deep extra cover, eventually coming around the bend and on to a straight line, generating a good head of steam en route, and emitting a climactic grunt at the point of release. The ensuing ball was unsurprisingly fast, and on the leg stump. By now it was definitely spitting rain again, and the light was atrocious. 'It appeared to be almost night,' Bill Edrich later recalled, 'but standing at slip I saw Pepper's front leg go down the track, the bat sweep, and the ball skid along the grass past Dougie Wright's outstretched hand.' Hutton then took up the chase, racing in from deep square leg, to fire the ball back to Griffith behind the stumps, but by then the batsmen had already crossed for two. Australia had won by six wickets. All else was noise. A minute later, the heavens opened again, and the players and officials tore back to the pavilion through a gauntlet of cheering fans. They could never have played cricket in the downpour that immediately followed. The weather had had the last sardonic laugh in the matter after all.

It was a climax for the ages, one that blended dazzling skill, unwritable drama, outrageous fortune and a sense of sheer collective joy at being able to see such a match being brought to such a conclusion, at such a time. To quibble, perhaps it wasn't so much a case of the better team, as of the one that played better, having won. There was no apparent rationing of either side's celebrations both in the Lord's dressing rooms and, in a few select cases, back at the snug bar of the Crown later that night, although Cec Pepper, the man of the hour, rather winningly deflated some of the more effusive back-slapping by announcing that he had somehow developed a plague of boils from his head to his feet, 'with one the size of a golf ball full on my arse'. The *Sydney Morning Herald* reported more decorously: 'Pepper was so tired when he reached his room that night that he declared he could not have completed another run had he tried.'

* * *

It's hard to say with any certainty how Keith Miller, or for that matter Graham Williams or Bill Edrich, or any of the other players at Lord's with recent or continuing experience of the war, dealt with the horrors they had seen while in uniform. But perhaps they did so by compartmentalising their lives; no matter how grim their ordeal, they were suddenly back playing cricket in front of a packed house at the game's headquarters. Years later, Miller would allow only that it had been a 'strange' and 'different' summer but preferred not to dwell on the specifics. Perhaps it was no wonder the players generally elected to simply fling the bat, in both the literal and metaphorical sense of the phrase. Miller was thought to have spent much of his time between 22 May and his next engagement on a cricket field, playing for an RAAF side against the RAF at Gloucester on 2 June, indulging his loves of the turf, romantic classical music, dancing and alcohol, sometimes in combinations of two or more of these enthusiasms at once. Cecil Pepper later cheerfully remarked that for his part he had 'put about ten points on the stock price of Johnnie Walker scotch' during the same period, while the Australian keeper Stan Sismey took the opportunity to travel to Scotland to marry a WAAF sergeant named Elma McLachlan in a service near her home town of Helensburgh on the Firth of Clyde, where his teammate Keith Carmody stood as best man. Adding poignancy to the proceedings, Sismey's younger brother Frank had been killed while flying an RAAF bomber that crashed on take-off from an airfield in Western Australia just days earlier.

On 23 May, the majority of the Australian party caught the breakfast-time train from Victoria to Dover, where, in marked contrast to the splendours of Lord's, they played a one-day match against a local invitation side at the Crabble Athletic Ground. On the way south, one or two of the players, Cecil Pepper prominently among them, stretched out on their backs across the seats, sleeping off something, or perhaps just contemplating the fixture ahead. For those who remained upright during the journey, a succession of large wooden signs, often still unnervingly phrased – 'Win the War on the Home Front', 'Air Raid Shelter', 'Be On Your Guard', 'DANGER – Small (Butterfly) Bombs Lie Hidden Here: KEEP OFF!' – flashed by the window. The Crabble ground necessarily lacked some of the racy metropolitan promise of the Australians' previous venue, but at least there was a well-stocked ale tent, reported to have been supplied with 200 crates of Watneys Red Barrel, a small military band pounding away at the start in front of the pleasantly gabled pavilion, and clouds that for once remained high in the sky. Batting first by arrangement, the Australian Imperial Forces, as they were billed, scored 151 all out in 45 overs, with the ruddy-cheeked Kent yeoman Claude Lewis, successively the county club's post-war coach and scorer, and one of those men whose lifelong devotion to cricket doesn't necessarily stem from statistical success on the field, taking a hatful of wickets with his slightly eccentric left-arm spin. The home team (playing on after winning) replied with 166. It was the mirror opposite finish to the one at Lord's just 24 hours earlier. The Dover side still needed 17 runs with their last pair at the wicket, but Lewis himself saw them home with a lofted drive over midwicket that Bert Cheetham misfielded, his irritated return then clearing the keeper for two overthrows. It had been anyone's match.

There was other cricket, too, that month, including a series of matches involving a New Zealand services side rotationally captained by 27-year-old Martin Donnelly, fondly known as 'Squib', a renaissance sportsman who had the distinction of playing cricket for, successively, Wellington, Canterbury, the Dominions, Oxford University, the Gentlemen, Middlesex and Warwickshire, while appearing once in the centre for the England rugby union side against Ireland at Lansdowne Road and serving as a wartime tank commander in North Africa and Italy along the way. No fewer than six of the New Zealanders were repatriated prisoners of war, sent to England for rehabilitation. When the Kiwis played a Lord's XI early in June, their 44-year-old Durham-born batsman Roger Blunt arrived at the ground on crutches. Somehow lacking the proper chit for admission, he had to talk his way past a pair of gate attendants whom Blunt, a classicist, thought 'might have given Scylla and Charybdis a run for their money' before eventually making his way to the visitors' dressing room. 'Cricket in those days could be gold and diamonds, but there were also bags of the other stuff,' he later reflected. After fortifying himself with a large scotch, Blunt discarded the crutches and hobbled out to the middle to score 73 out of his team's total of 178, which proved the highest individual innings of the day, at one point slashing a Bill Edrich bouncer square to the Tavern fence before jogging down the pitch to the next ball to crash it against the sightscreen. The match was a draw.

They were also playing at Bristol that last week of May, where Somerset's Harold Gimblett, the constant enigma of English sport, personally scored 65 in response to a total by the West XI of 67 all out. There was a full round of league cricket, too, with the middle-aged Learie Constantine, now primarily engaged by Bootle of the Liverpool & District Conference, turning out for a Lancashire XI in a limited-overs match against England. The county side won a low-scoring game, but the main talking point was the state of the ground. Whatever the Lancashire committee's ambitions for the future, Old Trafford remained a sorry sight in the summer of 1945, with a large bomb crater at the front gate, a skeletal-looking pavilion and an outfield similarly disfigured by the Luftwaffe. 'It was just barely adequate for a game of beach cricket,' Constantine remembered, adding that the 'spirit of friendship and goodwill' with which *Wisden* recalled the summer as a whole was all very well, but that 'not everyone in those days was as wise as they might have been', a reference, perhaps, to the action of the stupendously unintellectual spectator in the free seats at Old Trafford who had greeted the future high commissioner and peer on his way out to the middle by throwing a banana at him.

The state of repair of many other first-class cricket fields similarly left something to be desired that season. While there were some exceptions to the rule, those clubs unfortunate enough to lie in the direct path of the 'knock-for-knock' German bombing raids, as Hitler referred to the aerial offensive unleashed against the British homeland, were naturally the worst affected. At Kent the county secretary Gerald Hough, a decorated Great War veteran, at least managed to keep the lights on at the St Lawrence ground in Canterbury, although there were unavoidable reminders of what he called the 'late nonsense' in some of the ground's outbuildings. An army unit still occupied the upper floors of the Canterbury pavilion, there was a petrol store under one of the stands, and an explosives dump had been established in the ladies' lavatory at the Nackington gate. 'You could see the comic potential of that in a *Carry On* film, but it wasn't so funny at the time,' said Godfrey Evans, who even in 1946 remembered finding bits of shrapnel stuck in the Canterbury pitch.

Along the coast, the ground at Hove had lost most of its windows – sucked out of their frames by repeated explosions – while at Surrey, celebrating its club centenary that season, they were more concerned with the 88 metal stakes driven into the turf to erect cages for the captured German invaders widely expected in 1940, as well as with the state of an Oval pavilion roof 'whose structural integrity can no longer be guaranteed with any certainty', the 1945 yearbook reported. At Leyton, the journalist Alan Gibson remembered the ambient smell of the nearby soap-works and a ground that even before the attentions of any enemy aircraft was severely utilitarian, with 'some big three-stepped rough stone seating for the general public, solid as the rock of Gibraltar and trying to tender behinds'.

Meanwhile, the manoeuvring by which Pelham Warner all but singlehandedly mustered cricketers the length and breadth of Britain, frequently prising them from the grip of unsympathetic commanding officers or cold-hearted civilian employers, remained a Herculean feat by anyone's standards, let alone those of a 71-year-old man in indifferent health whose chief means of communication lay between a malfunctioning phone and a laborious exchange of letters through the post. There's no doubt that Warner had immense gifts as an organiser and leader, partly offset by certain flaws of character and temper. The 1945 cricket season could never have taken recognisable shape without him. In late May, George Pope replied on the stationery of his Chesterfield woodturning business to yet another letter from the MCC deputy secretary touching on his fitness and expenses. Though perfectly civil, with the note of deference then assumed to apply in a working man's relations with his employer, it nonetheless gave further proof of what Warner had privately called the Derbyshire player's 'absolute refusal not to cause me headaches at every turn'.

> Dear Sir,
> I thank you for yours, and I shall be pleased to accept your invitation to play at Lord's in the middle of July.
>
> I should like to know, however, as soon as you can, if the England–Australia match you mention will be a one-day or a three-day affair, as my club, in the Lancashire League, state that I can be released for a three-day fixture, but not a one-day one.
>
> My jaw has mended quite nicely and I am now feeling better in myself.
>
> Sincerely,
> G.H. Pope.

A somewhat more congenial exchange followed with Billy Griffith in his officers' mess at RAF Keevil in Wiltshire later that week.

> My dear Sir Pelham,
> I had a letter from you dated 23rd April asking me to play against an Australian XI on July 14th. I believe I wrote back to you accepting this most kind offer. However, I wanted to confirm with you that you still require me at Lord's on that day in order to fix my leave, etc, to coincide with the match.
>
> I did so enjoy that last game at Lord's – it was a grand game of cricket.

Warner's reply, sent three days later, and rather dramatically stamped STRICTLY CONFIDENTIAL, read:

> Dear Billy,
> Yes, I am expecting you to play for England v Australia on 14th July, and it is almost certain that the match will be extended to three days. It will be grand to see you again keeping wicket.
>
> In strictest confidence, *please do not breathe a word of it to anyone*, but I think the 2nd Army are going to play a game here at Lord's on Wednesday and Thursday, 27th and 28th June. General Dempsey sent over one of his officers and he lunched with me yesterday. If it should come off, I would be most pleased if you would keep wicket for My XI against them. It should be a delightful match.
>
> Kindest regards,
> Plum.

In the end, England did host Australia at Lord's for three days in July, although for various reasons George Pope elected to turn out for Colne in their league fixture against Nelson instead. Batting at number four, he scored 62 in half an hour's stay at the crease and then took four Nelson wickets for 73 off 22 overs, once again the fearsome pre-war bowler who could make his wicketkeeper's gloves crack like a pistol-shot, and leaving two of the opposition batsmen to sit out their next scheduled fixture with sore ribs. Perhaps his choice of team that week was all to do with MCC's definition of a professional player's 'reasonable' expenses, or perhaps just a case of reluctance on Colne's part to release their star all-rounder. A cynic might easily suggest that there was greed involved on all sides, and that special interests triumphed over an admittedly fuzzy concept such as the higher national good.

Pelham Warner's side duly went on to play the Second Army at Lord's in late June, although after a promising start rain again intervened to rapidly plunge proceedings into the futile. At the close Warner arranged for both sets of players to return for a limited-overs contest the following day, with the Army XI, hampered by dismal light, just failing in their chase of 271 to win in 70 overs.

* * *

On Monday, 28 May, some of the Australian cricketers braved the only fitfully efficient London Underground system to join a lengthy but subdued queue of men and women entering the latest *Daily Express* exhibition of German war atrocities, now housed in a previously bombed-out office block near Oxford Circus. The all-rounder Bob Cristofani had the strange experience of first feeling 'literally ill [as] one looked at the pictures of human skeletons, standing around on rickety legs with typhus faces', and then in turn of being harangued by a shrill, middle-aged lady standing nearby who heard someone use his surname and leapt to a conclusion, addressing him as a 'filthy Eytie', among other unappreciative terms. Cristofani, who had bravely served the Allies as a pilot in the RAAF, merely walked away from the encounter, which he later said 'wasn't unusual at that time for anyone suspected of being foreign, let alone a native of a hated Axis power'. Later that morning, the Australians walked over to Westminster Bridge to admire the captured German U-boat which had been tied up in a dock there in front of the Houses of Parliament. 'Strangely beautiful – and horrifying – when you think of the havoc it wrought,' Cristofani wrote in his diary.

'Wanting an early cashing in of the cheque of victory,' in Roy Jenkins's phrase, if also under pressure to do so from senior Labour members of his War Cabinet, Winston Churchill resigned that week and disbanded the coalition government. In due course he announced that parliament, which had sat continuously since 1935, would be finally dissolved on 15 June. Polling would take place on 5 July, although to allow the services' overseas vote to be counted the results were not expected until later in the month. Unlike his wartime deputy and now political opponent Clement Attlee, Churchill knew about the imminent availability of an atomic bomb for use against Japan, which he believed would bring about the final end of hostilities in the Pacific late in June or early in July, just as a grateful nation went to the polls. He was correct about the decisive effect of the bomb, but not about the timing of its deployment, which came about more than a week into the new Attlee administration.

* * *

While the Australians caught their train to play a two-day match against an Empire XI at Hove, Churchill, as tradition required, went up to his parliamentary constituency at Woodford on the north-east London border with Essex to announce the date of the coming election. It was a peculiarly English occasion. 'There were no flags, no parades as in Nazi Germany, no special presidential train as in America,' Harold Hobson wrote in the *Christian Science Monitor*, 'only a stoutish gentleman holding in his hand a high-crowned hat, addressing a few halting words, in a gentle shower of rain, to an audience of housewives out on a morning of shopping.' Churchill went back to Downing Street that evening, and the next day told the Cabinet that he was worried more than anything else on the world stage just then 'by the prospect of electors be[ing] away from their homes on 5 July as a result of Wakes and similar trade holidays' – particularly in Lancashire and parts of Scotland, 'which traditionally cease all normal activity during the first week of July'. Perhaps certain constituencies might delay their polling arrangements until later in the month, he suggested, before turning to consider the 'nearly equally troubling' matter of whether or not 'all *bona fide* candidates should be entitled to wear military uniform while engaged in politics, whether in their own constituencies or not'. It's somehow hard to imagine any other Allied head of government being quite as taxed as Churchill was by the technical arcana of an election (or, in Stalin's case, by any sort of democratic process at all).

Meanwhile, Bob Cristofani had better luck with the ordinary British public when later on that same Monday, the 28th, he went out to dinner with several of his Australian teammates at the art deco Lyons Corner House near the junction of London's Oxford Street and Tottenham Court Road. The cricketers' arrival in the small teashop with steamed-up windows and a framed portrait of the king on the wall quickly caught the attention of the other customers, particularly a group of boiler-suited young women at a nearby table. 'They looked too fetching in their blue blazers,' one of the party, an insurance-office clerk named Celia Holmes, later wrote. Winking at her companions, another pretty girl strode confidently across the room and kissed first Cristofani and then the recent batting hero Charlie Price on their cheeks. 'I shall never forget the look of mingled shock and embarrassment on their faces.' The wicked siren, too, must have felt that she had committed a faux pas, because she was blushing to her roots as she sat down again. Celia Holmes tried to laugh it off. 'It looks like someone just bowled a maiden over,' she offered, in the classic phrase. There was a bit of nervous laughter around the room, and then a middle-aged diner at another table stood up, raised his glass towards the Australian party and broke into a rendition of 'For They're Jolly Good Fellows', which ended in a communal round of applause for the now smiling cricketers. That latter gesture 'really summed up the overall reception we got in England', Cristofani wrote in his diary.

Later that night, he added another entry: 'So Herr Göring has been taken ill in prison. One tries to be generous to all God's creatures, but I hope it's nothing trivial.'

5.
Ealing Cricket Drama

A FEW days later, there were more problems for Pelham Warner about his selection of the England team, and about George Pope in particular. The secretary of Pope's league club at Colne wrote to Lord's on 6 June:

> Sir,
>
> Our professional, Pope, has informed me that he has been invited to play for England on July 14th, 16th and 17th, and has accepted provisionally.
>
> In the agreements between my Club and Pope there is a clause in which we agree to release him on suitable terms between the two parties concerned.
>
> On July 14th my club is engaged in its local derby needle match. Our very financial success turns on this match, when we usually have a good crowd. Much of our support depends on the quality of our professional. We also have 800 members to consider.
>
> In view of this we wondered if you would care to suggest or help us to find a suitable player who could take Pope's place for the occasion.
>
> I should be pleased to hear from you at your earliest convenience.
>
> S.A. Barritt.

Warner replied three days later, evidently not pleased to now be asked to add the recruitment of northern league players to his existing duties.

Sir,

Thank you for your letter. I note what you say about Pope, and your suggestion that we should help you to find a player who could take his place.

I am afraid I am quite unable to do this as I do not know of anyone at the moment, and, as you may imagine, it is not easy in these days to get a cricketer, particularly of the class of Pope.

May I say that the match here at Lord's in July is a very important one, looking to the future of English cricket? We have to begin to build up a side for international fixtures, and a game such as the one proposed is of great significance. It is played for charity – Red Cross and Australian war funds.

I note that your game on 14th July is a local derby, but may I venture to suggest, with great respect, that you consider the question of Pope playing or not from a wider angle; that is the future of our English cricket in the broadest sense?

I too should be grateful for an early reply.

Yours sincerely,

Deputy Secretary.

Warner's appeal to the Colne secretary's higher loyalties initially seems to have worked, because two days later Mr Barritt cabled back: 'Pope permission to play Lord's – Letter follows S.A.B.'

This was certainly magnanimous on Colne's part, although as we've seen Pope did in the end choose to turn out for his league club in front of a loyal but necessarily small crowd at the local Horsfield ground rather than appearing 200 miles away in front of a packed house at Lord's. By the end of the summer of 1945 Warner had come to the conclusion that his two top priorities – the need for a revitalised England Test side, and for a full resumption of domestic cricket – were entwined. If the Test team consistently failed, public interest in the game as a whole would dwindle. If the counties and leagues didn't prosper, there would be no match-ready pool of potential England players. The likes of Colne might be off-Broadway, as it were, out in the damp green margins of the game, but they clearly remained vital to its overall state of health. 'The chief thing about the job appears to be this,' Warner wrote in September 1945, 'to strike a fine balance between the daily course of cricket in this country and the needs of its highest manifestation at Test match level.' The same challenge might be said to still be the administrator's main point of concern today, 80 years later.

Meanwhile, there had been a closely fought match at Gloucester between the RAF and RAAF, in which Cyril Washbrook scored 50 and Keith Miller took two quick wickets but then, as if again running late for an appointment, scooped the first ball he faced from his fellow airman Bill Edrich straight into Les Warburton's hands at long leg. (It can surely only have been coincidental that there was a full card of racing that afternoon at nearby Cheltenham.) The RAF won by 16 runs. A somewhat improvised-looking England XI took on the West Indies in front of 11,000 spectators at Lord's that same day. The home side declared at 174/4 after 55 overs, and then the left-arm spinner Bill Roberts of the Army and Lancashire took six cheap wickets to remove the visitors for 84, 'a most likeable personality' *Wisden* wrote of the bowler on his untimely death just five years later, at the age of 36.

On 7 June, a Lord's XI went on to draw with New Zealand, who included four freshly released POWs in their side, but then the weather again intervened to spoil most of the following week's scheduled matches. On paper, at least, there was an impressively wide variety of teams eager to compete by this stage of the season, running the gamut from the various de facto Test sides down to the likes of the London Fire Force, United Hospitals, Civil Defence Services and Shoeburyness Garrison, and even a crew representing the navy shore establishment HMS *Defender*, near Liverpool. Rain was the dominant theme throughout much of the month. Players paced the dressing room as if in a cage, or merely reconciled themselves to the latest downpour over a game of cards, while for the young Godfrey Evans, at least temporarily released from army driving duties for a fortnight to play a half-dozen charity matches, the great trick was to be able to curl up in a corner and fall asleep for 20 or 30 minutes at a stretch, instantly snapping back awake again to remark to the first passing colleague he saw, 'Thanks very much, a large gin.' Forty years later, I asked him about his experiences that summer.

'Buggered about by the army, shortages, rationing, grey and wet,' Evans summarised, but immediately added: 'On the other hand, there were no more blackouts, no night terrors, cars back on the road, theatres lit up again, crowds queuing at the gates to get into Lord's, and, at least around the west end of London, a fair number of young ladies willing to express their appreciation for the returning heroes. Not the worst time to be alive and fit and in your twenties,' England's great post-war wicketkeeper noted, while flashing a boyishly happy grin to illustrate the point. And so the changes from war to peace happened, bit by bit, in miniature as well as in the great transformative shifts historians only tend to tell us about later. 'The thing I most remember from that whole summer is of being at Victoria station one morning on my way back to France and seeing a train full of evacuated kids with paper luggage labels around their necks being reunited with parents they might not have seen for years. *That* raised a lump in your throat,' Evans concluded.

* * *

On 9 June, the Australians divided into two sub-units: an RAAF side loosely captained by Keith Miller went up to Edgbaston to play a two-day match against a team led by Learie Constantine, while the Imperial Forces under Lindsay Hassett took the train back to Eastbourne to face the Sussex Cricket Association. In the latter game, the visitors, if they could be called that at the Saffrons that season, batted first and scored 224. Sussex began comfortably enough, with 16-year-old Ken Suttle opening the innings, the start of a 25-year-long association with the county, but then Charlie Price came on to enliven proceedings with his sporadic left-arm spin, hit a damp spot, and took 6-23 in a dozen overs. Impatient to get in on the act, Cec Pepper soon joined him, and in his first over knocked back Suttle's middle stump as the batsman tried to pull a long hop. After that wickets fell steadily, there was some typically spirited Australian appealing – 'We're not here just for our own amusement,' Pepper had perhaps needlessly informed the Brighton-based *Argus* before the match – and the last eight batsmen fell for 43 runs. Towards the end there was a cordon of five slips and two short legs, one in front, one behind, both standing as close as decency would allow. It was timely for the *Argus* to remind its readers the next day of what one of the Sussex batsmen had said of Pepper: 'He is always up to something.'

There was a small intramural party for the Australians that Saturday night held in a private room of the seafront Langham Hotel, where 'special provisions [were] made to stay open late' for the occasion. 'Late' was no exaggeration. It was 7am, and the bells of Our Lady of Ransom Church were calling the faithful to early morning Mass, when Pepper at last went back to the team's more modest overnight lodgings a mile or so up the esplanade, a journey he made while lying prone in a hastily requisitioned wheelbarrow pushed erratically up the front by two of his only slightly more vertical Australian colleagues.

Back in Birmingham, the RAAF side scored a respectable 275 in 90 overs. Most of the Australian batsmen emerged with credit without ever quite threatening to take the bowling apart, with Constantine himself plugging away, reduced in pace from his 1920s heyday but still capable of asking questions of the batsmen with his line and length, for figures of 4-46 off 12 overs. His own side began their reply at 11 the following morning, for once that month bathed in glorious sunshine. The openers were both club players, if that, but after them the line-up read: Eytle, Williams, Forde, Clarke, Christiani and Constantine, all established colony or county stalwarts, the last three of them current or soon to be Test caps. 'We'll never get the blighters out,' Miller remembered thinking. An hour late the score was 44/7, and Constantine's team were dismissed for 55. Miller himself didn't even bowl, but his friend Reg Ellis, the left-arm spinner from Adelaide who was flying Lancaster bombing runs from RAF Waddington in Lincolnshire just six weeks earlier, did so to some effect.

'I knew a total of three deliveries,' Ellis remembered towards the end of his life nearly 70 years later. 'A leg break, a googly and a top-spinner. The pick of the bunch was the top-spinner, because it used to hurry off the turf. It was all a matter of accuracy, of wearing a hole in the pitch, and that all came down to hours of practice. They sometimes used to call me a lucky bowler, and all I can say is that like a lot of pro sportsmen the harder I worked the luckier I got.' Ellis finished with figures of 5-17 in the first innings at Edgbaston, with 4-23 when Constantine's side followed on. Bob Cristofani chipped in with 5-23, and the visitors won by the tidy margin of an innings and 145 runs.

After the game there was what Ellis called a 'highly posh' civic reception for both sets of players, followed by a performance of Beethoven's *Eroica* and other classical selections by the Birmingham Symphony Orchestra. 'Keith [Miller] always had the knack of communicating his enjoyment, whether it be of sport, the ladies or music,' Ellis recalled. 'So it was all a delightful evening, very debonair and civilised. Quite a contrast to being banged around in a dark plane somewhere over Germany.' No party with Miller in its ranks could ever be entirely tranquil, even so, and Ellis remembered feeling grateful that he had then had several days off before his next appearance on a cricket field, which came at Lord's against an RAF side led by Bill Edrich. 'Looking back, I think the key to [Miller] was that he had a very low boredom level,' Ellis reflected. 'Doing nothing was torture for him, and it was when there was little else happening that the hijinks occurred.' One night in June Miller sought an interview with 51-year-old Keith Johnson, the regally aloof member of the Australian board of control and head of the RAAF's overseas public relations unit, who had just been appointed to manage his country's cricketers in Britain. Johnson may not have made an immediately sympathetic figure, but he had a genuine love of cricket, and had passed up the offer of an alternative posting to Paris because loyalty to the game and its players seemed paramount. When the moment came, Miller told him that he expected he and his teammates to be 'looked after' during their summer's tour.

'What does that mean?' Johnson enquired, perhaps bracing himself for the player's response.

'For one thing,' Miller said, 'I don't see why we shouldn't have our own plane to help us get around for a day out.'

'Out *where*, exactly?' Johnson enquired through gritted teeth.

'Oh,' Miller shrugged, 'you know ... Rome ... Bonn ... Places like that.'

'I think that is a matter the civilian and military authorities are unlikely to look on with favour,' said Johnson, with all the considerable dignity at his command. But Miller just laughed. 'I'll make my own fun, then, sport,' he said – which of course is what he did.

By mid-June there was also a certain amount of county, as opposed to Championship, cricket in England. At Chesterfield, Derbyshire took on Nottinghamshire in the first technically competitive match played on the ground in six years, although in the event 'competitive' might not have been the best word to describe the outcome. The home side managed just 78 in their one innings, a total the visitors passed with four wickets and several hours' playing time to spare. Glamorgan similarly crushed a Western Command team at Briton Ferry, and Hampshire in turn made short work of Sussex in between the rain showers at Southampton, where the South African-born Desmond Fell top-scored for the visitors with a gritty 61. Fell's technique was limited (although the watching *Southern Echo* correspondent wrote of one cover drive, 'all wrist and balance', that reminded him of Hammond), but he could at least console himself that by the time he departed he had driven the Hampshire seamer Lloyd Budd half mad by continually extending his front pad to him like a bomb-blast door, and more importantly by the fact that he was even on a cricket field at all. Fell had spent the previous two years as a resident of a 'not pleasant' German POW camp.

* * *

In the normal course of events, a midweek one-day fixture pitting the RAF (Uxbridge) against a Metropolitan Police B side would qualify only as a routine courtesy call by one team on another, watched over by a few dozen elderly or obsessed spectators, if even that. But by contrast the match played at Lord's on 14 June could boast at least one distinguished visitor looking on from a high-backed chair in the pavilion's committee room. This was no less than the freshly victorious Supreme Allied Commander in Europe, and future US president, 54-year-old General of the Army Dwight D. Eisenhower. Ike, as he was less formally known, was there as the guest of his wartime deputy, Air Chief Marshal Arthur Tedder, who in fairness knew only slightly more about cricket than his boss did. The supreme commander had come to England two days earlier in order to receive the freedom of the City of London and the Sword of Honour 'as a mark of appreciation of the part played by him in effecting the defeat of the Axis forces'.

On the 12th, Eisenhower made a triumphal progress from his west end hotel in an open horse-drawn landau in front of crowds who cheered him along the route down Oxford Street and High Holborn to the formal reception at the Guildhall. After a further hectic round of meetings the following day, he had expressed an interest in doing 'something quiet' in the capital before flying back to assume his new duties as the military governor of occupied Germany, based in the modernist Farben chemical plant headquarters in central Frankfurt, one of the few large buildings in the area to have survived the recent Allied bombing raids. A party or parties at the War Office placed a call to the recently retired Lt. Gen. Sir Charles Broad, a cricket man, who in turn rang first Tedder and then Pelham Warner. Warner thought that an hour or so watching some fellow servicemen going through their paces against a local police unit in front of a 'pleasantly drowsy' crowd might be 'just the tonic the Supreme Commander needs, [and] could serve to demonstrate those unchanging values our nations' armies have fought for these long years'; and so the arrangements were made.

Lord's has played host to some highly illustrious, and on occasion also disreputable, visitors over the years, both on and off the field, but surely few of them can have made as striking an entrance to the ground as Eisenhower did shortly before lunch that cloudy Thursday. He appeared this time not in a horse-drawn carriage but an open olive-green US Army jeep that for some reason bore the words 'Dream Boat' stencilled in bold letters on a sign stuck across its lower windscreen, and accompanied only by Tedder, an American military adjutant and a British driver-bodyguard. The car drove directly up to the back door of the pavilion, where the much-decorated general jumped out, a trim, uniformed figure with severely receding hair but a still youthful smile like that of a boy in a toothpaste advertisement, crisply saluting the elderly attendant who stood back to let him pass. Ike's strengths, it was widely agreed, were those of the Common Man. He exuded the solid values of the American Midwest: honesty, decency, simplicity, thrift and optimism. Something of an all-round athlete in his day, with a particular fondness for baseball, horseback riding and golf, like many Americans of that era he was not intimately acquainted with England's summer sport. After silently studying the proceedings for half an hour, Eisenhower turned to Tedder to summarise the spectacle as being 'tough and smooth' at the same time, and 'not for sissies either, when you watch those fellows stopping the ball bare-handed, and the batter not just smacking it around as hard as he can but steering it just out of their reach', an analysis many of the game's paid critics might not have disowned.

Eisenhower went on to tell his travelling aide, Col. Robert Stack, that he doubted cricket would ever fully take hold in the US, 'because the American likes everything to be done to a neat playbook, and these guys look to me as if they're making it up as they go along', another eminently sound judgement on his part, and one that perhaps spoke to the respective national characteristics involved as much as to the technical rules and regulations of the sports in question. There was time for the general to have lunch in the pavilion, surrounded by the well-tailored uniforms of senior War Office staff, before he left again in his jeep. 'That was England, just as it had always been,' he later wrote admiringly in his diary. It's an extraordinary thought that Eisenhower went directly from Lord's back to his base at Frankfurt and spent the following morning in what he called a 'gut-wrenching' tour of the recently liberated Buchenwald death camp, the scene of such barbarity, even by the most squalid Nazi standards, that hardened American GIs had blanched at the sight on first entering it. It's possible that he may have reflected that week on his being in such close proximity to the extremes of man's capacity for good and evil. Eisenhower's aide Col. Stack later remembered that his chief had privately said of the Germans that they inherently felt that they were superior to the rest of mankind, that the British by contrast liked to deflate everyone and everything, themselves included, with a dry joke, and that he, Ike, 'knew which of the two contrasting value systems he personally preferred'.

At Lord's on 14 June the last two policemen at the crease defied an air force attack that included England's Bill Edrich to play out time and save their side.

* * *

Pelham Warner could have been excused a sigh of exasperation when he opened yet another letter that week from the Colne club secretary regarding George Pope:

> Sir,
>
> I thank you for your telegrams and your letter.
>
> May I say here and now that there was never much doubt that we would *not* release Pope for your match on July 14th, 16th and 17th. We were only troubled about our obtaining a suitable professional in his absence. I am sorry you are not able to help in this matter, as we shall have to try our best within the scope of our somewhat narrow limits … I only hope that Pope may justify the confidence you have shown in honouring him.

There are times in life when the miseries of the world threaten to engulf us, when the precariousness of the human condition, so far from appearing a worthwhile and even noble struggle, seems an infinite rebuke. It's quite possible that Sir Pelham's own moments of inner despair that otherwise celebratory summer of 1945 coincided with his assistant passing him his morning basket of post, with an envelope bearing either a Colne or a Chesterfield return address conspicuous among it. As Warner later observed:

'There was that side of the whole business that involved serious and often elevated discussions about displaying our British values in a series of representative cricket matches', and then there was the relative banality that characterised so much of even the most senior MCC administrator's life, 'where one talked endlessly about hosting a great international pageant of sport, but actually spent half one's life worrying about the personal imbroglios and matters of expense, etc, pertaining to certain cricketers.'

There was a curious scene that week at a sparsely attended games field located on the other side of Wimbledon Park from the premises of the All England Tennis Club, where a side from the local King's College School hosted the Surrey Colts. The visiting team included two distinguished former or future England Test players in their ranks, with a significant 47-year age gap between them. The younger of the pair was Tony Lock, a left-arm bowler with a distinctive, whippy action who turned 16 only later that summer, while the side was captained by 62-year-old Sir Jack Hobbs, aka The Master, who also coached the youngsters, which must have been akin to having Mozart offer you free piano lessons as a teenager. We know only that Surrey batted first and scored 137/7, one report noting that Hobbs was 'content to score in the single figures before giving his wicket away', and that following this he had bowled half a dozen overs 'off a short run [with] a curving flight, and a gentle smile on his face as he probed the weak point in his opponent's armour' in the King's College reply of 56 all out.

There was a good deal of schools cricket elsewhere around the country that month, of which we need only mention a single-innings game played on 30 June between Harrow and Charterhouse. The visitors scored 195, with a fourth-wicket stand of 81 between two young batsmen listed as P.B.H. May and O.B. Popplewell, who went on to become arguably England's finest post-war batsman and a distinguished High Court judge respectively, with the future critic and playwright Simon Raven at the top of the order, while the already bucolic-looking Tory Cabinet minister-to-be Jim Prior managed to be out first ball and did not bowl, and a fifth man, the left-handed bat Anthony Rimell, would later play a single match for Hampshire before being lost to industry. Rimell once remarked that even the 'great cricketers of the day like Wally Hammond [had] managed to survive with no bodyguards, big houses or cars with tinted windows', and that in the same spirit he found that he could get by without such things, too, even as a globetrotting steel tycoon.

The next match involving the British Empire XI can only have come as a relief both for them and their opponents from the strains and stresses, to put it no stronger than that, of the previous six years. This was a single-innings tie with the Army at Westcliff, one of those agreeably flawed English outlying county grounds, if not on this occasion seen at its best, with a stiff breeze bowling straight up Chalkwell Avenue from the sea, a flock of assorted birds hovering above the nearby corporation landfill, and the sun only briefly deigning to appear in between two low clumps of trees on either side of the old pavilion.

'But at least we were all in one piece and playing cricket again,' as Captain Tom 'T.N.' Pearce, late of the army's Anti-Aircraft Command and himself a stalwart of Essex cricket, recalled. The Army also had the 44-year-old England Test veteran Maurice Leyland in their ranks, Pelham Warner's friend Billy Griffith kept wicket, one Michael Earls-Davis of Sherborne and Cambridge University rather disastrously opened the bowling, and a grey-flannelled post office delivery boy named Fred Grace ('no relation', he clarified), who happened to be leaning on his bike in front of the pavilion, was hurriedly called on to the field, stubbing out his cigarette en route, after the Army's Jasper Stuart-King pulled a muscle. When you add in the two well-stocked beer tents, the hand-cranked scoreboard, a roller that had first seen service in the reign of Queen Victoria, the various confectionery and whelk stalls and the mobile toilets, all part of a travelling circus the Essex club wheeled around between their county's grounds, the game was always going to have something of a festival air to it. Batting first, the Army managed 228 all out in 71 overs, Pearce top-scoring with 72. The Empire were always in the driver's seat after their opener Harry Crabtree, a native-born Yorkshireman who had come south as a schoolmaster, cracked 18 off the first over, more than once causing the square leg umpire to take evasive action, on his way to an unbeaten century. He was joined first wicket down by Robert Hunt, an occasional Middlesex all-rounder of the Jack Hobbs era, who himself hit 103 in slightly over an hour at the crease. *Wisden* was left to remark:

'The two took complete command. Driving freely and pulling with power, Hunt hit a six and seventeen fours in a delightful innings. He obtained 48 of the last 73 runs, which came in half an hour. Crabtree scored even faster at first.' Tom Pearce later said: 'If nothing else, that match had the wonderful effect of making it feel one was finally returning to something like normal life, even if the actual result was inconsequential at the time. Possibly its lack of importance was what actually made it worthwhile. We were really celebrating our essential normality again. Instead of fighting a world war, life was once more a thing of petty victories and minor losses. To me that was the real message of 1945: normality.'

As if to confirm the fact, the next day the British Empire side went out on a somewhat randomly mown field behind Ealing Golf Club in west London and beat the local Brentham XI by 71 runs. Neither Crabtree nor Hunt played for the visitors, but their sometime colleague Alf Gover of Surrey and England took 9-37, including the hat-trick. The small but contented crowd revelled in sunshine and the comings and goings of batsmen intent on whacking the ball hard, if not, in Brentham's case, that often. It was another small show of sanity, and one that gave rise to the inimitably British placard seen on the news vendor's pitch at the tube station later that evening:

> FOOD RATIONING CUTS
> US SHIP SUNK BY JAP TORPEDOS, 1000s MISSING
> EALING CRICKET DRAMA: LATEST

* * *

The England–Australia Tests which became part of that summer's mythology presented a curious contrast to other aspects of British life. More than any other event, they reinforced Tom Pearce's belief that something approaching normal peacetime conditions might be returning for a war-weary people. But perhaps part of their appeal was also that they came as a distraction from the continuing signs of national austerity, as seen by one of the last full sessions of Winston Churchill's Cabinet, held on the same day both sets of players took the train north to the second Test at Sheffield.

* * *

'SECRET', the minutes read. 'Memorandum by the Minister of Fuel and Power.'

1. In view of the fact that the restoration of full street lighting is due to commence on the 15th July, I must call the attention of my colleagues to the seriousness of the situation.
2. Even by the maintenance of maximum water gas production during the summer months, it will only be possible to build up stocks of coal at gas works to 4–5 weeks' supply by the end of October.
3. The restoration of gas street lighting causes me particular concern. It will require approximately 750,000 additional tons of gas coal in the present coal year. This clearly will make it even more difficult to maintain gas supplies to domestic consumers and to industry during the winter.
4. I have further ascertained that approx. 3,400 men are required to fit and maintain street lamps so that they operate as required. The Minister of Labour and National Service informs me that it is not possible to secure this workforce by the 15th July.
5. I feel compelled, therefore, to ask my colleagues to urgently consider this situation once more, and, at the least, to authorise the issue of instructions to local authorities that full street lighting may only be restored where and when adequate arrangements can be made.

For his part, Churchill's mind was concentrated less on the individual details of municipal coal stocks or street illuminations, and more on the unresolved global issues brought into focus by the coming election.

'The Prime Minister recalled that, when he agreed to meet President Truman and Marshal Stalin on 15th July, he had been proceeding on the assumption that in foreign policy there would be no divergence of view between the Government and the Labour party. His confidence had, however, been shaken by recent statements made by Professor [Harold] Laski, as chairman of the executive committee of the Socialist party ... Laski has persisted in the most strident terms in the suggestion that there would not in fact be any such continuity of policy between this Government and a Labour administration, a point he has made without drawing any protest or disagreement from Mr Attlee ...'

After five years of relative unity, domestic politics were clearly heating up again. With his high forehead, clipped moustache and wire-rim glasses, it was often said that Clement Attlee looked more like a provincial bank manager than a statesman capable of dealing with the affairs of a turbulent post-war world. 'A sheep in sheep's clothing,' Churchill liked to joke of his opponent, while to others the Labour leader's subsequent interactions with Joseph Stalin resembled nothing so much as a well-groomed English poodle attempting to dislodge a pit bull from its windpipe. But Attlee did have the one great redeeming virtue – almost always an insight to a man's character – of liking cricket. When the moment came, the new British premier's opening remarks to his fellow heads of government in the momentous tripartite conference later that summer at Potsdam took the form of an analogy between choosing the members of a Cabinet and selecting a 'good, all-round side of batsmen, wicketkeeper and bowlers', true enough in itself, if neither one of them a task the Soviet dictator was personally familiar with. Perhaps Stalin allowed himself a wry reflection on the curious ways of democracy. With hindsight, it had probably been counter-productive for Churchill to have told the British electorate that 'a Labour, or socialist, state cannot afford to suffer opposition – no socialist system can be established without a political police. They will have to fall back on some form of Gestapo.'

Even more so than at Lord's, the scars of war were all too obvious to the 21,000 spectators making their way into the Bramall Lane ground on the Saturday morning of 23 June. Long before the end of hostilities in Europe six weeks earlier, Sheffield was a sorry sight that bore not only the marks of the infamous two-night attack by the Luftwaffe in December 1940, but also the subsequent attentions of enemy planes on the city's steel and armaments factories. As a result, much of central Sheffield had been reduced to smoking hillocks of rubble and twisted metal, and would come to serve as a visual shorthand for the pity of war. Bramall Lane itself had, in the jargon of the day, 'bought it', leaving a meteor-sized crater in the outfield and a badly scorched bank of wooden seats at the Football Ground end that could only be called serviceable at best by the time of Test cricket's return in June 1945. Even without the additional intrusion of Hitler's bombers, Sheffield had sometimes seemed to vanish in a soupy haze generated by the city's many nearby industrial works, leaving C.B. Fry to comment of his appearance there for England against Australia in 1902 that by the time he batted in the late morning 'it was almost impossible to see the ball from the pavilion end', and that he had had to play 'purely from the bowler's arm' as a result. In a vivid passage that perhaps owed something to a ghost writer, but that undoubtedly caught the flavour of the place in 1945, Fred Trueman later wrote:

> Outside the walls of the ground, tramcars clattered along cobbled streets and hissed like ganders as they stopped to pick up passengers. The ugly fingers of soot-blackened chimneys forever pointing at the sky belched great fugs of yellow-brown smog into the atmosphere.

Nonetheless, as Pelham Warner himself noted, it was 'now more than ever vital to re-establish cricket on the widest front'; and there was also the 'eminently satisfactory point' that German POWs had been put to work in the days preceding the Test in 'knocking public benches back into order, and applying a thick coat of paint where called for'. Both sets of players stayed at the city's Grand Hotel, two to a room, which belying its name might have struggled to meet the most basic recreational or even sanitary requirements of the modern Test cricketer. 'There were two bathrooms for the twelve of us,' Keith Miller later recalled, 'one of which was reserved for the use of the manager. I was billeted somewhere up in the attic with Flt. Lt. Carmody.'

A dramatic, if only temporary change in the weather made its contribution to what Miller would later remember as a 'beautiful' game of cricket and *Wisden* depicted as 'the finest match of the season'. As we've seen, the early summer had been grim even by English standards, punctuated by steady rain and at times storm-force gales and heavy seas that lashed the country's east coast. The local Sheffield housewife Edie Rutherford, whom we last encountered enthusing about the prospects of revolution, and by now pining for the warmth of her native South Africa, wrote in her diary on 1 July: 'A pouring wet day again – paper says wettest June for 12 years. Husband saw in *Punch* this week about the American who was asked what memory of England he'd take home, and said, "The magical way in which spring merges into autumn ..."'

Other amateur meteorologists advanced the theory that the atrocious weather was the result of all the ammunition particles from the final assault on Germany entering the earth's atmosphere, while on a more spiritual note the vicar of Holy Trinity Church in Wallington, Surrey, whose high street was navigable only by flat-bottomed boat for parts of the month, saw the hand of divine judgement at play. In more prosaic terms, the Met Office records show an average daytime temperature in central London of 60.1°F (around 16°C), with 57mm of rainfall and a total of 186 hours of sunshine during June, compared to typical figures of 69°F (21°C), 42 and 199 respectively, which was sub-par, certainly, if not the full apocalypse.

But by the morning of 23 June there was for once oven-like heat, with a cloudless blue sky, for the start of the revived if now only single innings Oxford–Cambridge match at Lord's. Slightly more than 11,000 spectators were on the ground, of whom 9,507 paid at the turnstiles, generating gate receipts of £475 (£7,200 today) for the Red Cross. *Wisden* reported: 'Among the party entertained by Mr Stanley Christopherson, the MCC President, was Mr F.A. MacKinnon, 97, the oldest living University Blue and England player, who has attended every Oxford and Cambridge match from the 1870 contest.' This time around, Oxford scored 137 all out, a total Cambridge passed for the loss of only one wicket. The actual cricket, aside from a century by the light-blue opener Ian Bishop, who hit 15 fours in a stay of just two hours, but was never heard of again at first-class level, was relatively routine compared to the ground's inimitable atmosphere, which included a swelling beehive-like hum from the Tavern stand, the protracted if not lavish Harris Garden picnics, as befitting the only major organised sport whose sessions of play are intersected by meal breaks, and the characters who make the whole place what it is, among them the naval-blazered cove with his telescope balanced on the front rail of the pavilion fence, and the less vigilant posture of those of his neighbours who preferred dreaming through the afternoon. 'A wonderful English occasion,' Stanley Christopherson concluded. No one in authority then prohibited the likes of smoking, drinking or the occasional use of what might strike us as insensitive language among the crowd. In fact, those activities were rather encouraged.

It was similarly sunny and dry that same Saturday morning nearly 200 miles away in central Sheffield. The previous day the summer's principal tourists had let it be known that their Imperial Forces and Air Force contingents would henceforth function as one integrated unit known as Australian Services, although many individual newspaper sub-editors persisted with their own variants. It was at least agreed that the team would be known simply as 'Australia' for the purposes of the series with England. The visitors brought back Keith Carmody and omitted Ross Stanford from the side which had won at Lord's. Carmody assured the press that the small matter of his having been shot down over the North Sea and held captive by the Germans had not impaired his overall health, although, he conceded, 'the prison diet does not exactly qualify as an aid to fitness'. The Sydney-based journalist K.E. Hooper confidently informed his readers back home that the visitors had the 'freshness and spirit' to win again at Sheffield, and that in particular Reg Ellis, 'a protégé of the immortal Clarrie Grimmett' was, like his mentor, 'able to exploit to the full the timidity of British batsmen against left-arm googly bowling'. It was a fair point, although in the event Ellis took respectable but not match-turning figures of 2-66 in the English first innings and 3-47 in the second.

England had also made significant changes for the Test, replacing Ames, Robins, Stephenson and Gover. Errol Holmes, the Surrey amateur batsman, was brought in after Maurice Leyland, who had made his debut for Yorkshire in the era of starched shirts and skeleton pads 25 years earlier, strained his leg while practising in the nets. The Lancashire bowlers Bill Roberts and Dick Pollard, and the aforementioned George Pope – as always, 'talented but troublesome' as Pelham Warner characterised him – completed the side. As usual that summer, the selectors were forced to do without several first-choice players. Joe Hardstaff, Denis Compton and Alec Bedser all remained overseas, while the liberated POW Bill Bowes, with 67 pre-war Test wickets to his name, wrote to the MCC deputy secretary on 12 June:

> Dear Sir Pelham,
> I am prompted to write by the fact that I have received a query from Wing Commander W. Shakespeare 'would I be able to fill an unexpected vacancy at Sheffield', and, as this would imply that I am a certainty for the game [and] also the next match at Lord's, this letter is intended to correct any misunderstandings.
>
> The match at Lord's will be in approx. a month's time, and the weather up North has been so bad that last Saturday was the first time I have had a decent bowl – only about fifteen overs but I haven't recovered yet – and even as I write it is again raining.

I met Les Ames on Sunday, and if I had forgotten he refreshed my memory of those long Eng. v Australia matches when he told me how tired he was after the first day. I feel tired now after fifteen overs, and if I had to bowl again, and then again, well, quite frankly I do not yet feel equal to it … The doctors tell me it is ridiculous of me to expect to get over a three year period of under-nourishment in three months, so will you please consider me very doubtful for inclusion in any team.

If my performances in the matches between now and mid-July are not good enough for my name to be considered at Lord's, this letter will have been unnecessary, but, if I am considered, I shall only play if I feel equal to it and must not be considered a certainty.

Yours sincerely,
'Bill' Bowes.

Warner replied with good grace on 14 June:

Dear Bill,
Thank you for your letter. I quite understand the situation and I do beg of you not to attempt to play if you think it would be in any way bad for your health.

However, should you be absolutely confident in your own mind that you are fit, we shall be delighted to see you here at Lord's for the third Test. I will keep a place for you for the game, and perhaps you would kindly let me know, by 1st July, whether you think you are fit enough or not.

I am glad to hear you are putting on weight.

With kindest regards and all good wishes,
Deputy Secretary.

There was perhaps more of a professional feel to England's side at Sheffield, and less one of a VE Day festival party, as a result of the changes. Pope and Pollard were each making their first appearance at that level. It has to be said that the team's captain was only partly welcoming to his new charges. Before going out to practice, Pollard was hanging up his civilian clothes on a vacant peg in the communal Sheffield dressing room England shared with their opponents, when he looked up to see a bulky figure dressed in an RAF blazer and white flannels scowling down at him. It was Walter Hammond.

'You're in my space,' he grunted.

Over the years, the put-down had become Hammond's default position, a trademark almost as much commented on as his classic cover drive, a calling card as recognisable in its way as Winston Churchill's cigar or Hitler's moustache. Other than actually playing cricket, it was widely thought to be what he did best. The next morning, Hammond duly went out and scored exactly 100, batting for just over three hours, including eight fours and two sixes. 'He never neglected a scoring opportunity,' *Wisden* reported. England were all out for 286 half an hour before the close, and the visitors responded with 23 without loss at stumps.

Sunday was a rest day, so play resumed some 40 hours later on the morning of the 25th. In the now overcast conditions, it was suddenly a seamer's paradise, so much so that 20 wickets fell in three sessions. Australia collapsed to 147 all out, the England debutants proving their worth with Pope taking 5-58, four of the victims caught close to the bat, and Pollard bringing one back late to remove Hassett's middle stump. England reached 190 the second time around, Hutton top-scoring with 46 despite being hit by Miller on his foreshortened left arm with an inswinger that those who saw it (and Hutton himself, who didn't) described as a ball of electric speed. 'I don't think Keith ever cared for me very much,' the batsman was left to rue in his soft Yorkshire burr some 40 years later. Going in again on the dry but now cold final morning of the 26th, Australia were left facing 330 to win.

A young woman named Celia Horowitz was present in the crowd of about 12,000 at Bramall Lane on the last day. In September

1938, her German-Jewish parents had arranged for her to leave their home in Hamburg and be placed as a teenager with a foster family in the English midlands. She never saw her mother or father again, although she received occasional letters from them up until the middle of 1944. 'Be brave and good,' they urged her in the last message before they disappeared into Auschwitz. By then in her early 20s, Celia formed an understanding with an English soldier called Kenneth Lee, who was serving with the 9th Para Battalion. Lee wrote to her on 5 June of that same year: 'Tonight I am going to France, and by the time you receive this letter I shall be there, and you will be reading all about it in the papers. It all seems very unreal, even now ...' He, too, did not survive the war. In time, Celia began to write both stories and poems, often with a wistful air to them, and found that she was drawn to cricket, largely because of the 'cathedrals' in which it was played, and the fact that 'like life, it could be so often both romantic and sad', something every true lover of the game knows in their marrow. Taking her seat in the Football End stand that Tuesday morning, she wrote down in her journal an account of 'the little spouts of white smoke' rising from the terraced houses behind the ground, which was bathed by a 'timid sun' and a 'kicking breeze' that sometimes 'knocked over deckchairs and sent newspapers and empty paper bags eddying around, as if a fast train had just passed by the station platform'. Many years later, she would add that the experience of 'seeing the world awaken again' in 1945 had defined her entire later life.

In the drier terms of the match scores, Australia made another solid start with an opening stand of 108, while the jockey-sized Bill Edrich – a great battler, if an unlikely candidate to open the bowling for his country – was off the field with a torn muscle, but then folded to 288 all out. Hammond's side won by 41 runs, with roughly half an hour to spare. The 73-year-old Charles Fry, late of Sussex, Hampshire and England, dressed up in an antique naval uniform, was watching proceedings from the top deck of the pavilion, like his counterpart at Lord's using a telescope to follow the action.

Clicking this shut on Lindsay Hassett's dismissal, 'Fry poked his cap and monocle around the door of the dressing room and said, "Thought you might like to know what that one did, Lindsay – it swung from leg." He was gone again before the dejected Hassett could smile,' Dick Whitington later wrote. Pope and Pollard once again more than justified their inclusion, with three and five wickets respectively.

* * *

What might the modern observer have made of the sort of international cricket match played in 1945? It's always tempting to romanticise the past, almost as if slipping into a soothing jacuzzi of nostalgia. But perhaps it's still possible to convey some of the experience a spectator like Celia Horowitz would have had on a ground 80 years ago.

For one thing, the batting in those days was generally more measured, not to say textbook-inclined. Walter Hammond was admittedly a law unto himself, but his treatment of Cec Pepper's extravagant leg spin on the first day at Sheffield was a masterclass in the art of delaying the stroke until the last possible moment, and then extending a bat that Pepper himself would complain had looked almost absurdly broad. Hammond's driving off the front foot, in an action that was somehow both fast and unhurried, was a shot which had been old-fashioned even when W.G. Grace had delighted crowds with it in the early 1870s. It's arguable that in some ways Hammond's talent for accumulating runs and general disdain for the bowler actually increased with age, even as his ability to hit violently was retarded. Matching him in vigilance, if not always in the seemingly infinite amount of time at his disposal, men like Hutton, Washbrook and Robertson on the home side and Hassett, Whitington and Carmody for the visitors would all have made a strong claim for inclusion in a present-day Test XI. Each of them understood the merits of balance and economy of movement and that rarest of all batting virtues, true relaxation.

The typical bowling attack of the day might seem to us to be ludicrously top-heavy with spin. Captains often offered their spinners a fairly new firm ball which could produce disconcerting bounce for the batsman, and enticing opportunities for the close catchers. As a rule, the seamers were enthusiastic, often fiery and not infrequently wayward in direction. On anything resembling a lively wicket, bowlers like George Pope and Dick Pollard, and even that scurrying slingshot merchant Bill Edrich, could be an uncomfortable proposition. But in general they were men who tended to more or less just run in and do what came naturally, as opposed to following the dictates of computer technology or biomechanics, or exploiting the psychology of the opponent. Miller, of course, was a man apart, and was often genuinely fast, but even he seemed inclined to be guided by instinct rather than method. No one touched Miller as an attacking batsman, although it was said that he could look oddly hesitant in defence, which if true was a metaphor for the man.

In 1945, almost everyone trained on a diet of beer and cigarettes. Perhaps in consequence, the out fielding was an altogether looser affair than it is now, and once or twice even in the heat of a Test a ball would be spooned up so gently that it barely seemed equal to completing its journey to the man in the catching position, who quite often floored it again. Fielding back then wasn't all a case of missed dollies and giving chase at a gentlemanly trot to retrieve the ball – in the second innings, Hutton ran out Carmody with a flat throw that snapped into the keeper's gloves from the Bramall Lane cover boundary – but in general terms that component of the game hadn't evolved to the level of athleticism we expect today.

That aside, most of the action 80 years ago was as brisk as could reasonably be expected, often flickering away giddily as in some Chaplin-era hand-cranked film. The two teams bowled 121.5 overs on the first day at Bramall Lane, 120 on the second day and 102.4 on the third and final day, which was shortened by an hour. Despite or because of their greater affinity for the coaching manual, the batsmen tended not to linger, and at Sheffield more than one of them announced himself to the scorers by hitting the first ball he faced straight back against the sightscreen. Nobody went into a syncopated frenzy, or punched gloves, or showed any other particular emotion at any stage.

On the first day, the Australians all clapped dutifully when Hammond reached his ton, while at the other end Pope offered a quick handshake, but that was about it for any unseemly display of euphoria. As a race, batsmen instantly marched off when given out, and once or twice did so even before the official verdict. In all, it seems fair to say that you got your money's worth as a spectator. At Sheffield, *Wisden* reported that 'about 50,000 people' were present during the three days, perhaps 40,000 of them actually paying at the gate, generating receipts of £7,311, or the equivalent of £117,000 in today's money, a figure of roughly £3, adjusted for inflation, per admission. That would buy you about half a paper tray of vivid orange cheese slathered over a bed of chips like a slough of despond at a modern Test match venue.

No one in the crowd dressed like a banana or impersonated one of the entertainment stars of the day. Many of them smoked, however, with an intensity that over time caused a yellowing of the right-hand fingers down to the knuckle. On the whole, the available catering and toilet facilities were more redolent of a particularly uncongenial Turkish prison than at a present day sporting arena, and the Bramall Lane ground as configured in June 1945 would not have won any prizes for either its natural beauty or customer convenience. Perhaps to compare it to looking at a flickering lantern show depicting a vast open field, where top-class cricket was being played, filtered in sepia tones rather than today's blazing technicolour, might convey some of the flavour: not perfect, in short, but still pretty good.

* * *

After Sheffield, it began to feel something more like a normal first-class season. In the week of 25 June there were four separate matches at Lord's, teams representing Australia, the West Indies and New Zealand continued their own tours of British provincial grounds, some of them more well-heeled than others, the leagues and schools were in near-permanent session and Lancashire played a closely fought draw with Yorkshire at Old Trafford, where the visitors' veteran left-arm spinner Arthur Booth took ten wickets in the match and it rained a lot. When Pelham Warner's side had to abandon their game with the 2nd Army at Lord's due to the presence of ducks on the Tavern side boundary, Warner visited the two dressing rooms and arranged for the teams to come back the following day for a single-innings tie which brought over 500 runs in 140 overs and saw the return to the Army side of Leslie Compton, who ran up 52 in 21 minutes, if not that of his younger brother Denis, who was still serving with the Royal Engineers in India, where he scored an unbeaten 249 in that year's Ranji Trophy final.

The Australians were back at Lord's on 30 June, where an incident took place midway through the South of England innings that calls into question *Wisden*'s cherished belief that the servicemen's tour that year was invariably undertaken in an 'atmosphere of the utmost fairness and comity'. Certainly, as an exercise in mutual goodwill among the Allied nations it could only be counted a mixed success.

This is how the batsman involved, Gubby Allen, described it 40 years later: 'I played on to a ball from Mick Roper. Sismey, the wicketkeeper, who was standing up, and I both had a good look at the bails, and when we found them firmly in their grooves I threw the ball back to Roper as a friendly gesture saying "Bad luck". He promptly appealed to the umpire, Archie Fowler, a great pal of mine, and I was given out, handled the ball. Frankly, I thought it all a nonsense. The Australians subsequently claimed that they had called me back. But the only one who came near me was Keith Miller, and of course he wasn't the captain.'[6] If nothing else, the incident seems to prefigure the rancorous moment on the same ground in 2023, when at the end of an over the Australian keeper rolled the ball back along the ground while England's Jonny Bairstow incautiously wandered down the pitch and was given out stumped, although at least it could fairly be said that on the earlier occasion no one had leaned on his bat, or apparently exchanged words with his opponents, and nor, according to Allen, did anyone in the crowd start chanting. The dominant noise as he walked back to the pavilion was one of 'subdued mirth', he later wrote. Here some discrepancy exists with Roper's own account, in which he remembered being taunted with the words 'fatty' and 'coward' on his own departure from the field, although this last detail has proved difficult to corroborate, and, if true, would have been an unjust slur on a man who had served his country as a wartime fighter pilot.

* * *

The world of cricket had done its bit for the war effort, and now the upper echelons of the army were returning the favour. Following General Eisenhower's appearance at Lord's earlier in the month, another highly distinguished Allied commander now took the time to demonstrate his own long-term affection for the game, albeit in typically idiosyncratic fashion.

The officer in question was none other than General, later Field Marshal, Bernard Montgomery, who had been born in 1887 in a house immediately opposite the Oval, where Surrey won that year's County Championship, and a good enough player in his own right to be mentioned in the 1906 edition of *Wisden,* in a reference that presaged his later career, as having 'saved [a match] when a severe defeat

6 Miller had trained for the match in unusual fashion. Two days earlier, on the afternoon of the 28th, he had first declined his RAAF base commander's request that he take off on a training mission, on the grounds that 'I don't feel like it', but then eventually relented to go up in a Mosquito that had somehow caught fire shortly before landing. Whether through skill on his part or as another demonstration of 'Miller's Luck', he walked away from the wreckage unscathed.

had seemed impending'. Thirty-six years later, Montgomery would go on to lead the Eighth Army to victory in Libya with the famous injunction to his troops to 'hit Rommel [or 'Wommel', as Monty, a sufferer of mild rhotacism, put it] right out of Africa'. The general made no secret of his fondness for cricket and cricket terminology, and continued to make references throughout the war to the desirability of 'biffing' the Axis powers and 'bowling the opposition out'.

It in no way detracts from Montgomery's undoubted organisational genius and dedication to the cause of total Allied victory to say that in later years he enjoyed a somewhat equivocal reputation when it came to his dealings with young men. There was an odd and rather touching instance of this when, on 30 June 1945, the 57-year-old commander-in-chief of the British Liberation Army, fresh from taking the surrender of a million German troops in northern Europe, found the time to attend the annual schools match between Winchester and Eton, played this year at Winchester, where the visitors' opener Peter Blake scored an accomplished century, but rain once again prevented a result. Monty seems to have taken a particular shine to the 18-year-old Winchester captain, Hubert Webb, because after the game he treated him to a week as his personal guest at Osterwalde Schloss, the Saxony estate the British commander had requisitioned as his base. Webb later remembered being picked up in his host's Rolls-Royce, eating long meals together, and going sailing at Kiel ('idyllic, but for the bloated corpses floating in the water'), before being escorted around the ruins of Berlin.

Monty sent a long, typed letter to Webb after the teenager had returned to his family in England. 'Now we have made friends, we must not lose touch,' the general wrote. 'I may possibly be able to help you in times of difficulty, which do occasionally occur in life.'

In a hand-written postcard that followed a few days later, the conqueror of North Africa added: 'Dear Webb: You must always remember that cricket is the one imperishable gift. It was sent to us by the gods.'

Bill Edrich of Middlesex and England, whose experience as a wartime RAF Bomber Command pilot reinforced his view that life was there to be lived. He was eventually married five times.

Bill Bowes (l) who spent three years in a series of Italian and German POW camps, seen with his Yorkshire and England team-mate Hedley Verity. Verity fell in action during the Allied invasion of Sicily in July 1943, encouraging his men to 'Keep going' as he lay fatally wounded.

George Macaulay, another Yorkshire and England bowler destined not to return from the war.

Don Bradman, the greatest cricketer of his time - possibly of all time - who signed up to serve in the Australian forces in 1940, but was invalided out again the following year. To some surprise, a routine army physical revealed that the master batsman had 'distinctly sub-par' eyesight.

E.W. 'Jim' Swanton, who spent three wartime years in a Japanese camp. When Swanton finally returned to England in 1945, his father walked past him at the station, having failed to recognise his own son.

Walter Hammond, England's mercurially talented if aging captain in 1945, of whom a team-mate said: 'He took no interest in other people's lives, unless they happened to be pretty girls.'

Hammond's Australian counterpart in the Victory series, Lindsay Hassett.

George Pope (above, and far left, in a Derbyshire team photo), the England all-rounder whose correspondence with the Lord's authorities in 1945 saw a clash between an officer class on one side, and a gruff, free-thinking working man with a family to feed on the other.

Pelham Warner, seen in his playing days.

The Lancashire and England batsman Cyril Washbrook, who at the age of 30 hit his first century for England in 1945's fourth Victory match at Lord's. Eleven years later, Washbrook faced the unusual situation of finding himself both a Test selector and actually playing for his country against Australia at Leeds, where he scored 98 to help England win by an innings.

The Kent leg-spinner Doug Wright. Wright took ten wickets for England against the Dominions at Lord's in 1945, and no fewer than 2,056 over the course of his career.

Harold Gimblett, the constant enigma of English cricket on either side of the war.

Len Hutton, who overcame a wartime arm injury to score some 30,000 further first-class runs with a bat of a size usually only to be seen in schools cricket.

Les Ames of Kent and England in relaxed pose. 'We were still alive, and we were back playing the game we loved,' he later said of the 1945 season.

Australia's wicketkeeper-batsman Stan Sismey (left), who carried some two pounds of assorted shrapnel in his back as a result of being shot down by an enemy fighter while flying over the Mediterranean in 1942.

The Australians take the field against England at Lord's. Lindsay Hassett (second from left) is dwarfed by the newly liberated POW Graham Williams and the combative all-rounder Cecil Pepper.

Martin Donnelly, the cricket-rugby double international who rivalled even Keith Miller for big hitting in 1945.

Australia's openers Dick Whitington and Stan Workman.

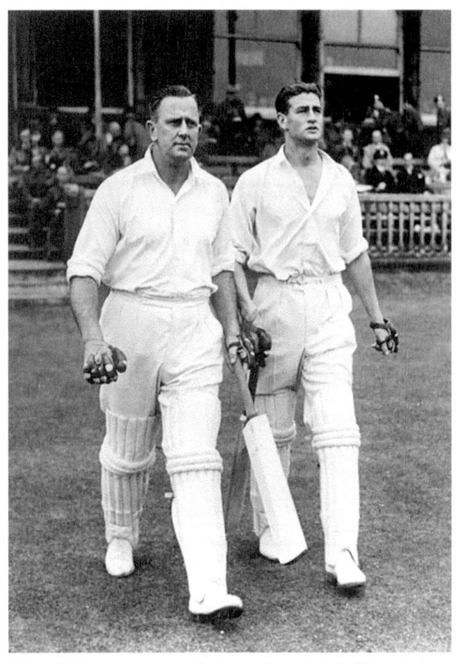

Cecil Pepper walks to the middle with Keith Miller. Both supremely talented all-round cricketers, neither one was a slave to authority.

Lindsay Hassett (l) with Stan Sismey. Although Hassett acted as the Australians' captain in the field, he was nominally under Sismey's command thanks to the latter's military rank.

6.
High Summer

AS USUAL in the 1945 season, Pelham Warner played the grand ventriloquist, operating at arm's length. In a steady flow of letters, cables and phone calls, he transmitted his wishes to county and league secretaries, frequently reminding them of the need to consider the demands of the de facto England Test side alongside their own commercial interests, and as often as not communicating direct with individual players to invite them to a match. Even so, Warner's name rarely if ever appeared in print in connection to any of this activity. Like God, the MCC deputy secretary appeared to be everywhere that summer. As England's captain Walter Hammond admiringly wrote: 'Plum's method of dealing with every little thing down to the bill of fare at the players' lunch was always most careful and conscientious, [but] one wondered if it sometimes cut him off almost completely from the real happiness of simply enjoying the spectacle of a good and full list of summer's cricket.'

By now it *was* full, too. As we've seen, the two-day Roses match at Manchester in early July was drawn, but the 41,000 spectators who generated gate receipts of £6,135 (£92,000 today) were further welcome proof that aspects of normal life might be returning to that devastated area, where German bombs had not only cratered the Old Trafford pitch but also flattened much of the nearby football stadium. Left to score 100 in as many minutes, Yorkshire had finished 18 runs short with five wickets in hand. Pollard was Lancashire's best bowler, but the most poignant sight of the day had been that of Bill Bowes representing his county again for the first time in nearly six years. As noted, Bowes was far from match fit, and at nearly 37 had reached the age when a seam bowler naturally tends to lose some of his fire. He was also playing with strained muscles in his neck and back, and, thanks to the gastric issues he carried as a souvenir of his three years in captivity, restricted himself to a slice of dry toast and a glass of water at the lunch interval. Despite these various handicaps, Bowes returned the eminently respectable figures of 1-20 off 15 overs in the first Lancashire innings, and 0-24 off 17 in the second. The home crowd stood and applauded him on and off the field.

Not long afterwards, the momentum of the cricket season was briefly overshadowed by two distractions, one of them financial and the other political. Both are worth touching on before we return to the field.

To take the more pressing, if also less publicised, first: it seems that at some point between the summer's second and third Tests, several of the Australian servicemen came to express a distinct lack of enthusiasm for their tour contracts. One or two of these documents still survived many years later, and what most strikes the modern observer about them is their simplicity. Instead of a fussily embossed paper, adorned with sub-clauses about performance bonuses and product endorsements, one reporter described the basic form as a cheap-looking sheet of paper in faded yellow, granting the player, who remained 'subject to King's Regulations', only his basic travel and meal expenses, while the individual's military unit continued to pay his modest base salary. In other words, men like Pepper, Miller and the rest played as many as 50 days of competitive cricket that summer effectively for free. There seems to have been some muttering about this by around the first week of July 1945, because Keith Johnson, the Australian manager, wrote a note for the file indicating that 'there [had] not been a good spirit abroad' amongst some of the team as they prepared for the next Test, and that this had required both an 'urgent wire home to the Board, and an audience with Sismey', who as a serving squadron leader was technically the commanding officer of the group. Johnson handled the matter with a discretion the tabloids would never allow today. Always highly conscientious in such affairs, he thought it 'of signal importance that nobody knows of the issue outside the circle'. No sooner was the matter apparently resolved, however, on mutually acceptable terms, than there were similar troubles in the England camp.

Somehow inevitably, these involved George Pope. As we've seen, Warner and his fellow selectors had long lobbied for Pope's release to play in the summer's third representative match, at Lord's, which had increasingly come to be seen as the centrepiece of the series. 'We here all assume that he will be present [and] fit to both bowl and bat to the required standard in a match of such magnitude,' William Shakespeare had written on 3 July. Such assumptions were to underestimate the player's talents as a contrarian, which at times matched his undoubted gifts as an all-round cricketer. 'I had not reckoned on his incomparable mastery of prevarication and selective understanding of the facts,' Warner himself later wrote, with some warmth, after reading Pope's cable to him of 4 July. 'Cannot Play July 14th Test. Letter Follows', it read, an already dire turn of events made worse by the fact that Pope had arranged for the message to be paid for on delivery by its recipient.

Pope's subsequent letter to Warner read:

> Dear Sir,
> Following my telegram to yourself re. the Test Match, I am very sorry to inform you that owing to business reasons I cannot afford to have six days away from my place of work at present. It would mean six days away, as I would have to leave Chesterfield on the Friday and return home the following Wednesday ... I am sorry as I would have liked to have played, [but] I also cannot see my way clear to play on the 6-7-8th August owing to having previously fixed a week's Tour with Mr C. Leatherbarrow of Liverpool. I have asked to be released from this, but he is not willing to do so.

> The same applies to the September fixture at Lord's, Over 33 v. Under 33. I have other engagements arranged, and they will not release me from same to play in your match.
>
> I hope that you have good weather at Lord's and that you exceed [*sic*] the amount of money taken at the gates.
>
> Yours sincerely,
>
> G. Pope.

The press picked up the story as filtered through what then passed for the media relations arm of MCC – essentially Warner himself and his deputy Hugh Henson – blandly reporting that 'Pope has informed the selectors that he will be unable to appear at Lord's next Saturday', and that the player had for some unknown reason 'vacated' his place in the side. It was left to the *Daily Express* to publish the full story on 11 July, with its back-page scoop that 'Pope has evidently been told by the Colne club that should he choose to play for England on the dates in question he would have to pay for a quality professional to take his place in the league side.' Reluctant to do this, the paper added, 'Pope has made a stand on behalf of his fellow professionals [and] declined the honour of the MCC invitation.' In light of the paper's report, perhaps the line in Pope's letter hoping for a healthy return at the Lord's box office was ironic. Either way, Warner was not pleased, writing back overnight:

> Dear Pope,
>
> Thank you for your letter. I note that you cannot afford to have six days away from work [and] also cannot see your way to playing in August, owing to having previously fixed a tour with Mr C. Leatherbarrow, that you have asked to be released and that he is not willing to accede to your request … Speaking privately, I should have thought that a rather important fixture such as England v Australia, especially in these days when we are trying to build up a side for the

> future, might perhaps have been given more sympathetic consideration.
>
> I hear that you bowled very well at Sheffield and also batted well, and I am very sorry that you are unable to play in these matches.
>
> Yours sincerely,
> Deputy Secretary.

There was apparently no further direct exchange of correspondence, nor comment on the matter of any sort, prior to the start of the Test on 14 July. But the MCC archives at Lord's do hold a clue which suggests that Pope's non-appearance was not well received by at least one of those on the selection panel. A typed note dated 6 July shows a total of 18 possible players under consideration for the following week's match. Pope's name appeared on the list, only to be crossed out again by a slash of someone's pen. It's impossible to know if this was Warner's way of reacting to Pope's news, but it's also impossible to doubt its impact on him.

The other matter besides the players' remuneration to now briefly intrude on the season was that of the general election. As noted, this was held on Thursday, 5 July, just as, in one of those matches then held at Lord's that fell short of the first-class, Berkhamsted School beat Bishop's Stortford College by 116 runs, while, at Shirland Road in Chesterfield, George Pope was sitting down to expound on his own willingness or otherwise to play at headquarters.

The conventional wisdom, repeated ad nauseam in the cottage industry of books and articles on the election, insists that this was the single greatest earthquake of 20th-century British politics, and one that overnight marked the arrival of a dynamic, confident, populist Labour administration bent upon social action, and the humiliation of their Conservative opponents, whom they derided as reactionary, hidebound, senile, bellicose, discredited, divided and defective. At a stroke, Churchill's wartime administration was decisively rejected in favour of the immediate construction of a socialist utopia as prefigured by the terms of the 1942 Beveridge Report, with its promise of nothing less than a cradle-to-grave welfare state.

The whole question of Britain's post-war social and political development perhaps overruns a book about the 1945 cricket season, but it's fair just to note before moving on that not every observer was as floored as was later claimed by the result of the election announced on 26 July, and that at least one well-placed media commentator stood far enough outside the consensus to go into print accordingly. This was none other than 28-year-old John F. Kennedy, then a roving European correspondent for a US news agency, who on 24 June had written a story published on the front page of the *New York Journal-American*: 'There is a definite possibility that Winston Churchill and his party will be defeated. This may come as a surprise to most Americans, who feel Churchill is as invincible at the polls as he was in war. However, he is fighting a tide that is surging through Europe, washing away monarchies and conservative governments everywhere ... Britain is moving irresistibly in this same direction, if not in this election then surely at the next one.'

After visiting the ruins of Berlin, Kennedy was back in London in the week of 2 July to record the final rites of the campaign, both large and small: Churchill's unquenchable optimism about the result; the slow, backfiring procession of loudspeaker vans spluttering up and down Oxford Street; and the queue outside the St John's Wood Road teashop where the future US president was eventually able to enjoy a meal of 'metallic-tasting cod, advertised on the bill as salmon, doused in a sticky white sauce that resembled hair oil, three or four bullet-like potatoes and a slice of sponge cake with yellow ersatz cream oozing on top ... Cost me nearly 10 bob [50p, or £7.50 in today's money], with a cup of cold, acorn-flavored coffee – undrinkable.'

On 3 July, Kennedy, an anglophile, and thus speaking more in sadness than anger, went on to tell the readers of the *Journal-*

American that 'while Mr Churchill and his men have let Britain drift perilously close to the economic rocks, the Laborites have been free to promise everything to everyone, which they have. The farmer, shopkeeper, housewife, small businessman and worker have all been led to expect better days ahead ... Actual [government] may be Labor's greatest crisis,' Kennedy concluded. Further refuting the bolt-from-the-blue interpretation of events, a Centre of Public Opinion poll published in the *Daily Express* on 2 July showed the two main parties locked in a statistical dead heat at 45 per cent, while the Gallup Poll in the *News Chronicle* had Labour and the Conservatives on 47 and 41 per cent respectively, which was within a point of the final outcome.

The urge to seek some respite from the coverage of the election – and for that matter of the continuing war in the Far East – appeared quite widespread, because there was a full house at Edgbaston that week to see Walter Hammond's XI beat the New Zealand Services by seven wickets, largely thanks to a run-a-minute 132 from Bill Edrich, while 15,000 spectators were on hand to see the RAAF thrash the British Army by 183 runs in a single-innings game at Lord's. The primary reason for the lopsided result was Bob Cristofani's leg-break bowling. Coming on third change from the pavilion end with the Army score at 62/5, chasing 254, he took four of the last five wickets which fell at a cost to him of only three runs.

That same day, the RAF scored 181 in 64 overs against a British Empire XI in front of a full house at Westcliff. Jack Andrews of Hampshire then hit an even-time 125 for the Empire, generally favouring the short forearm punch through the covers. This was all impressive in itself, but, coming as part of an opening stand of 175, his innings inevitably let some of the steam out of the contest. Right at the death, Andrews was caught on the rope off the veteran Surrey spinner Stan Squires. The bowler was one of those county yeomen whose tireless commitment to the game doesn't necessarily stem from any personal distinction on the field. Born in Kingston-upon-Thames in 1909, Squires had left school at 16 to work as an office boy in a City stockbroker's firm, but within two years had talked his way into a trial in the Oval nets. Considered a promising young all-rounder, and signed on wages of £2-10sh a week, 'he never appeared to impart any force into his batting', *Wisden* reported, before adding that 'as a slow bowler he specialised in off-breaks, although in later years to suit his county's needs he turned to the leg variety'. Throughout his career, Squires wore thick, jam-jar glasses, and despite this impediment was one of the first to sign up for the RAF on the outbreak of war, reaching the rank of flying officer. As a cricketer, it seems fair to say that he was neither born to greatness, nor had it thrust upon him. In fact, he had no greatness recorded of him at all, just a dozen years of unstinting service to his county which brought him a total of 19,000 runs at an average of 31, and 306 wickets at 35 apiece. The accident of the English weather saw him wheeling away that July afternoon at Westcliff in for once blazing sunshine, finishing with figures of 1-34 off just three overs.

Engaged as an 'energetic and conscientious' south London publican in the winter months, Stan Squires, who was married with three children, succumbed to pneumonia just four years later, at the age of 40. 'No more popular player every wore the Surrey colours,' *Wisden* said in his obituary.

* * *

It seems almost everyone in Britain obsesses about the weather to some degree or another, and 1945 was no exception to the rule. 'Changeable' might be the polite way to describe the year as a whole, which broke records at both ends of the scale for heat and cold. Many of the great British films of the period, like *Brief Encounter*, are played out in mackintoshes under grey skies, while the work of contemporary artists from R.S. Lowry up or down to the young Lucien Freud seems to specialise in figures stooped under the weight of a howling northerly wind. Perversely, much of the south and midlands had sweltered in a heatwave, punctuated with regular rainstorms, earlier in the spring, before turning more consistently wet just as the cricket season got underway. By the second week of July it wasn't only grim throughout much of the country, but on the afternoon of the 9th day literally turned to night in a full, three-hour solar eclipse of the sort the ancients believed might have been caused by a giant turtle devouring the sun. It was just one of those years. In another wild fluctuation of the thermometer, the south-east saw readings of 93°F (34°C) in the week of 2 June, leaving even Keith Miller to complain of the heat in his inter-services game with the RAF at Gloucester, with a daytime high as far north as Bradford of 88°F (31°C), while *Wisden* went on to write of a two-day Yorkshire match in the latter city that Len Hutton had 'batted in semi-darkness and in between drenching showers'. It was the same story during July, with intervals of tropical heat invariably followed by the return of pewter-coloured skies and poor visibility, and the rain-stops-play headline an almost daily aspect of most match reports. Even someone like Walter Hammond, who led a comparatively well-off existence and travelled around the country in a heated car, was affected by the 'woefully unsettled' conditions. 'The rain is appalling, and makes a mockery of batting,' he wrote on the eve of the third Test, by then also suffering one of his recurrent bouts of lumbago. It's a remarkable fact that there were still record crowds at many cricket grounds, perhaps as people sought at least the illusion of warmth evoked by the summer sport.

The Park Avenue ground in Bradford was saturated at the start of the Yorkshire v Australian Services match on 11 July, before drying out in response to a fresh wind on the second day and then assuming biblical-flood dimensions again ('You waited for it to come down with frogs,' Len Hutton remembered sardonically 40 years later) at the end. Batting first, the Services scored 204, with the home seamers John Whitehead and Alec Coxon not surprisingly doing the damage. In turn, Graham Williams continued his rehabilitation by taking 5-41 for the visitors, but the large crowd at least had the memory of Hutton's faultless innings of 82 – representing more than half his side's total score – to take home with them before yet another storm settled the issue.

It's a strange thought that while his countrymen were playing cricket at Bradford, Keith Miller was still an on-call RAAF pilot attached to 169 Squadron at RAF Great Massingham. There were rumours as late as the middle of July that his unit would be deployed to Burma to help fight the Japanese, and in the meantime he continued to lead an almost clinically schizophrenic double life between the cricket field and the cockpit of a Mosquito fighter-bomber, dispatched on reconnaissance missions at the pleasure of the squadron's commanding officer, Wing Commander Neville Reeves. In time, Reeves came to find his admiration for his famous subordinate's undoubted coolness under fire tempered by certain reservations about his relaxed approach to military discipline, while Miller in turn found his CO tiresomely 'tight-arsed'.

Following his earlier show of reluctance, Reeves now again ordered an unimpressed Miller aloft on a training flight one hot July afternoon while, as if to rub salt into the wound, he took several of the other men under his command to practise in some cricket nets set up just off the end of the base's main runway. Soon enough, Miller's green-and-brown-camouflaged Mosquito appeared overhead. It did not go unnoticed by his colleagues on the ground that the plane's starboard engine appeared to be on fire, and that thick clouds of smoke were pouring past the fuselage. There had been a mechanical malfunction of some sort, and now the plane spiralled down at a sickeningly steep angle for what seemed from the ground to spell certain doom for both Miller and his navigator, who were already far too low to bail out. 'It looked like curtains for them both,' Reeves later confirmed.

Back in the base's control tower, Miller's unmistakable voice came over the intercom. 'I'm sorry, boys,' he announced evenly, 'but the plane's buggered.' As if in illustration, a few seconds later the Mosquito ploughed into a field just opposite the nets, its port wing shearing off in a ball of fire when it hit a steel fence post.

Emergency vehicles raced to the scene, with Wing Commander Reeves at the head of an animated posse of men in cricket whites following close behind. By some twist of fortune, both the plane's occupants were able to hurriedly unstrap themselves and walk away from the burning aircraft seconds before its fuel tanks exploded in a spectacular plume of jet-black smoke, with shards of twisted metal and bursts of sparks shooting up like an early fifth of November firework display. Wiping the grime from his face, Miller looked at the flannel-clad airmen gathered anxiously around him, nodded back to the smoking wreckage of his plane, and remarked casually, 'Nearly stumps drawn that time, gents, I think.'

* * *

Miller's pre-Test adventure at RAF Great Massingham may have been the most striking single example of how differently certain top-class cricketers prepared for a big match than they do today, but it was far from the only one. There was also the perennial British matter of 'class', which meant that a player was judged as much on his good manners, and having a proper sense of his place in the social pecking order, as on his actual proficiency with bat or ball. It was a fact of life that was always likely to be quite pronounced in any team led, like the England side of 1945, by Walter Hammond.

In an age when surnames were the normal form of address between a captain and his team, who in turn called him 'Sir' or the comparatively relaxed 'Skipper', English first-class cricket might strike some modern observers as resembling an extended country-house soap opera. Deference, a word that invites scepticism or even satire in the 21st century, was a significant force in almost any group of men, military or civilian alike. Hammond, although still a peerless cricketer on his day, was perhaps not so well cast for the man-management aspects of captaincy as we might understand them, and certainly not known for his motivational skills as they applied to junior colleagues. 'I admired him, but he was about as welcoming as a clenched fist,' England's Godfrey Evans remarked of him after one overseas tour together. Hammond's batting, which gave such joy to thousands, seems to have given him no pleasure at all, while his many dalliances with women ('Well, Wally liked a shag,' Lancashire's Eddie Paynter once commented when asked to sum up England's captain) also brought him little solace, and according to at least one source may have been responsible for a major illness. Hammond's biographer David Foot has suggested that his subject was suffering from what was known euphemistically as a 'social disease' contracted on a tour of the West Indies in 1925/26, and that this accounted for his erratic mood swings later in life. It remains a viable, if unproveable, theory. What's not in doubt is that Hammond played as a professional cricketer for nearly 20 years before declaring himself an amateur in order to satisfy the prevailing social requirements of an England captain. It has to be said that he responded to his new role as a patrician authority figure with something of the zeal of a convert.

England made three changes for their next match against Australia at Lord's, replacing Jack Robertson, Errol Holmes and George Pope with the largely unknown quantities of John Dewes, Donald Carr and Luke White, all of whom were aged just 18 and making their first-class debuts. It was a bold move to draft in a trio of what amounted to no more than promising schoolboy cricketers, and, statistically speaking, not a success. The three newcomers scored only 47 runs between them, and Carr, the bowler, failed to take a wicket. But at least their inclusion served to highlight the elaborate etiquette of finely tuned social protocol that then pervaded English cricket, and in particular its lack of any spurious egalitarianism. None of the new recruits to the side would have dared address the captain by his Christian name, and even the impeccably blue-blooded Hon. Luke White, late of Eton and the future 5th Baron Annaly, would come to reflect on his skipper as a 'very great cricketer who could frankly be a touch on the cool side with his men'. Accounts of Hammond's petty takedowns of his juniors and his tendency to treat them not so much as valued colleagues but as necessary accomplices on the field and useful servants off it, were quite striking even at the time, and might well reach the level of a sackable offence today.

John Dewes, then embarking on national service in the navy before going back up to Cambridge, long remembered the Saturday night after the first day's play of the Lord's Test.

> We batted first, and I managed to get my head down and stayed at the crease with Len Hutton for a while, until Miller clean bowled me. I got 27, and frankly I thought I'd done all right. Hammond was the next man in, and when he passed me on his way out to the middle he muttered, 'Try moving your feet next time, Dewes.' That was it. But then about half an hour after stumps the new boys were all told to report downstairs where a taxi was waiting at the gate, and the next thing I knew we were at the White City dog-racing track. Well, that was a first for me, and I don't think old Luke White or Donald Carr usually moved in those circles, either, although I remember Luke telling me with a straight face that his family actually owned most of that part of London and had given it its name.
>
> When we got there we all sat down to a meal in the stadium, which was packed like Wembley on Cup Final day. The skipper was at one end of the table, Bill Edrich and one or two others in the middle, and the three youngsters down at the end. Then the racing itself began. From then on for the rest of the night we were basically Hammond's runners. 'Dewes!' he'd call out. 'Put a quid on dog number 5 for me.' I'd walk up, collect the pound from the skipper, go to the window, pass it over, then go back and hand Hammond the slip. His dog didn't win. Next race it was the same thing, only this time the skipper shouted, 'Carr! Put this down on number 4,' or whatever it was. And Carr did so. Hammond kept that up for about six races, alternating between the two

> of us, I might add with never a winner among them, and then on the final heat he shouted out 'Mr White!' as if just now remembering his name. And Luke White said 'Yes, sir?', went up, took the skipper's money, passed it through the window for him, and trotted back with the slip. Still no joy for old Wally. He was getting pretty tetchy by this stage, ripping up the betting slips and tossing them over his shoulder each time his dog lost. Looking back now, Hammond's mood probably darkened as his losses mounted, but also because he was suffering from a pretty bad go of lumbago. It eventually kept him off the field at Lord's. But that's hindsight. At the time it just seemed like you were back on your first day at school and being persecuted by your headmaster. I suppose we could have said no. After all, putting money down on the greyhounds had nothing to do with our duties as Test cricketers. But that's how it was in those days. I should say that like everyone else I admired Hammond the cricketer to the ends of the earth. He was one of the true giants of the game. But he could also be pretty snooty to those he deemed to be small fry, including some of his own teammates.

In terms of the Test itself, Hammond won the toss at Lord's and England batted, or at least they did once the rain let up at around noon on the first day. Hutton alone rendered the innings vertebrate, scoring 104 in three and a half hours, which proved to be almost half his team's total. First wicket down, the left-handed Dewes came out, wearing a striped Cambridge Crusaders cap, gave a few exploratory swipes of the air with his bat, took guard, half a dozen fielders crouched around him, and gazed somewhat optimistically down to the deep square leg boundary. The Australian spinners Pepper and Ellis had come on early, but now Miller appeared at the pavilion end, took a perfunctory run, and sent down a ball that sailed far over the batsman's right shoulder and was still on the rise when the keeper took it above his head while dancing backwards into the deep.

Dewes knew little of several subsequent balls, Hutton not much more. But then Bert Cheetham returned, right-arm medium, at the other end, which for the sorely pressed batsmen must have felt like facing a steady-as-she-goes Morris Eight after dealing with a runaway lorry. Hutton twice pulled him through midwicket, both strokes that suggested business. When Miller reappeared he soon removed Dewes's off stump, on his way to figures of 3-44, all three victims clean bowled, off 18 overs. Hassett's placing of his field still bore no obvious relation to the saving of runs, with several wide open spaces on both sides of the wicket should the batsman be able to exploit them. Alas, few did. Miller did Hutton for pace immediately after tea, leaving England on 169/5. Listed as 'Repton School' on the scorecard, Donald Carr came out to replace him, trying imperfectly to control the violent shaking of his knees, and walked past the bowler waiting for him on his mark at the pavilion end.

'Good luck, kid,' Miller said.

'Thank you, Mr Miller,' Carr replied.

If the new batsman thought this exchange of courtesies might earn him one off the mark, he was badly mistaken. 'I got three balls from Miller, and I didn't see any of them,' Carr recalled. 'The next one I just jammed my bat down on, and to my utter amazement made contact. The next thing I knew the ball was flying past mid-off for four. "Well played, son," said Miller. A few balls later he knocked my leg stump over, and I didn't see that one, either. A couple of the Australian chaps shook my hand as I walked off.'

Edrich and Griffith, both holders of the DFC, put on a spirited 66 in 70 minutes, but after that the last three men departed in brisk succession, leaving England 254 all out. Few of the home batsmen had imposed themselves on the proceedings, several catches went down, and the bowling, Miller excepted, only rarely got any life out of the pitch or moved the ball off it. Hutton had done wonderfully well, back to his pre-war best, but for long periods it might have been a club, or, for that matter, a school match.

At least there could be no complaints about the Monday morning gate of 26,000 paying customers, although as it happened one important figure was missing – Walter Hammond, whose lumbago had worsened over the rest day, leaving him confined to his top-floor room at the Charing Cross Hotel, with a hot-water bottle strapped to his aching lower back. Warner's friend Billy Griffith took over the team's captaincy in his absence. It had rained again over the weekend, but Monday was dry, with a fresh northerly breeze, the teams' flags snapping noisily from the twin turrets rising up at either end of the sturdily Victorian pavilion brickwork. In Pope's and Bowes's absence, Bill Edrich opened the bowling at one end, making up in sheer energy what he lacked in physique and finesse, with the yeoman Dick Pollard at the other. The Manchester *Guardian* said of Edrich that, while far from the ideal choice to lead a Test attack, 'he hurls himself at the bowling crease as though he has a personal grievance against it'. Australia were all out for 194, of which Hassett made 68 and Pollard took 6-75, leaving some to wonder what Pope might have managed.

England had a tidy lead of 60, but little went right for them the second time around. With Washbrook nursing a sore thumb and Hammond *hors de combat* at his hotel, Dewes was pressed into service to open with Hutton. In the first innings, Miller had removed the teenager's off stump, but he varied the routine here with an outswinging yorker that the young batsman tried and failed to scoop out before it flattened middle and leg. England finished the second day at 118/3, which given the absences in their line-up perhaps sounded better than it was. But at least the match was alive, and for once the sun was beating down on the third and final morning, when the word was that Washbrook would bat if required, but that Hammond would take no further part. 'Neither his own temperament, nor external comment, could rouse him to the cause,' the *Guardian* wrote in a sardonic later review.

England's remaining six wickets went down for 46 in just 70 minutes' play that morning. Hutton, with 69, again made nearly half his side's total. Edrich weighed in with a few thumping strokes to reach 58, Washbrook, coming in sixth wicket down, managed an unbeaten 13 with his right hand strapped into what looked like an oven mitt, but the middle order of White, Carr and Griffith made a total of just five between them. Playing his first representative match of the series, Bob Cristofani did most of the damage with figures of 5-49, confirming what was already widely suspected – that English batsmen in general didn't care for the well-flighted leg break on anything like the sort of turning wicket Lord's generally presented around the midway point of a three-day match. In the end Australia had five hours to make the 225 needed to win. Pollard was soon peppering both the openers, bowling to a ring of five slips, and had Whitington caught behind without scoring, but the tourists' keeper Stan Sismey, promoted to number three, kept on the move with quickly run singles and put on a second-wicket stand of 82 with Jim Workman. Keith Miller, complaining noisily of both a migraine and a sore back, the latter of which may or may not have resulted from playing cricket, then limped out with the score on 104/3, with two hours left to play.

If this was Miller under the cosh, one could only imagine him at full tilt. After a few minutes of reconnaissance, he went down the track to crash Wright back over his head for a first-bounce four. It wasn't all histrionics on Miller's part, though. He could mix it up with dead-bat play and adept pad-play, together with the most astute judgement of the quick single. It was said that spectators sometimes looked up at the board and were amazed to see that Miller's score had suddenly advanced by 20 or 30 runs since they last checked. He hit an unbeaten 71 here in just over an hour and a half, including one blow off Roberts that sailed far over the square leg umpire's head and climbed steadily into the earth's troposphere, where it seemed to hang motionless for an instant before beginning its long descent into John Dewes's hands just inside the deep midwicket rope. Dewes dropped it. The repartee that ensued from the Tavern was for once not marked by its air of civility or deference to the young gentleman cricketer. Miller seemed to forget about his headache and his bad back after that, launching two more blows into a Tavern crowd which by now was all jeers and satirical applause. Australia got home by four wickets with ten minutes to spare. The winning runs were four leg-byes that were missed by Griffith but competently fielded by a London policeman stationed on the Nursery End boundary. Miller went off, flicking the hair from his eyes, with a speed that suggested he might again be running late for a previous engagement. The result gave the tourists a two-one lead in the series with two to play. *Wisden* wrote: 'Pollard always toiled hard, but he badly missed the support of George Pope. About 84,000 people were present during the match.'

Pelham Warner seems to have agreed with this assessment of England's pace attack because, even as the two teams were leaving the field at Lord's on 17 July, he sat down to fire off a letter to Charles Leatherbarrow, Pope's sometime employer at his family's wholesale dried-fruits business in Liverpool.

> Dear Sir,
> I apologise for again worrying you … but may I with great respect venture to ask you to consider your decision about releasing Pope to play cricket? These matches between England and Australia at Lord's are of great interest and importance, and, incidentally, all the proceeds go to charity … Now Pope, as you know as well as I do, is a good all-round player; and we should very much like to have him in the England side. Although it is [a matter] of some higher importance than that, his inability to play must upset the balance of our XI.
>
> In the circumstances, therefore, I wonder if you would kindly give Pope leave to play? The Committee of M.C.C. would be grateful to you and so would I, to whom falls the job of getting up these teams.
>
> I should be glad of an early reply.
>
> Deputy Secretary.

Warner's appeal to the fruiterer's better nature seems to have worked, because Pope himself cabled Lord's four days later.

'Thank you invitation to play August 6th against Australia. Pleased to accept. Leave expense question to you.'

In a reply sent that same day, Warner tempered his satisfaction at the news of his leading all-rounder's decision with a certain degree of ill-concealed pique apparently triggered by the player's reference to finances.

> Dear Pope,
>
> Thank you for your telegram, saying that you will be able to play for England v Australia here at Lord's on 6th, 7th and 8th August.
>
> As to the question of money: I saw in the Daily Express that in an interview it was stated: "Pope declined to play in the last match, in which England was defeated by four wickets, because his expenses were not guaranteed. Now he is leaving the question of expenses to the M.C.C." In regard to this, you never mentioned finances in any of your communications with me, so how could you have said in the newspaper that your expenses were not guaranteed?
>
> The fact is that when a cricketer plays here in these big matches, his railway fare, cabs, hotel bills, etc. are paid in full, and I personally ensure that players will not be out of pocket, but indeed rather the reverse.
>
> I am glad to hear you will be playing here at Lord's. I take it that you will make your own arrangements for hotel accommodation?
>
> Deputy Secretary.

Meanwhile, Mr Leatherbarrow himself replied to Warner, in so doing revealing a personal affinity for cricket, along with the suggestion that Pope's most significant defect as an employee might be an independence of spirit that verged on the truculent:

> Sir,
> I only received your letter last night. It had been sent on specially from my Liverpool office to my home. I have been away at Blackpool this week playing cricket. In the circumstances, and to avoid any unpleasantness, I have today telephoned [your office] to make a point of personally seeing you to explain the position first hand, from which you will also gather that Pope was wholly wrong in [his assessment], and is entirely free to play in the next Test game.
>
> I personally think with an incident of this description, it is better closed with only a selected few knowing the full story and thus prevent any possible ill will being caused. This will also particularly apply to yourself as you will only want Pope playing at his best. Therefore, I think the wiser policy is to let him imagine that the matter has been amicably arranged.
>
> I have today written to Pope that I have received your communication, and of course have automatically released him from his engagements with me on the 6/7/8th August.
>
> Yours faithfully,
> C. Leatherbarrow.

Warner in turn replied on 23 July:

> Thank you very much for your letter of the 19th, the tone of which I very greatly appreciated.
>
> I would only say this: that Pope seems to have got everything all wrong!
>
> I quite agree with you that an incident of this description is better closed, with only a few people knowing the whole

story, and I, for my part, will say nothing more about it, and certainly will not bother Pope further on the matter.

Kindest regards,

P. Warner.

* * *

It seems fair to say that there are really two ways of looking at the Australian cricketers' progress around the United Kingdom in the summer of 1945. On one level it was what Keith Miller would later fondly recall as a sort of victory lap of 'the country's loveliest parks, celebrating all that was good about England, and about cricket', with ample opportunity for the sport's female spectators, in particular, to make known how positively they would react to any romantic overtures the craggily handsome athletes might care to make to them. And on the other hand, there were the trials of a cash-strapped tour of an impoverished and war-weary nation which involved dreary nights spent in unprepossessing town centre or seaside digs, and long days travelling between fixtures over what were among the worst-maintained roads even in the Europe of 1945, or else on the sadly reduced rail network.

In that latter context, there was the logistical nightmare awaiting the tourists – billed for the occasion as the RAAF – as they set off to fulfil an engagement with the local invitation side expecting them at the Courtaulds ground at Mercia Gardens, Coventry, shortly after the Lord's Test. Miller himself sat the game out, and was thus spared the ordeal of a four-hour drive up the A5 and its tributaries through the early morning hours of 21 July. The Australians' northward journey was interrupted when their hired motor coach broke down around the hamlet of Weedon Bec, the birthplace in 1886 of the distinguished actor Leo G. Carroll, but not, in fairness, known for either its raw energy or lavish amenities for the stranded traveller. A replacement bus, hurriedly dispatched south from Rugby, also failed them when it was found not to have sufficient fuel to continue to its final destination. At that point a third vehicle was summoned, and at least proved adequate to the job of conveying the dozen or so cricketers and their small entourage to the Courtaulds ground, where they arrived two hours late, promptly lost the toss, and took the field without having had time for lunch.

The Australians were still out there some four hours and two sessions later, when the home side declared their innings at 273/7, Kent's Arthur Fagg having scored exactly 100 and Cristofani, following up his good form at Lord's, taking 5-83 off 33 overs. There was still no rest for the weary tourists at the close, because Ross Stanford remembered the team then being asked to assemble in the pavilion to be formally presented to 'some big nob at Courtaulds and his lady wife', the latter clutching a purse-sized dog to her chest, and both parties going down the line 'with some little words of welcome for the plucky Aussies', before releasing the visitors back to the unappealing cold supper awaiting them on their hotel lounge's sideboard.

Under the circumstances, it must have been galling for the Australians, and many others besides, to read in the next day's press of the dining arrangements of the 'Big Three' heads of government in their conference at Potsdam, where, according to the *Daily Express*, 'several dozen crates of chicken, game and cakes', as well as a large suckling pig borne in on a pallet by four soldiers as though carrying a human corpse, along with 'copious amounts' of vodka, gin, brandy and other spirits were being laid on for the Allied leaders and their staffs. The media did not similarly report on the arrival in Potsdam on 21 July of a Pentagon military courier bearing a coded message for President Truman with the details of the world's first nuclear detonation, a test which had taken place earlier that week in the New Mexico desert. The president's paper mentioned the fact that the ensuing fireball had mushroomed into a cloud of smoke 10,000 feet high that could clearly be seen 200 miles away, before continuing, in tones departing from those of the normally arid government brief: 'All present seemed to sense immediately that the explosion far exceeded the most optimistic expectations.

and wildest hopes of our scientists. The whole surrounding country was illuminated by a searing light with an intensity many times that of the midday sun … It was golden, purple, violet and blue [with] that great beauty the poets dream about but describe most poorly and inadequately. Thirty seconds after the explosion came first the air blast, pressing hard against all observers, to be followed almost immediately by the strong, sustained, awesome roar which warned of doomsday.'

Five thousand miles away from these events, the Australians drew their match in the drizzle in front of 6,000 spectators at Coventry, where 35-year-old Tommy Armstrong, George Pope's occasional county teammate at Derbyshire, but then primarily employed as an accountant at the nearby Jaguar Cars plant, took 7-52 in 20 overs of orthodox left-arm spin.

Keith Miller was back in the side now advertised as Australian Services for a two-day match starting the following morning against Yorkshire at Bramall Lane, where he announced himself by scoring an imperious 111. That particular figure is usually imbued with a mystical horror for Australians, but didn't seem to be an issue on this occasion. Nearly half Miller's runs came in boundaries, including a blow off the famously thrifty spinner Arthur Booth that pinged off the metal shutters of the groundsman's hut and rebounded more than halfway back to the aggrieved bowler's outstretched hand. One or two teammates prodded away at the other end, and the Services were all out for 232 by tea, a collective scoring rate of a run a minute.

Len Hutton then also made 111 for Yorkshire, an innings devoid of fireworks but based solidly on first principles, neat, vigilant and precise, and always in line for anything there to be hit. The batsman had now taken 366 runs off the Australian bowlers in four consecutive innings, which if nothing else seemed to settle the matter of whether or not his injured left arm was still up to it. Cecil Pepper had figures of 6-69, turning it sideways at slow-medium pace, and, in spasms, genuinely fast, restricting the home side's lead to 11. It would have made a cracking limited-overs contest, but instead of that the sides were meant to get through four full innings in just two days, with rain a constant factor. Even before the first ball had been bowled it was almost unanimously accepted that the match would end in a draw, barring some excessively creative declarations of the sort not then normally associated with Yorkshire cricket or more particularly their veteran captain Maurice Leyland, fond as he was of a dry joke. Everyone shook hands just before six on the Tuesday evening, at which point the sun perversely came out, and the large crowd swarmed like ants across the pitch. For Yorkshire the figures of 4-48 off 25 unerringly accurate and often hostile overs against Bill Bowes's name was probably the most satisfying takeaway of the match. There were 16,500 spectators over the two days.

Between the drama of the Lord's Test and the individual contributions of men like Cristofani, Pepper and Miller, it had been a 'grand week for the Australian Services, and for the fortunes of cricket in all parts of the Mother Land', *The Times* reported on 25 July. Even so, no sporting season involving the stage-management of nearly 50 tour matches, five of them at international level – not to mention navigating the minefield of a system that allowed some home players to be paid for their services, and others to notionally claim only expenses – could be entirely trouble-free for the game's administrators. The name Pope again crossed Pelham Warner's desk late that month, though on this occasion it was that of George's older brother and fellow Derbyshire all-rounder Alf. 'I do not believe that either my brother or I will be appearing in County Championship play for much longer,' he informed the *Bradford Telegraph and Argus*, adding that it was an 'altogether better proposal' to be contracted to a northern league side 'who will consider the player's welfare alongside their own financial interests'. Warner forwarded a suitably annotated copy of Pope's interview for William Shakespeare's attention, before turning his thoughts to the troubling matter of the state of health both of the England captain and certain of his colleagues.

Winston Churchill in characteristic pose.

British soldiers temporarily leave their weapons to play an improvised game of cricket in May 1945.

The reason why The Oval wasn't called on for any of the immediate post-war matches. Refitted as an internment camp, with barbed wire strung across the playing area, the ground was ready again in April 1946.

V-E Day scenes in central London. Reporting back to his air force base 100 miles away, Keith Miller first learnt of the end of the war 'not from some big speech at Buckingham Palace, but by seeing toilet rolls flying out of windows in the Norfolk countryside.'

John Dewes, seen here seated second from right in a Cambridge University team, was one of a trio of largely untested teenagers brought in by England for the summer's third match against Australia at Lord's. It was a bold move, but statistically not a success: the three newcomers scored just 47 runs between them and failed to take a wicket.

Walter Hammond and Lindsay Hassett go out to toss before the third Victory match at Lord's in July 1945.

The Australians seen before taking the field for the third and final day at Lord's, 17 July 1945. Back row, l-r: Keith Carmody, Graham Williams, Cecil Pepper, Bert Cheetham, Keith Miller, Dick Whitington, Ross Stanford. Front row l-r: Jim Workman, Stan Sismey, Lindsay Hassett, Bob Cristofani, Reg Ellis.

Clement Attlee (seen with the king at Buckingham Palace immediately after his landslide victory in the July 1945 general election), and Generals Bernard Montgomery and Dwight Eisenhower, all three of whom found time to visit Lord's in the summer of 1945. Attlee and Monty were both long-time cricket lovers, but Ike picked the game up quickly.

Part of the overflow crowd for the fourth Victory match at Lord's in early August 1945. A spectacular lightning storm disrupted play on the first morning, while at around the same time 6,000 miles away the Americans dropped the world's first atomic bomb on Hiroshima.

Lord's officials hold back spectators trying to force the ground's Grace Gates open after being locked out. There were 34,000 present on the first morning, although some estimates put the day's total attendance as high as 45,000, at a time when people took a more relaxed attitude to health and safety regulations.

Australia's Bob Cristofani drives Doug Wright to the boundary in the fifth Victory match at Old Trafford, while on his way to a score of 110 not out. E.W. Swanton emerged from captivity that week to wander in to the Thai village of Kanchanaburi, where a large radiogram standing incongruously on the mud floor of a makeshift café brought him the news that 'England were playing Australia at Manchester, and a gentleman called Cristofani was getting a hundred.'

Learie Constantine, the legendary West Indies all-rounder, and future high commissioner and peer, who captained the Dominions to a last-minute victory over England to round off the 1945 season at Lord's.

Keith Miller appearing to perceive the virtues of attack. He scored a better than run-a-minute 185 in the Dominions match.

Teatime at the end-of-season Scarborough Festival.

Richie Benaud pays his respects, one great Australian cricketer to another, at Miller's 2004 funeral in Melbourne.

> My dear Wally,
> I hope to Heaven your lumbago is going or, at any rate, is passing off as we want you very badly here on 6th, 7th and 8th August. If by any chance you are not fit enough to play (and I pray daily that this may not be so) I would venture to suggest Gimblett might take your place. He played very well here on Saturday, making some perfectly glorious drives.
>
> It was a fine effort, especially as he had an attack of cramp in his calf about ¾ of the way through his innings. This was probably due to lack of exercise.
>
> Meanwhile, Dewes writes to me and says that his commanding officer will not let him off to be 12th Man, but would do so if he is actually playing.
>
> Now, who would you propose as 12th Man, supposing the original side stands? Would you like me to try and get young Carr, or who would you suggest?
>
> All good wishes,
> Plum.'

Hammond's hand-written reply, sent from his modest home at Brimscombe, near Stroud, again demonstrated how far removed were the concerns of a senior England Test player from those of his modern counterpart.

> My Dear Plum,
> I seem to be unfortunate these days. There has been a death in the chief party responsible for my box at Lord's, and I have been asked to cancel it. If you have any difficulty in placing the box in other hands let me know and I will pay for it.
>
> At least you will be pleased to hear that my back is improving, and I think I shall be free to play, but if there is

> any doubt about this quite frankly I should prefer Wyatt.[7] As to 12th Man, I agree that it is a good idea to get a coming young cricketer.'
>
> Forgive haste,
>
> Wally.

On the Thursday afternoon following this exchange, Hammond was walking down a street in central Bristol with two motor-trade acquaintances when a loudspeaker van drove by them with the announcement that the town's northern parliamentary seat, held for the previous 14 years by the moderate Liberal National MP Robert Bernays, had been won by the Labour candidate William Coldrick, a trade union activist who could, and did, boast of having been imprisoned for his role in the General Strike of 19 years earlier. England's incumbent Test captain was not as a rule one for open vulgarity, but he allowed himself an exception here. 'Fuck me,' he muttered to his companions. Each time another van passed by it bore news of further Labour gains around the country. The full scale of the landslide came to be known at around six that evening. Labour had a net gain of 239 seats, for a majority of 145 over all other parties. Most people in Bristol itself seemed to contain their emotion at the result, although 'one young chap and his girlfriend performed a strange little dance of joy right there in the street', according to an eyewitness.

Hammond was not alone in his initial reaction to the news, which, if not wholly unexpected was sufficiently dramatic for him to fret in a letter, 'Will all one's money now be pinched by the

7 The 44-year-old Bob Wyatt, himself a former England captain, had scored an unbeaten century earlier that week playing for the RAF against a Walter Hammond XI (in which Hammond himself didn't appear) at the Abbeydale Park ground in Sheffield. This letter showed magnanimity on the current England skipper's part, because the two players, though mutually respectful, were not close. 'Of course Wally was a brilliant batsman,' Wyatt reminisced towards the end of his long life in the 1990s. 'But he should never have been appointed captain of his county, let alone of England. He was out of his depth, and he didn't deal with lesser mortals very well – he could be bloody rude, cracking jokes about the younger players out in the middle. I didn't much care for that.'

socialists?' It didn't happen, or at least not in the way he might have imagined, although there were soon to be other, perhaps better-founded, concerns that the state might impose itself on certain previously neglected aspects of British life, including the proposal of 53-year-old Ellen Wilkinson, the new Labour secretary of education, that all returning service personnel wear a compulsory armband so that young females could avoid them for fear of catching the sexually transmitted diseases said to be 'rampant' among repatriated soldiers. We needn't linger on the broader question of the United Kingdom's political development in the period from 26 July 1945 until the return of a Conservative administration under a then sadly reduced Winston Churchill in October 1951, except to say that, by wide consensus, this was a golden era of 'planning' in all walks of public life, and as such the logical extension of the enhanced government apparatus that had grown up to direct its citizens to do anything in the national interest as it was defined by the war, rather than a sudden outbreak of ideologically pristine socialist principles for their own sake.

Walter Hammond might have been a hopeless Test captain, but in some other ways he was the voice of reason. Like many people whose lives appeared to have been in a state of near-constant turmoil for the previous six years, he seems to have viewed the events of that last week of July with a mixture of enthusiasm and apprehension. Finding himself back at the White City dog track on the Saturday night following the election result, Hammond turned to remark to his new fiancée, and soon to be second wife, Sybil: 'I don't suppose we will ever be allowed a flutter again, will we, by our new lords and masters?' 'Of course you will be,' she replied. 'You're having one now, aren't you? They may take a bit more of your winnings in tax to help build schools and hospitals, but that's just as it should be, isn't it?' 'No it's not,' said Hammond with some vehemence. 'I should be free to do as I like with my own money. I earned it, not them.' Somewhere in this brief betting-window exchange there surely lay a larger point about the continuing debate of whether it should be the proper role of a government to solve seemingly intractable problems by mobilising and directing people and resources to collectively useful ends, or conversely, in Hammond's words, 'The buggers [in office] should just leave us alone.'

* * *

Thirty-six hours after hearing the election result, the Army and RAF teams went out to play cricket against one another at Lord's. The 37-year-old Sgt. Charlie Harris, a sometime Nottinghamshire opener, was, like Harold Gimblett, one of the game's enigmas, a batsman as likely to block a full toss as to knock an unplayable delivery out of the park. Harris was also something of a comedian and was known to walk out to the middle and hang a sign saying 'Do Not Disturb' on the stumps. He scored a brisk 73 here, Les Ames replied with 93 for the airmen, and the match was drawn. There was also a full round of county fixtures in that last week of July, even if none of them were officially deemed first-class. Cricket had now 'awakened again at all levels of the game, and in all parts of the land', *The Times* wrote on the 30th. It was 'wonderful to behold' this renaissance, 'now that we may all begin to recover from Hitler's blood-thirst and enjoy our simple pleasures again'.

Seeming to confirm the point about the game's universality, the Australians continued their northern journey through Durham and over the border into Scotland, where at Selkirk the All-Scottish Services side proved sufficiently elastic to include 'Hopper' Levett of Kent and England, Lancashire's current Test seamer Dick Pollard and the bowlers Austin Matthews and Arthur Creber, both of whom were Welsh, in its ranks. From there the tourists went on to a one-day match at Greenock, 'the tie starting late in the afternoon', according to *Wisden*, 'through the visitors' motor transport again breaking down on the way from Selkirk that morning'.

The Australians then beat a full-scale Scotland representative side in front of a Saturday crowd of 8,000, many of whom had come expressly to see Keith Miller in action, at the Hamilton Crescent ground in Glasgow. In the event it wasn't one of those Miller performances for the ages – out for 9, and never coming on to bowl – although at least one local admirer, an unmarried, 27-year-old schoolteacher named Clare Morey, got full value for her 2-shilling ticket, as she vividly remembered 50 years later.

'There was a party, or at least drinks after [stumps] in the pavilion, and I knew someone who knew someone, so I went up there and after a bit I turned around and found myself staring into the most hypnotic blue eyes I had ever seen on a man … He smiled at me. My reaction was right out of a ladies' romance novel. Literally, my knees shook. I turned beetroot red. Mr Miller then introduced himself and asked me if I had liked the game. I really knew nothing about cricket, I admitted, having just wanted to see the servicemen everyone was talking about in action.

'"Never mind," he said. "I'll teach you everything you need to know."

'And I have to say he did,' she added.

7.
'You've Had a Revolution'

NOWADAYS, MOST people might imagine a major overseas tour involving luminaries of the sports or arts world to be a relatively smoothly organised affair, the principals themselves shepherded around in comfort, lodging on the upper floors of some exclusive city-centre hotel or beachfront resort, accompanied throughout by a team of media sherpas and steered through a few carefully stage-managed press conferences which resemble one of those quaintly deferential political interviews of the 1950s where the 'moderator' kicks off by asking the PM if he minds terribly answering a question or two. But in the straitened circumstances of 1945, the Australian cricketers had a very different time of it. The tourists' manager Keith Johnson frequently had to improvise as he went along, whether in hurriedly securing backup transport following the latest breakdown of his team bus, or personally negotiating the terms of the side's overnight accommodations with the landlord of a roadside pub with no pretension to luxury and little else to commend it but its proximity to the next day's venue, which itself often fell short of the top flight of sports arenas. Even Pelham Warner was astonished, and deeply impressed, by the sheer feat of logistics involved in conveying the visitors around the country. 'Their journeys were often undertaken at night, and achieved on roads that in many circumstances were far from ideal,' he wrote.

When it came to the players' financial compensation, the authorities tended not to overdo it. Twenty-five years later, the Australians' Jim Workman could still vividly recall that he had been paid just £57 (around £850 in today's money) to cover his basic expenses for the 20-week period from late April to mid-September

1945, from which he was expected to meet the cost of any additional blazers, caps, flannels or boots he might require over and above the standard issue. If he or any of his teammates happened to crack their bat or rip their trousers in the course of a match representing their country, it was down to the player himself to make his way to Jack Hobbs's sportswear shop in London's Fleet Street or one of its regional counterparts and buy a replacement.

The tour's makeshift arrangements and that particular touch of the haphazard surrounding the actual itinerary continued through late July and early August. In due course, most of the team who had played Yorkshire at Sheffield made their way overnight 250 miles down the pre-motorway road network to Chichester, where they drew a one-day game played in the rain against a scratch Sussex XI, before immediately reversing course to lose comprehensively against a Metropolitan Police side at Westcliff, and then heading south again to fulfil their two-day engagement with the Royal Navy at Portsmouth. Here Lindsay Hassett hit the Australians' highest individual score of the season, 189 out of a total of 331, opening his account with a flourish of strokes before dropping down a gear, but still treating the crowd to recurrent and violent onslaughts against the spinners. Hassett was at the crease for just 220 minutes, and his innings included a six and 18 fours. The Australian captain acquitted himself with his usual air of determination bordering on obduracy, with an affinity for dispatching anything loose into the distant areas wide of mid-on. The home team boasted John Dewes and the future Test all-rounder Ken Cranston in its line-up, but still followed on, 127 behind, before batting out time for a draw. Perhaps the one inescapable lesson of the match was the familiar one that, even on an uncovered pitch, any two sides would have difficulty in bowling the other out twice in only 11 or 12 hours' total play. Nonetheless, there was still plenty to admire at Portsmouth apart from Hassett's Olympian calm, such as the batting of Cranston and the bowling of Pepper, even if the Navy's Trevor Bailey extended the run of disappointing all-round performances that had begun earlier in July when going wicketless for Pelham Warner's XI against New Zealand, and continued in his next match for a Lord's XI against the Public Schools. Here he was bowled for 0 in the first innings and managed 28 against his teenaged opponents in the second, displaying what *The Times* called 'sound enough technique, if one also rather limited in ambition'. Though not the critical terminology prevalent at the time, one or two cricket writers had already come to wonder whether Bailey might yet catch a break, or, conversely, if the sinkhole spiral of his recent form would send him whirling further downwards in its unsparing vortex, never to see him resurface again at anything above the Sunday afternoon knockabout level: if so, a misjudgement for the ages.

Meanwhile, the Australian Air Force detachment had completed its circular tour of the Highlands before doubling back to play Sussex at the County Ground, Hove – a journey of some 500 miles, undertaken by a combination of train and bus, from their previous engagement. It was a limited-overs fixture, for once played in bright sunshine and thus brought to a finish. Batting first, Sussex reached a respectable 199 all out in 78 overs. The 44-year-old Bob Gregory, who curiously enough played in the Championship for Surrey, made 56, and the RAAF's Jack Pettiford took 5-43 in 19 overs of probing leg spin. The visitors knocked off the runs with two wickets to spare, Pettiford now doing the honours with the bat by thumping an even-time 63. As he also took a flying, one-handed catch in the leg trap to dismiss Sussex's Eddie Harrison – the sometime All-England squash champion, but present here in his capacity as a free-swinging lower middle-order bat – it was hard to see what more the Australian all-rounder could have done short of staying behind to sweep up the stands after play.

There was a modest dinner that night for both teams a mile or two away in the terrace restaurant of Brighton's venerable Grand Hotel. The 39-year-old Harry Parks, one of the distinguished Sussex cricketing dynasty, was there 'and behaved very properly, too', he once assured me, which was more than could be said of a 'certain red-blooded Aussie bowler I shan't name who was going at it hammer and tongs all night with our young waitress. She was a nice girl – an English girl – better spoken than most people you met working in service those days. I seem to remember a black dress, quite short, and a pinny. Very fetching, she was, but of course that's no excuse for this bloke's behaviour. Each time she came round with the soup, or whatever it was, it was the old hand-up-the-leg routine by the Aussie ... [His] manners were really terrible. In fact, he didn't really have any manners at all, in the sense of knowing when to give over. Finally old Jack Langridge leant over and told him in no uncertain terms to leave it off and let the poor woman do her job. He was good as gold after that, even if he knocked it back a bit in the bar afterwards. Quite talkative he became. I could take a few myself in those days, but this was in a different league,' Parks added, deeming his opponent's lubricated dialogue 'rich stuff, all about Churchill and Attlee and that gang, until he suddenly went out like a light. After that they had to sling him in between two blokes, one walking ahead, the other behind, and get him back to his digs like he was literally dead. A day later he was walking out to play for his country at Lord's.'

Australia made only one voluntary change for the fourth match of the series beginning on the bank holiday Monday of 6 August, bringing back the middle-order batsman Ross Stanford, lately of the 617 'Dambuster' Squadron, in place of Keith Carmody, himself a former German POW, and more recently serving as captain of the RAAF side on its tour of north Britain. The second change was forced on the selectors by the all-rounder Bert Cheetham's decision to sail home to attend to family business in Sydney. He was replaced by Jack Pettiford, fresh from his triumph at Hove, who was making his first-class debut at the age of 25. Pettiford could count himself unlucky not to have played in the previous Test, on a wicket that gave Cristofani match figures of 9-92. When the two leg-spinners subsequently appeared in tandem, not least at Lord's, it was Pettiford who generally asked more questions of the English batsmen.

The England team as announced shortly before the start wasn't without interest. There was a record crowd of 34,000 packed together under a pale blue sky flecked with cement-coloured clouds, with many more would-be customers locked outside, to see the home side's names go up on the Tavern board. The first in the frame was that of Surrey's Laurie Fishlock, an estimable left-handed bat, but, at the age of 38, not a player who could be said to advance the selectors' youth policy. The more familiar names of Hutton and Robertson followed, and then after a painful delay that of Hammond. All three of England's schoolboy recruits from the previous match were dropped, in Luke White's case never to return at international level, but George Pope reclaimed his place to lead the bowling attack. It later transpired that, after representations from William Shakespeare, a public-spirited Derbyshire butcher had compensated the Colne club (for whom Pope took 8-65 in his last league match before the Test) so that he could be released to play for England.

Given what was going on elsewhere in Britain that Monday morning, they were lucky to at least get off to a prompt start at Lord's. In the north they experienced both soaring temperatures and torrential downpours that swamped the Aigburth ground in Liverpool, with jungle-like clouds of steam swirling around the turf at Jesmond as play was hurriedly abandoned for the day. In Scotland, thousands were suffering from flooding, including a small but hardy group of Glaswegian cricket supporters who had gathered in the pre-dawn hours at the city's Central Station intending to catch the express to Euston before continuing their journey by public transport to St John's Wood. Even under normal circumstances, this might have proved a reasonably daunting prospect in the summer of 1945, but it became one of near-Homeric proportions here, as one of the travellers, an insurance broker named Kenneth Rose, found when the party's train finally reached its destination some ten hours later, 'only to discover that all the London bus drivers had withdrawn their labour, leaving us with a three-mile walk to the ground'. There were several other such wildcat strikes around the country that day, leaving the police to intervene to disperse crowds who became irritable while waiting for their own transport to get away for the bank holiday. A week's cricket festival in the midlands got off to a miserable start, with *Wisden* reporting, 'Rain, which limited play to 100 minutes, ruined what promised to be an interesting match' at Edgbaston, which was still better than they managed for an inter-services game at Portsmouth, where a hand-drawn sign hung on the gated archway to the United Services ground showed only a crude but expressive image of a dark cloud with jagged lightning streaks beneath it, and an exclamation mark added for further emphasis.

Australia won the toss at Lord's and batted. After 70 minutes' play the score was 33/1, made in such languid fashion that a smattering of slow hand-clapping broke out among the crowd sprawled six deep on the outfield, perhaps already sensing that the visitors might be primarily there for the purpose of avoiding defeat rather than actively pressing for victory. At that stage, play was suspended not so much by rain as by a brief but spectacular tropical storm, which saw the players and officials race for the pavilion and the three-man Lord's ground staff struggle to roll out the covers through the spectators packed around the boundary rope. Chester Wilmot, commentating on the match for the BBC, later described it as 'quite alarming in its ferocity ... One flash of lightning appeared to strike at the wicket itself, and the claps of thunder [were] uneasily reminiscent of the cricket played in the days of the buzz bomb.' But though impressively violent, at least the squall was short-lived. Play resumed with eight minutes to go before lunch, with Whitington and Sismey on strike. 'I was bloody miserable,' Sismey later recalled, 'and my back [which carried two pounds of enemy shrapnel] was killing me. But at least I was playing cricket.'

Pelham Warner was personally on guard at the Grace Gate shortly after the interval for the arrival of General Montgomery, taking time away from his German headquarters to pay another visit to the cricket. 'As his car entered the ground he was at once recognised, and on his way to the Committee Room he was cheered to the echo, the pavilion standing up to welcome him,' Warner later wrote with some gratification. For the next two hours, Monty nonetheless proceeded to spread first indignation and then mounting anger among his hosts as he roundly criticised the performance of the England team – 'none of these men appear to me to be putting their backs into it' – while lamenting the fact that so many of their number seemed to his hawklike eye to be inadequately turned out, with stained flannels or a button 'hopelessly adrift' on someone's shirt. 'He lectured us on the players' unacceptable turnout on parade,' Warner was later forced to admit. 'But at root he loves the game and has only the team's best interests at heart.' The hero of El Alamein was again applauded as he left the ground after tea, although there was a regrettable incident when a spectator seated in the upper reaches of today's Allen Stand, immediately above where the official party stood saying goodbye, took the opportunity to tip the contents of his glass of beer on Monty's bald patch directly below. The offending party was promptly identified and removed by the police.

As it happened, the news of Montgomery's visit to the cricket took second place to that of events taking place that day some 6,000 miles from Lord's. Coincidentally, at around the time the lightning storm broke with such violence over north London, the headlines flashed up on the midday newspaper hoardings around the ground that the Americans had dropped the atomic bomb on Hiroshima. The explosion that killed upwards of 140,000 people, most of them civilians, was revealed in Clement Attlee's dry words explaining to the British public that 'The problems of the release of energy by atomic fission have now been solved, and a device has accordingly been dropped on Japan by the United States Air Force.' Elsewhere, reaction ranged from the rightly apprehensive, Winston Churchill writing in near-mystical terms that 'This revelation of the secrets of nature, long mercifully withheld from man, should arouse the most solemn reflections in the mind and conscience of every human being capable of comprehension ... We must indeed pray that these awe-striking agencies will be made to conduce to peace among the nations, and that instead of wreaking measureless havoc upon the entire globe, they may become a perennial fountain of prosperity,' to the more robust tone of Noël Coward: 'The papers are full of the bomb which is going to revolutionise everything and blow us all to buggery. Not a bad idea.'

Bill Edrich, though never backward in taking the fight to the enemy over the years, confided in his diary: 'I must say [I am] both pleased and shocked by [the] news. People here are now talking about little else ...' In another example of the necessary compartmentalisation of life between the extremes of terror and joy familiar to so many people who had experienced the war, Edrich added: 'It seems strange to be gaily playing cricket on a day such as this.'

* * *

Perhaps in the end playing sport represented a psychological compensation for the horrors of war, and now more particularly of Hiroshima, or perhaps it was all just part of the British gift for carrying on. Twenty-four hours after the Lord's match began, the US president Harry Truman, breaking his homeward journey from the Potsdam conference, met with King George VI on board the battlecruiser HMS *Renown*, at anchor off Plymouth. Truman's first words, referring to the recent election, were 'You've had a revolution, I see,' to which his host quickly replied, 'Oh no! We don't actually do those here. We *evolve*.' The king may have been no orator, but nonetheless impressed Truman sufficiently with his 'British commonsense' for him to record the line in his diary.

The monarch's aphorism certainly seemed to fit the deliberate pace of the cricket at Lord's, where the Australians eventually scored 388 all out, which included an unusually measured century by Miller. Perhaps it was due to the developing bulletins from Japan successively chalked up on the news pitches, but to the correspondent of the *Yorkshire Evening Post* it seemed as if 'the vast crowd was strangely quiet'. Towards the end of the innings a certain amount of barracking again issued from the Tavern area, including the shouted remark of one persistent critic who evidently went with the first draft of his review and repeatedly bellowed, 'Get on with it, mate!' Perhaps, too, Miller's innings appeared slow only by his standards, because his century came up in just short of four hours and contained ten boundaries. When the batsman left the field, all 11 Englishmen stood and applauded what each of them seemed to recognise as the work of a master hand.

While not personally inclined to the bold socialist project on which his nation had embarked, Pelham Warner had no insuperable objection to hosting the great and good, of whatever political stripe, as witnessed in the mandarin tones of the letter he wrote on 4 August:

> Dear Prime Minister,
> The Committee of M.C.C. would be greatly honoured if you could see fit to pay us a visit at Lord's during the England v Australia match.
>
> We should be delighted if you would take lunch in the President's Box on any day. If luncheon is out of the question, perhaps you might be able to come to tea? I need scarcely say that your presence at such [an] occasion would give great pleasure to us all, and you may be sure of a warm welcome.
>
> I need hardly add that we should be delighted if you could bring Mrs Attlee with you.
>
> Perhaps your Private Secretary could telephone to me and let me know whether you will be able to come, and, if so, the time of your arrival?
>
> Respectfully,
> Deputy Secretary.

Like most national leaders even in that prelapsarian age of deference, Attlee sharply divided public opinion. Some said he was a dangerous Marxist, others that he was the epitome of bourgeois respectability, privately educated, with a substantial villa surrounded by laurels and rhododendrons in the London suburbs and a penchant for solving *The Times* crossword puzzle. Terms used to describe Britain's first post-war premier were: characterless, authoritarian, interventionist, bureaucratic and dour, but also: loyal, modest, compassionate, patriotic and even in his way drily humorous, a man who chose as his epitaph:

> 'Few thought he was even a starter
> There were many who thought themselves smarter
> Yet he ended PM, CH and OM
> An earl and a Knight of the Garter.'

What all sides agreed on is that Attlee, even or especially at the great crisis points of history, rarely needed an excuse to watch cricket.

Even as the monstrous cloud was clearing to reveal the unimaginable carnage that had befallen Hiroshima on the morning of 7 August, the premier arrived by taxi at the Grace Gate, wearing his habitual homburg hat, wing collar and unassuming smile, umbrella at the furl, to be seen momentarily rummaging for change to hand the steward on duty before Warner arrived at a brisk trot from the direction of the pavilion to escort his guest back to the downstairs committee room. 'The PM was roundly cheered, although there were a few dissentient noises to be heard from the free seats,' Warner later noted.

Attlee saw Australia, now again batting under heavy skies, all out at lunchtime, with Pope the pick of the England attack, not only a fine swing bowler of his type, but, according to the visitors' Ross Stanford, also something of a pioneer in the art of ball-tampering.

'Pope was bald,' Stanford later recalled, with a wry smile at the memory. 'But he had Brylcreem in his cap and of course in between bowling he would rub one side of the ball in his cap with this stuff, to get it to move around … He could swing it a yard in the right atmosphere.'

Forty years after these events, Keith Miller told me that he, too, had made note of Pope's cranial technique, and adapted it for his own future use.

'Old George used to shine the ball in this stuff, and I thought well, why not? From then on whenever I played cricket I used to quiff up my hair with as much grease as I could get away with until I looked like Elvis Presley doing "Hound Dog",' Miller said, which if nothing else goes to prove that the player's distinctive pomade of the later 1940s and 50s was as much by way of a professional aid as a fashion statement on his part.

England passed the Australian score for the loss of four wickets, noticeably accelerating from there to finish at 468/7 declared, with Washbrook 112 and Edrich unbowed on 73. In fairness, the visitors experienced several challenges in the field, most notably behind the stumps. Their regular keeper Stan Sismey had been hit on the thumb while batting, forcing his teammate Jim Workman to pull on the gauntlets. Workman did his best, but it was said that the chief characteristic of his keeping lay in his emulating the Ancient Mariner's tendency to stoppeth one in three. A total of 39 byes and leg byes, among 57 extras as a whole, ensued. Stanford remembered that there had been some spirited back and forth about this in the visitors' dressing room, where just before the start on the third morning 'Old Wally Hammond put his head round the door, which was unusual – he wasn't exactly one for fraternising with the opposition – and said to Lindsay Hassett, "Do you know, Lindsay, if you asked me, I could let Keith Carmody keep wicket." Well, Keith was actually our 12th man that day, but he was a fair middle-order bat and more to the point not a bad keeper, either, back home in Sydney. "Oh?" said Lindsay. "Thanks, Wally. I didn't know that.

But since you ask, will you let Keith Carmody keep wicket?" And Wally said, "Yes, he can go out there with my blessing." Well, Keith went out there and did bloody well, too, catching Washbrook behind the sticks. I always remember that about Wally. Funny bloke. You could never tell which side of his face you might get.'

Whatever else you made of him, Hammond was clearly one of that small number of cricketers who, apart from questions of records and averages, have a lasting place among the immortals of the game. By the end of the summer, so was Keith Miller. People increasingly came to watch Miller play as much to relish his combination of enterprise and unorthodoxy as to enjoy its material results. At Lord's, the crowd was amused by the way he elaborately bowed and doffed his cap after being beaten by a ball from Pope, or by the moment he turned to address the noise from the Tavern by swinging his arms about as if conducting an orchestra. Miller was always as ready for a bit of fun as for suddenly unleashing a bouncer or hitting a six. He was numerically modest, but never boring, with the ball at Lord's. The Australian journalist Ray Robinson wrote of him: 'No stage villain looks more melodramatic than Miller the bowler, staring at an umpire who refuses one of his whirling appeals. Once he toppled over backwards and appealed sitting on the pitch.'

At Lord's, another critic archly referred to the Australian attack as 'strangely carefree', and to Jack Pettiford's leg spin as 'little more than a joke'. If so, it was at least a practical joke, since Pettiford had figures of 3-62 off 18 overs. Australia went in again on the final afternoon and lost four wickets knocking off their 80-run arrears, but in the end it was the story familiar to much of that season's cricket, with the weather having the last derisive laugh as the players walked off under rapidly darkening skies to share the honours of a match, watched by 93,000 spectators over the three days, that finished in a different world to the one it began in.

They at least got back on the field at Lord's the following day, Thursday the 9th, for the annual Southern v Northern Schools grudge match, with the-then thin and gawky, if precociously gifted,

Peter May appearing for the South but managing only a single run. It was still raining in Birmingham, and at the Stanley Park ground in Blackpool the New Zealand Services drew with a team raised by George Pope's sometime employer, the fruit merchant Charles Leatherbarrow. Pope himself, having spent most of the previous night sitting on a hard bench in the third-class compartment of a northbound milk train, took 2-24 in a spell of five overs sent down at noticeably reduced pace. The Americans dropped their bomb on Nagasaki that same day. Mr Leatherbarrow wrote to Pelham Warner to say that the match at Blackpool had 'gone off alright', with 'Pope deporting himself well enough', but, like many others, wondering about the state of the world. 'The *Daily Express* published a photograph seeming to show Jap scientists at work developing a terrible new device of their own … What does this all herald for the future? Or is there even to be a future?' Leatherbarrow fretted.

The press in general saw it all as a critical moment in man's affairs, writing 'acres of rot', according to Keith Miller – never one to indulge in metaphysical asides on his or anyone else's ultimate destiny – 'twaddling on about the Japs also having the bomb and being about to blow the whole world to smithereens'. But then came the superbly measured response of 44-year-old Emperor Hirohito, speaking to a silent public, many of whom stood to attention, often in tears, to hear their supreme ruler's singsong voice coming over the loudspeakers positioned up and down Japan's city streets. 'The war situation has developed not necessarily to our advantage,' the emperor was forced to admit, as the initial smoke cleared at both Hiroshima and Nagasaki, with the Red Army also then swiftly making their way through Manchuria. George Pope, hearing the BBC report of the speech back home in Chesterfield, thought the overall mood strangely subdued, with 'no sign of public cheer – all very different to VE Day'.

A Cabinet meeting at Downing Street on Friday, 10 August, debating these events, concluded: 'It would be inexpedient to insist on the terms of surrender of Japan involving the abdication of His

Majesty the Emperor if this would have the result of delaying substantially the end of the conflict in the Far East.' And so it proved. Although, under pressure from the Allies, Hirohito formally renounced his divinity, he remained unmolested on the throne of Japan until his death from cancer 44 years later.

In cricket terms, one immediate result of the suddenly diminished Japanese enthusiasm for the war was a series of hurriedly arranged – and technically premature – 'VJ' fixtures up and down the British Isles. While admittedly not in the absolute first rank of sporting events, Bournville, for instance, played Sparkhill in a 'Great Victory Fête' at the former's ground adjacent to the Cadbury factory in Birmingham on 11 August, while the Public Schools marked the occasion by being comprehensively routed in a two-day match with an invitation XI at Lord's, John Dewes hitting a run-a-minute 78 for the home team, but Peter May continuing his disappointing recent run of form with scores of 0 and 1 for the visitors.

The Australian Services in turn went up to the combined football-and-cricket ground at Northampton, where they lost in the final over of the day to the county side, the 33-year-old part-timer Reg Partridge taking 5-43 with his previously only modestly effective bag of seam and leg spin. There was a convivial dinner held for both teams on the night of the 11th at the timbered Bantam Cock pub in the town centre. *The Times* that day warned presciently that 'the accounts for the nation's victory [will] assuredly soon come due', and indeed would involve Britain's transition from her status as the world's largest creditor state to that of the world's largest debtor as she struggled to pay off her huge accumulated US dollar loans from what proved a sadly reduced national income. But these longer-term tests of the country's social and economic fabric failed to dampen the spirits of the cricketers who sat down at the Northampton pub that night to enjoy a ration-busting carvery dinner rounded off by half a dozen bottles of recently liberated Hungarian brandy of such potency it was considered unwise to smoke in the same vicinity. Cecil Pepper later remembered the event as a 'well-provisioned beano that [had] gone off smoothly enough' until the point where someone had asked someone else to pass him a jug of water, 'and he airlined it'. A good deal of beer was also consumed, some of it ending up being poured over Pepper's head, and he recalled experiencing a 'wavy feeling' during the train journey the next morning to High Wycombe, where the Australians managed to beat Gubby Allen's XI, thanks in large part to Hassett's century, while Pepper restricted himself to just seven runs – a six and a single – before giving the charge to a local council clerk named Tomkins who, drafted in for the day, made the most of his hitherto unexplored skills as an off-spinner to finish with 1-82 off a dozen overs.

Up at the Lowerhouse ground in Burnley on 13 August, two sides culled from the local leagues played each other in what was modestly billed as a 'VJ Day Grand Challenge Gala', with George Pope, who must by then have been thoroughly sick of the fine print of the British Railways timetable, taking 7-71 for the home side. There was also a notably lopsided two-innings match beginning that same day at the Sportpark facility in Haarlem, suburban Amsterdam, where an improvised Netherlands XI scored 277/9 declared before dismissing the British Liberation Army side led by Bryan Valentine of Kent and England for 52 and 67, to win by the small matter of an innings and 158 runs.

George Pope was back in action once more two days later for the North against the Australian Services at Blackpool, where he took another six wickets to add to his season's haul. Neither anxiety about money, nor his terms of employment with Charles Leatherbarrow, nor the sheer fatigue of commuting around the country seem to have come as a deterrent to his cricket that month. 'On tomorrow a.m. at Todmorden, so have to pack up now and run for it,' he scribbled in a postcard to his brother Alf, mailed from 60 miles away in Blackpool on the evening of the 17th. Pope had also made himself available for the summer's climactic Victory match at Old Trafford and signed up both for the Over 33s (he was 34) v the Unders at Lord's, and a late-season Empire XI tour of Ireland. 'Still hanging on to job [despite] every team in England wanting me to play for them!' he wrote in another family postcard. Nor was this mere bravado, as the opposition found when Pope took eight wickets against them in the Irish tour's first fixture at Lisburn.

On 18 August, the Royal Navy beat the Army in a single-innings game at Lord's by no fewer than 117 runs. It was a Saturday, the ground was all but full, and for once the teams toiled under a hot sun with only a token rain shower, somehow *de rigueur* that season, thoughtfully restricting itself to the tea interval. John Dewes had a big reception on his arrival at the wicket, opening for the Navy, getting under steam with a clipped three from his first ball on his way to a chanceless 90, at which point he set off for a single through mid-off he might have been better advised to forgo and was run out by a direct throw from 18-year-old Billy Sutcliffe, son of Herbert, sprinting in from cover. Further down the list, Trevor Bailey continued his lacklustre form with a scrappy knock of 11 but made partial amends when it came time to bowl by taking 3-48 in 12 overs, including the prize Army wickets of Gloucestershire's Denis Moore, and the once and future Test player Freddie Brown. Charles Palmer of Worcestershire at one point hit Bailey through the covers off the back foot and then pulled a long hop just wide of the man at square leg for four, but fell in the next over when Bailey himself acrobatically caught him close in off the fast-medium bowling of Kent's Tony Mallett. The future England all-rounder chiefly remembered his life that summer being divided between 'cricket, lovely cricket', and 'living in those ghastly 1940s wooden hutments'.

At Old Trafford, in what amounted to a dress rehearsal for the final Test starting on the same ground 48 hours later, the RAF played the RAAF; a serious match, obviously, but not without a certain boyish exuberance in Bill Edrich's good-natured mimicry of the umpires, or in the collective scramble for souvenir stumps at the end. Cyril Washbrook, first in for the RAF, always remembered the sight of the visitors' wicketkeeper and slips smartly retreating in lockstep as he took guard, ready to face the normally medium-paced Mick Roper. Roper greeted the Lancashire and England opener with a swift one to the jaw, but the umpire called it a no-ball for overstepping the crease. Four more such shouts then followed in quick succession. After that, some of the fire seemed to go out of the visitors' attack as a whole, with Washbrook and in turn Edrich and Wyatt all amongst the runs. Ross Stanford scored an unbeaten 79 for the visitors, but 'Ellis Robinson bowled his off-breaks with deadly effect,' *Wisden* reported. Robinson was a then 34-year-old all-rounder who had broken into the Yorkshire side before the war, and in the normal course of events might have considered himself unlucky never to appear for England. Always ready for a bit of fun of the sort not invariably linked with northern cricket in the 1940s, the story was often told of him standing at slip, with his dour county teammate Arthur Mitchell alongside him in the ring, when Robinson suddenly brought off a flying catch that involved a leap, a dive, and ended with a double somersault before the happy fielder bounced up again, holding the ball aloft to bask in the acclaim of the crowd, at which point Mitchell muttered out of the side of his mouth: 'Gerrup. Tha's makin' an exhibition o' thissen.' The RAF beat the RAAF at Old Trafford by 44 runs.

It says something for the importance then attached to any fixture involving Yorkshire playing Lancashire that the sides' meeting at Bradford that week was the only county match of the 1945 season to be awarded first-class status. *The Cricketer* described the ensuing contest as 'competitive', which was the polite phrase many of the press used for a game that was characteristically a blend of brute force and brilliance. Batting first, the visitors scored 239, with another assured performance by Washbrook. Bill Bowes managed to bowl 18 overs and take 3-22, but then pulled a muscle and had to drop out of the match. Yorkshire passed the Lancashire total by 20 runs, thanks largely to a studious 88 by their veteran Wilf Barber, the holder of two pre-war England Test caps. This was clearly cricket for connoisseurs, appealing to those who see more to the game than a man hitting a ball or a series of numbers flicking round the scoreboard like a fruit machine. Things looked promising for Yorkshire when they had their opponents at 93/3 in their second innings, but as so often that summer the weather had other plans. Rain restricted play to just over an hour and a half on the third day, dashing any hopes of a result. There was at least a mildly comic touch to the proceedings when the local *Telegraph and Argus* newsstand pitched at the ground's Hirton Park end on the second evening read 'Nutter Goes Mad', referring to the visitors' Bert Nutter's achievement in taking 5-57 with his right-arm seam. Himself the son of a professional cricketer, the easygoing Nutter was small in stature but upright in style and, like Ellis Robinson, thought unlucky not to have been noticed by the Test selectors. Instead, he joined the RAF, serving for six years, and towards the end of his career transferred to Northamptonshire. It was a tribute to the enduring popularity of Hedley Verity that the Roses match at Bradford raised over £3,000 (£45,000 today) for the fallen Yorkshire and England bowler's dependents.

Bert Nutter then found himself with a week off before playing his next match, appearing as the professional for Nelson in the Lancashire League, and spent part of the time visiting family friends in Englewood Road, south London, by coincidence just a few doors away from Jack Hobbs's home during the years of his greatest fame with Surrey and England. One untypically hot and dry afternoon in mid-August, Nutter took the proverbial Clapham omnibus up to Oxford Street and paid 2 shillings to walk around the waxwork exhibition displaying models of Hitler and his circle ('Laughably bad likenesses overall', he wrote in his diary), and then an additional charge of sixpence to enter the small-scale mockup of a German concentration camp. 'Stark sign hung over the entrance recording the 1943 words of Herr Himmler,' Nutter added, sufficiently moved by what he read there to make a note of the words: 'By the end of the year, the Jewish question will have been settled in all the occupied countries … All of us have asked ourselves: What about the women and children? I have decided that this too requires a clear answer. I did not consider that I should be justified in disposing of the men only to allow their children to grow up to avenge themselves on our sons and grandsons. We have to make up our minds, hard though it may be, that this race must be wiped off the face of the earth.'

From there it was a ten-minute walk between largely boarded-up shops through another rain shower to the corner of Newman Street, to tour the site of the equivalent Japanese exhibition. Unsurprisingly, there was something of a vogue for such displays in London that summer. 'Dank and humid inside, with gramophone playing cries of wild birds and animals,' Nutter wrote. 'The sounds and feel of the jungle ... Further in, large pictures hung up everywhere of English prisoners seen in most pitiful state. I prefer not to elaborate,' he added. Later that afternoon, in something of an immersive tour of Axis wartime artefacts, Nutter, now joined by two friends, retraced his steps back along Oxford Street to Hyde Park, where they saw a row of former Luftwaffe Heinkels and Messerschmitts, with two or three RAF officers on hand to explain each plane's technical capabilities. 'Some had visible bullet holes in their fuselage or wings,' Nutter wrote, 'and I imagine were brought down to earth with a bump by one of our boys. What things they must have seen!' A defused V-1 rocket was also on view. 'Infernal!' was Nutter's one-word review. As he noted later, echoing his fellow serviceman Bill Edrich's words, 'Curious to think of us all happily at our sport again, having just got through the very worst of hells life could throw at us. Never again shall I protest at playing cricket for a living!'

* * *

At the stroke of midnight on Tuesday, 14 August, a sonorous BBC radio announcement asked listeners to stand by for 'news of the utmost national gravity'. To the war-weary public, it must have sounded ominously like another unwelcome turn of events from somewhere around the world, but in fact it was a characteristically subdued address from Clement Attlee in Downing Street to the effect that the Japanese government had seen fit to accept the terms laid down in the recent Potsdam accords and give up the struggle. The king's own speech on the subject was broadcast over the radio the following morning. 'Three months have passed since I asked you to join with me in an act of thanksgiving for the defeat of Germany,' he remarked. 'We then rejoiced that peace had returned to Europe, but we knew that a strong and relentless enemy still remained to be conquered in Asia ... Our sense of deliverance today is overpowering, and with it all we have a right to feel that we have done our duty ... The war is over. You know, I think, that those four words have for the Queen and myself the same significance that they have for you. Yet there is not one of us,' the king added, 'who has experienced this terrible conflict who does not realise that we shall feel its inevitable consequences long after we have all forgotten our rejoicings of today ...'

The pace of events proved to be swift during the remainder of that third week of August. The 15th was officially designated VJ Day, with crowds again gathering to dance the hokey-cokey under the drizzly skies of central London. 'City not at its best, with scores of morons wandering about,' the foreign office minister Alexander Cadogan noted testily in his diary. On the 16th, Winston Churchill, now leader of the Opposition, spoke in the House of Commons for the first time of an 'Iron Curtain' falling across Europe. On the 17th, George Orwell's definitive allegory of that same state of affairs, *Animal Farm*, was published. And on the 18th, a Saturday, there was a full round of what Warner and the other authorities deemed to be only 'miscellaneous' cricket matches, but which included an appearance by a touring West Indies XI at Southport, and a one-day, two-innings Derbyshire v Leicestershire fixture in which George Pope took nine more wickets. Among several other contests that failed to reach the same technical heights, there was the one between Sefton and Liverpool Police that featured an unusual break in play when one of the visiting fieldsmen glanced up from his position at deep long leg and noticed a spectator, standing just a few feet away at the entrance to the beer tent, with whom he had unfinished professional business. At that, the fielder stepped smartly across the boundary rope to feel the man's collar, and then to escort him back to the pavilion, where he was detained until a uniformed officer arrived to take the suspect into custody. When play resumed, Sefton won the game by 68 runs.

The Australian Services team spent much of that Saturday sitting in a hired, cream-coloured Crossville coach, festooned with an irregular, hand-painted black stripe, which with a certain inevitability broke down en route while travelling in slow stages between Blackpool and Manchester, where they were due to again face the England side the following Monday morning. Sunday the 19th was officially designated a national Day of Thanksgiving for the return of peace, with a service in St Paul's Cathedral attended by the royal family, and more ad hoc events marking the nation's deliverance held at churches and chapels up and down the country. The touring cricketers reacted to the mingled solemnity and carousal of the occasion in various ways. Keith Miller later remembered that he had been too busy 'packing up all the flying gear in Norfolk' and then 'humping it across to Blackpool' before in turn bussing to Old Trafford – 'all a bit like getting to the dark side of the moon in those days' – to allow much time to celebrate. Set against this, there was the experience of Miller's friend and sometime flying colleague Bill Edrich, who had the advantage of already finding himself in the Manchester area prior to the Test, having appeared for the RAF against the RAAF at Old Trafford on the 18th. It was later authoritatively said that the England player had appeared for breakfast with the rest of the team, prior to going out to play in front of another full house on the morning of the 20th, still wearing his dinner jacket but missing his two front teeth.

The series with Australia hung in the balance. With the possible exception of the last Test at Lord's, the four matches thus far had rivalled anything an official Ashes series might have to offer as a pinnacle of international sporting competition. None of the players ever took the games less than seriously, even if, as noted, Miller sometimes liked to leaven the proceedings with a bit of fun out in the middle, such as his habit of drop-kicking the ball back to the keeper at the end of an over. But they would have been less than human had they completely ignored the unique atmosphere that prevailed in Britain that August. Laurie Fishlock of Surrey and England was one of the home team players thought to have taken advantage of the collective Mancunian good cheer over the weekend of the 18th–19th, when many local publicans, swept up in the general tide of euphoria, had temporarily given up accepting payment or regulating the number of customers on their premises. 'There was a joyful chaos on the streets throughout these last two days,' with many individuals 'ultimately failing to maintain their vertical posture', the local *Empire News* was left to report, while *Wisden*, restricting itself to the technical details of the ensuing cricket, was not impressed by the performance of certain home players. 'Fishlock was not at his best ... and mistimed a slow yorker,' the almanack noted, while a spectator in the pavilion was heard to mutter, 'You're plainly still pie-eyed' to the returning batsman, a slander that was refuted only with difficulty.

Perhaps the most poignant fixture that week, besides the one played for the benefit of Hedley Verity's widow and children, was the match between Glamorgan and a West of England XII captained by Wally Hammond at the Arms Park in Cardiff as a memorial to Glamorgan's pre-war captain Maurice Turnbull. Turnbull had been an all-purpose sportsman who was a champion squash and hockey player, a fencer, and to this day the only man to have played international cricket for England and rugby for Wales. He was also a scholar of racing form, a shrewd bridge player, knew his poetry and music, scrupulously attended the nearest Catholic church each Sunday, ran a successful insurance business, and wrote two well-received books. To the women of south Wales, Turnbull must have cut a dashing figure with his elegant tweed suit, oiled black hair and slightly disreputable smile, his close-cropped military moustache completing his resemblance to the actor David Niven. He (Turnbull, not Niven) had married immediately before leaving to serve with the Welsh Guards on the outbreak of hostilities in September 1939, and, as we've seen, fell to a sniper's bullet while at the head of his men during the Allied breakout following D-Day. Maurice Turnbull was 38 at the time of his death, and in addition to his wife Elizabeth he left behind three small children. The West XII easily won the testimonial match at Cardiff, where their opening bat Tom Barling was unlucky to fall to an aerial catch by the man on the deep square leg fence, narrowly avoiding the boundary rope on his way down, with his score on 99. The day raised some £2,200 (£33,000 in modern money) for Elizabeth Turnbull and her family.

Britain's cricket-loving premier Clement Attlee had at one time told Pelham Warner that he planned to take the train to watch the first day of the match at Old Trafford beginning on the 20th. Instead of this, Attlee found himself chairing a Cabinet meeting held in his room at the House of Commons scheduled to last just an hour, but which in the event ran from the lunch interval until past teatime. Among other things, it was noted in the minutes that there would now have to be a 'transition period' while the government 'in carrying out its industrial policy will have power to introduce by regulation various provisions, in [addition to] the very wide and drastic powers which had been required for war purposes'. It's a matter of debate whether Attlee's reforming new administration went too far, or not far enough, down the road of imposing its Keynesian economic vision on the country, but on a purely human level anyone with sport in their blood can surely sympathise with Attlee himself as he was forced to spend that sun-baked afternoon navigating the rhetorical wasteland that then as now characterised so much ministerial discourse, rather than enjoying the life-affirming pleasures of a day out at the cricket.

For their part, the Australians had spoken of making two changes at Old Trafford from their side in the previous Test at

Lord's, but in the end made do with one. Keith Carmody replaced Jim Workman at the top of the order, but Stan Sismey, described as 'absent, on honeymoon' earlier in the previous week's Manchester press (with less formal variants of this circulating among his Services' teammates) returned from Scotland just in time to take the field on 20 August. The newly-wed wicketkeeper was not quite at his best, even so, because he took a single catch behind the stumps while missing at least three others, and when it came time to bat, said *Wisden*, promptly 'discarding the monumental patience he showed at Lord's, attempted to hook the wrong ball and was leg-before'. Later in the proceedings, Sismey was not embarrassed to go down on his knees in a corner of the dressing room and pray that Australia might 'fuck up the Poms' in their second innings, but, alas, this appeal seems not to have moved the game's ultimate authority.

For Keith Miller, meanwhile, love of God was, like the love of a woman, a romantic convention for which he had little use in the traditional sense. It would be hard to say if Miller was 'demob happy' as he reported for duty at Old Trafford, or if this was merely a natural extension of his habitually breezy approach to life. Quite possibly it was a bit of both; but Miller did, nonetheless, have specific grounds for a certain amount of celebration that week, having been released from active duty at 169 Squadron (as opposed to separating from the RAAF itself) on the same day Japan surrendered. He had spent some 600 hours in the air since being promoted to the rank of flying officer in November 1944, and in time would receive a chestful of medals for his service. Although Miller remained in uniform until June 1946 his active combat days were now over.

Perhaps Miller's experience had given him a sharpened perspective on life, as expressed in his famous talk-show aphorism about the comparative pressures of playing cricket and having a Messerschmitt up the arse. Or perhaps his own survival at a time when so many of his comrades had perished was a source of guilt. As his future Test opponent and kindred spirit Denis Compton once observed, 'I think Keith had more of a doubting side to him than he let on. He was not a real he-man. He *pretended* to be. He worked hard at it. In actual fact he was someone who loved his books and his music, and I saw him in tears once when we went to see Jimmy Stewart in *The Glenn Miller Story*. And the fact that he came through, that most of his real adventures in the war were dust-ups with authority, not with the enemy, that so many of his pals never came home while he was out there being cheered on the cricket field, I'd say that really nagged at him.' Rarely one to descend into the briar patch of psychiatry, Compton allowed himself an exception in this case. 'It was bilge, of course. I know for a fact that he was as brave as they came in the war, but the fact remains that he went home unscathed and I think that really bothered him in later life.'

* * *

Old Trafford did not look at its best immediately prior to the start of play on the Monday morning of 20 August. As we've seen, the ground had taken several direct hits during the northern Blitz, and after that the pavilion had been requisitioned first by the Army and then by the Ministry of Supply, who had stuffed it to the rafters with an array of packing cases, surplus military hardware, discarded uniforms, several thousand mismatched kitchen utensils and other assorted debris, 'a cross between a wholesale goods supplier and a rundown boarding school on moving-in day', according to England's Billy Griffith. With a certain aptness, 60 German prisoners of war had each been engaged at a rate of three farthings an hour (the equivalent of 40p, in today's money, for a full day's shift) to repair the damage to the ground's main stand, erect the scoreboard, wash the dishes in the downstairs kitchen and make good the damage to the members' dining room inflicted by a Luftwaffe oil bomb. A sub-unit of POWs meanwhile took turns with an archaic paint-rolling device marking out two concentric circles around the outfield. The inner ring defined the playing boundary, and the outer ring the furthest limit for the several hundred members of the public seated on the grass. Old Trafford as a whole still had more of the character of a field to it than a stadium.

'After six years of transport restrictions the sight of dozens of special omnibuses labelled "Cricket Ground" was something remarkable,' *Wisden* reported. There were 28,000 spectators in the ground on the first day, queuing up at the turnstiles from 5am, part of a total attendance of 72,463 during the match. The POW workforce had given most of the seating areas a coat of bright green and white paint – in certain visible places, still wet – and erected crudely fashioned signs bearing phrases such as 'Please This Way To Stand'. The *Manchester Evening Chronicle* later informed its readers that the crowd had consumed 12,000 meat pies and upwards of 30 36-gallon barrels of beer on each of the three days' play. Ground admission was 5 shillings, or the equivalent of £3.75 in today's purchasing power. The weather was dry and mostly warm on the first day, intermittently wet on the second, and then fine again at the close. 'It was really a wonderful occasion,' *Wisden* concluded.

Hammond tossed, and Hassett correctly called heads. Australia batted first on a pitch 'Groundsman Williams calls full of runs and likely to play well throughout the game,' John Kay wrote in the *Manchester Evening News*. It's sometimes hard to fully imagine the scene when compared to that of a present-day Test match. Reading the spectators' diaries and published accounts is a bit like peering through a sheet of gauze at a diorama depicting some late Edwardian garden party. There's an innocence, and also a class-consciousness, to the contemporary newspaper reports as archaic in their way as the actual press facilities at Old Trafford, which consisted of a wooden hut craning out at an angle over the boundary like a significantly more modest – and benign – version of Hitler's Berghof. The *Evening News* reported that there were 'many personages who attended in uniform, while others preferred business attire, or demure jackets and flat caps', the 'ubiquity of rolled umbrellas' being the unifying link between the classes, 'with many juveniles disport[ing] themselves in school colours round the ice-cream caravan'. The youth factor increased significantly later on the first day, nobody bothering in the general teatime commotion to keep out the small boys who thronged at the gates. To get everyone in the mood, there were also 'marching bands and decorous applause amid the sunshine ... even a few parasols for the ladies, and vendors selling straw boaters to strolling young gents,' said the *Chronicle*. 'Not an inflamed crowd,' as George Pope summarised it. 'Nice.'

Pope and Eddie Phillipson, right-arm medium of Lancashire, coming in for his county teammate Bill Roberts, opened the home attack. England used only one other bowler on the first day – Dick Pollard, the young man of the trio at 33 – Hammond shrewdly using his seamers in short four- or five-over bursts to keep them fresh off the leash. At lunch Australia were in some trouble at 104/5, and not looking very happy with life: at one point Pettiford called Carmody for a quick run, which ended in a skidding U-turn and an ungainly dive for safety by the latter, followed by what the *Chronicle* called 'a long and unappreciative stare down the wicket' at his partner.

In the end Australia lasted just 59 overs, for a total of 173 all out. Miller was in for more than quarter of an hour before he scored, once taking a blow to the ribs from Phillipson, but then as if awakening from a coma danced out to Pollard with a swing of his left arm, and suddenly mid-off was running a losing race to the boundary with the ball. Demonstrating the fallibility that was a significant part of his charm, he was almost out next ball, holding his bat out absent-mindedly to a long hop and just failing to give a catch behind the wicket. In the end Miller finished unbeaten on 77, which was all highly laudable even if his innings included another Australian unforced error, this time with fatal consequences.

'Keith walked over when I came to the wicket,' Ross Stanford recalled. 'Their Eddie Phillipson was swinging the ball a mile and Nugget generously said to me, "Get off strike as soon as you can and I'll take Phillipson." Thanks, mate, I thought. So I hit one straight away to cover, took off for a single that wasn't there, Len Hutton's throw came in like a ruddy tracer bullet, the bowler whipped off the bails and I was back in the pavilion again before you could say Waltzing Matilda. That was a bad blow for us, because if Keith and I had stuck together we might have put on enough runs to make a game of it.' As it was, England would enjoy a first-innings lead of 70, with Hutton and Hammond, the former technically solid, if tending to score runs almost in a spirit of apology, the latter with a more definite note of intent about him, to the fore, and Bob Cristofani taking a pleasingly symmetrical 5-55 for the visitors.

Australia resumed at the start of the third day on 37/3 with their top two batsmen, Miller and Hassett, at the crease. The opener Dick Whitington had come and gone for 10 the previous evening, acrobatically caught behind – the first of six dismissals Griffith took in the innings – later rather curiously writing of the event in the third person: 'At that, he strode disconsolately from the ground to the accompaniment of organised hooting from the Old Trafford members', who had formed a 'guard of dishonour to usher him off.' *Wisden* says nothing of any such incivility, but notes that inside half an hour of the restart both Miller and Hassett had similarly been caught by Griffith for the addition of just nine runs. After that the only resistance was an extraordinary unbeaten 110 by the visitors' number nine, Cristofani, which was roughly a third of the total number of runs he had managed to score in 18 previous matches that season. Cutting and hooking with apparent disdain, he reached his century at a fraction less than a run a minute, with a six and 13 fours, to the accompaniment of the usual cricket crowd cheers for tail-end heroics. Dick Whitington, who later became an accomplished journalist, said that Cristofani's innings was 'one in which even Victor Trumper would have taken pride'.

Needing 141 to win in even time – 'a light task in ordinary conditions', said *Wisden* – England were now back in the series, even if they managed to lose Laurie Fishlock with only five on the board. Fishlock would play two post-war Tests for England without ever asserting himself at that level. Edrich bustled out to join his captain at 70/3, and these two took England towards the line with a stand of 54. Hammond was out after the visitors' substitute Eddie Williams chased and caught a skier just in front of the sightscreen with 17 still needed, but after that Washbrook and his partner dug in to see England home with roughly half an hour to spare. Hassett, tacitly conceding defeat, brought himself on to bowl what proved to be the final over, just as he would when graciously accepting the inevitable as Australia's captain eight years later at the Oval, when England regained the Ashes after nearly two decades' worth of failures. The match at Manchester characteristically ended in rain, although for once arriving too late to spoil the result.

After that the crowd gathered in front of the pavilion to hail both sets of players in raucous, if not especially tuneful, style, and then the teams went back inside to a room where Miller remembered with some distaste that a plate of 'sweating pink mutton and pastries, with a jug or two of warm beer' awaited them on the sideboard. 'We continued our festivities elsewhere,' he recalled. The summer's final Test had raised £11,627 for charity, and its result meant that the Victory series was drawn two-all.

Six thousand miles away, E.W. Swanton had emerged from three years' captivity that week to wander in to the Thai village of Kanchanaburi, where a large radiogram standing incongruously on the mud floor of a makeshift café brought him the news that England and Australia were even then facing off at Manchester and that Cristofani was en route to a maiden century, in its way a surely definitive case of the sensation of passing, almost as if bodily pushed, from a world of darkness into one of light. Swanton's account of this event appeared under the headline 'Cricket Under the Japs' in the following year's *Wisden.* He sustained his animosity to his fellow captors, often expressed in drily humorous style, for the rest of his life. In time, Swanton and the other liberated British prisoners were each given a cursory medical, a £50 gratuity and an issue of civilian clothes invariably too big for them. As a final parting gesture, the former prisoners were then handed a military pay book which was uncompromisingly stamped with the words 'Unfit for future service.' Few people beyond the narrow confines of the BBC Outside Broadcasts unit had then so much as heard of Swanton, but he made good this shortcoming over the next 55 years to wield as much influence on the game as any cricket writer before or since him.

* * *

Compared to a sold-out Old Trafford, the Cambridge Avenue ground in New Malden must almost have seemed like someone's agreeable if somewhat randomly maintained back garden. It would have been hard to recognise the bucolic setting, with its small wooden pavilion at one end, and a tree-lined boundary marked by a slow-moving brook at the other, as part of the same sport being contested 200 miles away at the hurriedly patched-up ground in central Manchester. 'Events [move at] a measured pace hereabouts,' the *Sutton Post* correspondent commented of a match in mid-August 1945. There was generally a crowd of a hundred or so men in dark suits and women in full dresses for the midweek club matches featuring the Malden Wanderers, for whom the Bedser twins, Alec and Eric, sometimes turned out in the later war years. Never in the absolute top flight of sports arenas, Cambridge Avenue presented 'a decent wicket', although the outfield, popular with local dog-walkers, was 'bumpy and bare in places', the *Post* said.

It was nonetheless here that, the Oval still being converted back from its intended role as a wartime internment camp, a full-strength Surrey side hosted Sussex in a single-innings game on Saturday, 25 August. In keeping with the slightly haphazard feel of the game as a whole, Surrey's 27-year-old all-rounder Stuart Surridge was deputised at the last moment to play for the opposition, who had reported for the day a man short. Surridge still remembered this experiment in team-swapping towards the end of his life nearly 50 years later, if not necessarily for strictly technical cricketing reasons. 'It was spitting down rain and an army lorry dropped me off at the corner by the front gate, and lying right there by itself at the side of the road was a large bag of potatoes, apparently shed by some truck going by up or down the road into town. I'll have some of them, I thought, and stuffed as many as I could into my kit bag. There must have been ten pounds in weight's worth of them. In those ration days you could live off that for a week. That wasn't a bad haul for me, and the Sussex boys liked a drop or two at the close, too. When I think back on [New Malden] I don't think so much of scores but of a lovely big bag of spuds and propping up the bar at the Royal Oak with John Langridge. Anyway, a good day out, nice crowd, can't remember the actual score,' Surridge concluded.

Wisden confirms that 'despite a dismal morning and intermittent rain before and after lunch, quite 2,000 people visited the well-equipped picturesque ground. Sensations marked the cricket from the start, when Pierpoint with his first ball got the visitors' opener Sunnucks caught at point and, after a leg hit to the boundary, bowled Jones.' Sussex never fully recovered from these early blows, managing just 76 off 40 overs. Surrey passed this total for the loss of three wickets, before batting on for a further hour and 73 more runs to entertain a crowd now basking in the mid-afternoon sunshine. Fred Pierpoint, right-arm fast, played only four more matches for Surrey, finishing with the modest haul of 13 first-class wickets at 45 apiece, before disappearing back into the leagues, one of the relatively anonymous but indispensable 'nearly men' of cricket whose own career highlight was capturing the wicket of the highly regarded Peter Sunnucks with the first ball of the day in front of a damp but enthusiastic crowd that grey Saturday morning, whose report in *Wisden* set him for ever apart, separated by a thin film of distinction from lesser players. Sunnucks himself went on to play a total of 68 first-class matches not for Sussex but Kent, once scoring 162 for them in a county match at Trent Bridge. Stuart Surridge would play 221 times for Surrey, leading them to the Championship title in each of the five years in which he was the club captain.

That same Saturday a three-day fixture that crowned the year as much as even the Victory matches began at Lord's, where Walter Hammond's England played a Dominions side led by Learie Constantine. There are times when one can only defer to the *Wisden* correspondent present on the ground to convey something of the flavour of the proceedings:

'Lord's, August 25, 27, 28. Dominions won by 45 runs with eight minutes to spare. One of the finest games ever seen produced 1,241 runs, including sixteen sixes, a century in each England innings by Hammond, and grand hundreds for the Dominions by Donnelly, the New Zealand left-hander, and Miller of Australia. In addition, the result was a triumph for Constantine, who, in the absence of Hassett through illness, was chosen captain by the Dominion players just before the match began. Both sides experienced various changes of fortune and the issue remained in doubt until the end.

'The final stage', *Wisden* continued, 'will be remembered chiefly for the glorious driving of Miller. He outshone everyone by his dazzling hitting. In 90 minutes he raised his overnight 61 to 185, and in three-quarters of an hour of superb cricket he and Constantine put on 117. Though travelling at such a pace, Miller played faultlessly. One of his seven sixes set the whole crowd talking. It was a terrific on-drive off Hollies, and the ball lodged in the small roof of the broadcasting box above the England players' dressing room.'

In all, Miller hit 20 boundaries, and his 185 took him only 168 minutes. The blow off the unfortunate Hollies was among the longest carries ever seen at Lord's, and came within only a foot or two of emulating the legendary shot by his fellow Victorian Albert Trott when he cleared the pavilion chimneys batting for MCC in July 1899. *The Times* correspondent was left to wonder whether Lord's was a big enough ground for Miller, who would finish the 1945 season with three centuries and three fifties in just seven first-class matches, at an average of 72.50.

For the record, the team scores at Lord's were: Dominions 307 and 336, England 287 and 311. Among other points of distinction, it was Walter Hammond's last batting exhibition of real virtuosity for England. Unusually, he was twice out stumped, if only after he had scored 121 in the first innings and 102 in the second. Unmentioned by *Wisden* was the moment when Miller, who was suffering from a sore back, returned to the visitors' dressing room immediately after his better than run-a-minute century to be met by a dark-suited Pelham Warner, bowler hat in hand, offering his congratulations with the prescient words, 'My Lord, Keith, we shall be hearing more of you in the future.' 'Cheers, mate,' Miller replied, genially enough, before suggesting that the MCC deputy secretary join him in a bottle of beer he extracted from a large supply in his bag. The offer was declined. 'And that was my last sight of Flying Officer Miller for the year,' Warner recalled, 'one arm bidding farewell, the other employed in quaffing a long draught of ale from the bottle,' which, proving his timing wasn't restricted purely to his batting, the Australian followed by letting rip with not so much a conventional belch as a sustained gastric oratorio. It seemed to take on a life of its own and to change in pitch and volume halfway through. Warner appeared to pause momentarily in his departure through the dressing-room door, but in the end continued on his way without further comment. He was followed in turn by Gubby Allen, who vigorously shook the batsman's outstretched hand and asked, 'But tell me Keith, how do you belt those sixes?'

Cricket can be a hard game, and many of its practitioners are only too pleased to expound on the many technical intricacies of their craft. Miller was not one of them.

'Oh, you know,' he replied, with an offhand shrug. 'You just shut your eyes and swing.'

The players' party that night was held in the Boomerang Club, which Miller himself fondly remembered as a place of 'low entertainment, set in a basement under Piccadilly Circus'. It was the 'best-looking dive located below street level you could hope for', he later told me, with a well-stocked bar and a dancefloor 'where several of our guys accosted the local English girls with some success'. Lindsay Hassett had recovered from his illness sufficiently to join his sometime colleagues for a double celebration of the successful outcome of the match at Lord's and his own 32nd birthday. Wally Hammond later looked in to toast his Australian counterpart with a glass of sherry, but said little beyond offering the mandatory minimum congratulations to Miller and one or two of the others present. It was sometimes said that England's captain struggled to make taking an interest in other people seem less of an obvious effort. As a rule, Hammond rarely offered direct blame or praise, and revealed his current opinion of his teammates only by the act of bringing them on or off to bowl, or moving them around the field by means of a few grunted remarks from his position at slip. His colleague Godfrey Evans thought that 'Wally was really like a set of Chinese boxes. If you made it through the outer wall, then you faced another one, then another, ad infinitum.'

A few miles away in Whitehall, Clement Attlee sat down at his desk early the next morning to read a voluminous report prepared for him on the pressing needs of the United Nations Relief and Rehabilitation Administration, the predecessor organisation of the UN, which had sent the Allied heads of government an urgent request for 'personnel, transport, medicine, clothing and food' to distribute among the civilian populations of the defeated Axis powers. After reading of the particularly distressing state of affairs in Germany, where 'as a matter of basic survival 44,000 tons of matériel will be required from the UK and USA by the end of September', among a host of other fussily detailed statistics concerning Britain's own parlous state of affairs, with the threat of 'wholesale cuts in power [and] supply of foodstuffs' over the coming winter, Attlee had turned to his private secretary, 37-year-old Leslie Rowan, a former all-rounder at Tonbridge School and Cambridge, to remark sadly that the world seemed to be confronted by the 'same insoluble passions and selfishness' that had produced the war in the first place.

'And to think that one could actually be out in the fresh air watching the cricket,' Britain's prime minister concluded, with some feeling.

8.

Endgame

IN A normal English summer, a two-day match between a middling county side and some overseas visitors at the end of a long tour, starting on a wet Friday morning at Trent Bridge, might qualify only as a contract-fulfilling call by one set of cricketers on the other. However, Nottinghamshire's fixture with the Australian Services from 31 August–1 September took on an unusually compelling aspect, for a variety of reasons. Batting first after losing the toss, the visitors managed only a sub-par 194 in their first innings. Apart from the weather, the headline news was the return to county colours of the 36-year-old Bill Voce, the tall, tousle-haired right-handed bat and left-arm bowler who in the pre-war years had formed one of England's great pace duos with Harold Larwood.

Voce's career trajectory reflected, and in some ways epitomised, the professional cricketer's life of that time. After starting work in a colliery when he was 14, he had been noticed in the nets one afternoon by Fred Barratt, a Nottinghamshire seamer, and joined the Trent Bridge staff in 1926. Success in the second XI brought him into the county side in June 1927, at the age of 17, in a home match against Gloucestershire. Voce seized the moment by taking 5-36 and followed this by adding six more wickets the following week against Essex. The bowler's Test debut came in January 1930 against the West Indies at Barbados, where he opened the tourists' attack with the Hon. Freddy Calthorpe of Cambridge University and Warwickshire, a stereotypically upper-class toff to look at and listen to – it was said his voice could have shattered glass – if also capable of some rueful half-lights when commenting on Britain's straitened circumstances in the inter-war years, which among other privations had seen his family forced to temporarily shutter the west wing of their ancestral estate in Norfolk. In the event, these richly contrasting emblems of the British class system did not flourish as a long-term bowling partnership, although Voce himself went on to take 98 wickets in 27 Tests, including 15 at 23 apiece in the notorious bodyline series of 1932/33. It was said that he was not only genuinely fast, but that he had the stamina to bowl unwaveringly through the longest spells in the heat of the midday sun. In later years, Voce revealed hitherto unknown skills with the bat, with a particular affinity for the lofted blow over square leg. He finished with four first-class centuries, and no fewer than 26 fifties.

Voce had last played for Nottinghamshire in August 1939 and returned six years later only after a bitter pay dispute with his county employers, who had offered to re-engage him at a rate of £390 p.a. (£6,000 today) from April 1946 onwards. Even after protracted haggling, the player's contract still remained below even the modest norms of a professional England Test cricketer of the day, and was said to have led to an exchange of harsh words in the Trent Bridge committee room. So perhaps Voce had something to prove when he walked back out on the springy green Nottingham turf to bowl to the Australians in front of a crowd of 12,000 spectators that damp Friday morning. He seems to have made his point, because he took 5-46 in the visitors' first innings and 6-67 in the second, while scoring a belligerent 80 runs for once out. In the event, he would play his last first-class match only in July 1952, by which point he was nearly 43, going out with a single expensive wicket at home to Middlesex.

Perhaps it was all a case of Voce's legendary control of bounce and swing that accounted for the Australians' lacklustre performance that first day at Trent Bridge, when the visitors were saved from total ignominy only by a stand of 61 for the ninth wicket between the bowlers Charlie Price and Mick Roper. Or possibly there were other, non-cricketing factors to consider, too, such as the extended pre-match dinner held for both teams at the Council House in

Nottingham's town centre, where the Lord Mayor had thanked the visitors for 'all you have done in service during the war, and for your efforts to bring the British people and the people of your country together in affectionate friendship through sport', and Keith Johnson, the tourists' manager, had said in reply, 'We felt it was our duty to help protect this beautiful country which we regard as our Motherland … and thank goodness that when England is in danger in the future it will only be when playing a Test match against Australia.'

At nine the next morning, Johnson was obliged to tell the local press that of his team's ideal starting line-up, Hassett, Stanford, Pepper, Carmody, Workman, Sismey and Ellis had all come down overnight with 'stomach trouble' and in the end the last four men named were replaced in the side by Craig, Price, Roper and Bremner, a 'deeply regrettable state of affairs', Johnson was forced to acknowledge, although as it turned out one with generally beneficial consequences for the match's final outcome. One or two cynics around the ground were left to wonder whether the officially stated stomach issues might conceivably have been a euphemism for the impressive liquid consumption thought to have characterised the previous evening's civic dinner, while no less an authority than Keith Miller recalled many years later that several of his teammates had resorted to the evolutionary survival tactic of expelling toxic wastes from the body, in Carmody's case by 'hanging his head over the thunder box all night long'. Apparently himself immune, Miller scored 12 and an unbeaten 81, including a further two sixes and five fours, at Trent Bridge, where in the end the visitors pulled off an unlikely result by bowling out the home side for just 176 on the final day, Cristofani taking 6-59 and Pepper 4-71 to secure victory by 103 runs.

The traditional end-of-season Scarborough Festival, also getting underway that week, had been originally designed to combine competitive sport with the overall air of a late-summer carnival. Godfrey Evans later chiefly remembered of the occasion that the local pubs, of which there were many, usually opened their doors at 10.30am, while play typically began no earlier than noon, leaving ample time for the cricketers to slake their thirst on their way to the North Marine ground. This being early September in the north of England, there was generally a damp, faintly leafy back-to-school feel to the proceedings, though there were often glorious exceptions to the rule. 'The sun shone and there was the usual large and appreciative crowd spilling over the mound near the main gate,' *The Cricketer* wrote of the last pre-war Scarborough tournament. 'The town band played the "Eton Boating Song" and selections from *Rose Marie*, with the brio and that reckless disregard for their conductor which had made them famous.' In addition to the musical accompaniment, there was also a row of marquees dotting the Scarborough outfield, the one reserved for the committee and their guests furnished by tubs of palms and exotic plants, with a champagne cup in the adjacent members' pavilion and trestle tables groaning under the weight of barrels of beer and plates of brightly coloured cakes in the outlying tents laid out for the benefit of the fee-paying customers. On this occasion, there were also generous amounts of bunting and flags around the field, along with patriotic slogans advising the public of the need to conserve water, and to eat carrots to improve their eyesight. The ground's heavy roller had been previously requisitioned to help lay out improvised landing strips in the North African desert, but two men in brown overalls had repeatedly pulled its replacement up and down the toast-coloured pitch, which looked good for days of cricket and thousands of runs.

So began one of only 15 matches to be deemed first-class in 1945, pitting New Zealand against a side chosen by 72-year-old Henry Leveson-Gower (pronounced Looson Gore, and popularly known as 'Shrimp'), a four-time Oxford blue in the 1890s, MCC stalwart, and more to the point for the last 45 years the principal organiser of the annual Scarborough festival. His team's batting line-up on the day was impressive: Hutton, Washbrook, Wyatt, Fishlock, Edrich and Robins occupied the first six places, with

Arthur Wood of Yorkshire and England at the age of 47 perhaps stooping more than actively squatting in his position behind the stumps. The bowling was another matter, with the new ball in the hands of Alec Coxon of Yorkshire and Glamorgan's rugby-playing all-rounder Austin Matthews, both triers, certainly, if of only modest pace. Yorkshire's Brian Sellers captained the side and chipped in with a few overs of his rather approximate off-spin. Rounding out the XI was the 32-year-old medium-pacer Jack Parker of Surrey. Though never gaining international recognition, Parker's ability to extract bounce on hard wickets made him a bowler who was well suited for export, and he was unlucky to have been named a member of the MCC party scheduled to visit India in the winter of 1939/40, only for the tour to be cancelled due to the war.

New Zealand's captain Ken James won the toss and batted; literally so, as he opened the visitors' innings with Martin Donnelly. The duo made 1 and 100 respectively. 'Beginning with 51, including nine fours, out of 71 in an hour, Donnelly batted altogether two hours and a half for his century, with fourteen fours among his brilliant strokes … Perfect timing enabled him to drive, cut, and hit to leg, besides pull, with a minimum of exertion,' *Wisden* wrote. None of the other visitors lingering long, New Zealand were all out for 220 at tea on the first day. Len Hutton then played a not insignificant part in the Leveson-Gowers' reply, with 188 out of a team total of 472. It was perhaps this innings, as much as the same batsman's century in the third Test at Lord's, that went furthest to reassuring the selectors of his recovery from his wartime injury. The *Yorkshire Post* correspondent Jim Kilburn felt moved to tell his readers that Hutton's 'driving, his forcing back-foot shots, his hooking and his late-cutting represented batsmanship of his own standard, and there is no higher'.[8]

---

8 Shortly before his death, Hutton told me that he felt he had never been the same batsman again after March 1941, although he continued to score immense amounts of runs until his final first-class appearance, playing for MCC against Ireland at Dublin in September 1960, when he made 89 before discreetly allowing himself to be stumped.

The visitors came out a second time. After a wet weekend, Scarborough had woken up to bright blue skies on Monday morning. The good weather seemed like a shock at the end of a summer widely remembered for its rain. 'What a glorious start to the month of September,' the *Post* wrote elsewhere in its pages, 'with the scent of hay and mown grass, and also that hint of crispness in the morning air.' This time around, Donnelly hit a six and 13 fours in making 86 out of 142 in a hundred minutes, a sort of left-handed version of Miller at his most imperious, with something of that player's ability to reduce tiring bowlers to the role of so many handmaids, seemingly there merely to serve him.

Ken James entered into the Scarborough spirit by declaring when his side reached 312/7, which set Leveson-Gower's XI a target of 61 in just over half an hour. The home team crossed the line with four minutes to spare. A flayed cameo of 27 by Washbrook in a couple of overs helped the cause. He batted in a style that could be called correct-aggressive, but then ran himself out going for a suicidal single to mid-off, leaving Laurie Fishlock and the hurriedly promoted keeper Arthur Wood to finish the job. The middle-aged Wood wasn't normally one for the headlong dash between wickets and was apparently none too pleased at being called upon to pad up and hurry out again to face the New Zealand quicks in the now fading light, complaining that he could hardly see the ruddy ball and that his lumbago was murder. The first ball Wood faced was bowled to him by Tom Pritchard, right-arm fast. It rose sharply from a length and passed by perilously close to the Yorkshireman's averted head on its way through to the keeper. After that, Wood walked around in a tight circle for a bit, visibly muttering, though whether it was to himself or the opposing bowler was a matter of debate. The next delivery from Pritchard was straight and low, and the batsman gave it his trademark shot, a lusty heave of the blade that all but completed a full circle in its execution, but on this occasion failed to make contact. The next one came in equally fast, swinging to leg, and Wood again launched himself on to the front foot, got a nick, and sent the ball flying in the general direction of fine leg and across the rope for four. The shot after that was its mirror opposite in terms of angles, but achieved the same result, with a thick edge that flashed past gully and crossed the deep backward point boundary. That concluded Pritchard's over, leaving Fishlock to do the honours against 48-year-old Ted Badcock – something of a cutup in his heyday quarter-of-a-century earlier opening the attack for Wellington, but reduced here to a sort of comic butler's role, shuffling up bowed at the waist to be promptly carted through midwicket for two. The Leveson-Gower side had won by eight wickets.

The Australians in turn came to Scarborough on 5 September, crushing the home team by an innings and 108 runs. Miller scored an even-time 71, but the real plaudits this time belonged to Cecil Pepper, who hit 168 in 146 minutes. His innings included four sixes that were content merely to cross the rope, and a fifth one resulting from a full, long-armed slash of the bat that sent the ball high in the direction of the Scorebox End. There was a fielder down there, and the ball flew about 12 feet above his head and bounced off the steel drum of the replacement roller parked nearby that promptly shot it back again like a slip-catching net. The sheer abruptness and audacity of the stroke caused the non-facing batsman, Lindsay Hassett, to momentarily sit down on the grass and laugh. Shortly after that, Pepper launched another one so high and hard that it cleared the roofs of the nearby houses on Trafalgar Square, 'so repeating an effort by C.I. Thornton in 1886, when batting for Gentlemen of England against I Zingari', *Wisden* informed its readers. Reg Ellis, trotting up with his neat, tiny steps, sent down 34 overs of left-arm spin and took 10-67 in the match.

Later that day, Walter Hammond put his name to a news agency article that paid generous tribute to the summer's principal tourists, along with the merest hint of professional disdain for some of their cricket.

'I am sure the players will not be sorry to say goodbye to the competitive game for a few weeks,' Hammond wrote. 'Although I know they have thoroughly enjoyed their matches over here, they have probably found the long programme something of a strain. They have been playing nearly every day for some weeks. Before the war, most of them were of course only Saturday afternoon cricketers ...'

Back at Lord's, meanwhile, an Over-33 team captained by Jack Davies of Kent took on the Under 33s led by the occasional Nottinghamshire wicketkeeper-batsman Cecil Maxwell.[9]

The again atrocious weather prevented any definite answer to the question of whether this would prove a triumph for the vitality and spirit of youth, or the accumulated wisdom and patience of age, as in the end both sets of players, old and young alike, ran from the field in a thunderstorm, with the Overs leading by 14 runs with half their second innings wickets intact. With the exception of a few remaining Cross Arrows and Colts games, one of them featuring the 16-year-old Tony Lock, that concluded the season's fixture list at Lord's.

Press censorship controls in Britain formally ended that week, exactly six years after the nation's editors had first been warned under the government's Defence Regulation No. 3 against publishing 'matter calculated to foment opposition to the prosecution of the war', or even to 'obtain, record or communicate to any person information which might be injurious [to] the interests of His Majesty's Government'. There was little immediate risk of such dissent from among the ranks of the summer sport's critics and correspondents, who for the most part then remained stout established pillars of respectability. We've touched on the wonderfully *ancien régime* musings in *The Cricketer* of Sir Home

9 Something of a sporting polymath, Jack Davies (1911–92) played rackets, squash and lawn tennis at club level, appeared in a rugby union trial for England, and won the OBE for his work as a wartime military intelligence officer before going on to serve, in what he always regarded as a logical series of promotions, as a governor of the Bank of England, a privy councillor, and president of MCC.

Gordon, whose reports combined a certain amount of technical data about scores and averages with lengthy digressions into the world of the correct headwear for a fielder in the Gentlemen v Players match, or the desirability for the square leg umpire to equip himself with a collapsible shooting-stick that placed Gordon alongside P.G. Wodehouse as among the century's most inspired fantasists of the English language. Next to him, even E.W. Swanton, soon to embark on his 30-year tenure as cricket correspondent of the *Daily Telegraph*, seemed like a hopeless radical.

Elsewhere in cricket's fourth estate, Neville Cardus was still living in self-imposed exile in Sydney, where quite coincidentally he had taken up residence shortly after the outbreak of war in Europe. The 31-year-old John Arlott, a former clerk in a Hampshire mental hospital, and a still-serving Southampton-based police sergeant, was just starting out as a trainee BBC books and sports producer as an alternative career. Evelyn 'E.M.' Wellings was meanwhile in the seventh of what became a 35-year spell as the increasingly influential cricket correspondent of the *London Evening News*, where it was said he habitually dipped his pen less in ink than in vitriol. A stern critic of any lax post-war falling-off in standards of either technique or decorum, Wellings was in some ways the southern counterpart to the impressively austere Jim Kilburn of the *Yorkshire Post*, where for 42 years he filed copy with a Parker fountain pen filled with green ink on press telegram forms which were then borne away by a messenger to the home office in Leeds. Kilburn never employed a typewriter, which he called 'the devil's own invention'. Nor did he ever write about off-field events, which earned him the gratitude of many cricketers. *The Times* said in its obituary of him that his reports were 'always precise, frequently elegant, sometimes stern, and invariably fair and accurate. He never wrote an unpolished piece or an unidentifiable one, although he was only occasionally analytical.' Kilburn's stature at the *Yorkshire Post* was such that sub-editors did not dare touch anything he wrote, even if it happened to contain a mistake.

At a slight remove from the nuts-and-bolts recording of a match's scores, there were whimsy merchants like Ronald Mason (1912–2001), a career civil servant who in his spare time wrote evocatively of cricket and cricketers in a graceful, if at times also mildly flowery style, and Herbert Farjeon, a diminutive Anglo-Irish playwright and author who regarded his cricket sketches as the pinnacle of a career that had also seen him compose the popular air 'I've danced with a man, who's danced with a girl, who's danced with the Prince of Wales.' Farjeon had written poignantly of the longed-for reawakening of the sport after the war, but sadly died, aged 58, in the week Germany surrendered. We've noted some of the strangely divided life of the combat veteran and soon to be BBC fixture Brian Johnston, who would take some beating when it came to bringing a pervasive sense of fun, if not always of technical exactitude ('and he plays that one there') to the commentary box. But R.C. 'Crusoe' Robertson-Glasgow, variously attached to *The Observer* and the *Sunday Times*, if really of no fixed journalistic abode, was probably the best of the lot, a sharp and graceful writer who was less interested in retailing the dry accountancy of a match than in capturing its quaint or absurd aspects, to which he himself in no small way contributed. Crusoe's press box colleagues knew him for his sometimes manic exuberance, his taste for a drink, his casual dress, his seemingly effortless and lapidary prose style (of a lively wicket at Southend in 1945 he wrote, 'the pitch, like Jezebel, was fast and unaccountable') and not least his cavalier way with deadlines. He was an ineffably British *bon vivant.* Tragically, he also suffered from an illness that would probably now be diagnosed as bipolar disorder, once remarking that his life consisted of intervals of helpless mirth interspersed with moments when 'I feel horribly trapped' and 'not quite normal'. The impact of that latter line was deepened by Crusoe's suicide in March 1965, at the age of 63, when he found himself isolated by a late-winter snowstorm at his home in Berkshire. After helping his wife clear a pathway to their front door, he had calmly gone back inside the house, climbed the stairs to his bedroom, and swallowed a massive cocktail of alcohol and barbiturates. Depression, for all his long struggle to deny it, had the last bitter laugh.

* * *

After Scarborough, the Australians again climbed in their fitfully reliable Crossville bus for the 200-mile journey back south to the prim Leyland Motors ground in Kingston-upon-Thames for a match against Surrey. It was a green pitch, and over the two days a total of 37 wickets fell for just 327 runs. Freddie Brown had figures of 4-17 and 4-16, and even Miller managed to score only eight runs in two visits to the crease. In the end Surrey needed barely 50 to win, and managed to lose seven men before doing so. From there, the tourists returned to Hove, where they beat the county side by three wickets with two minutes to spare. The returned POW Graham Williams and Mick Roper, an estimable fast-medium bowler with no great pretensions with the bat, were together at the end. The home team's Eddie Harrison, a pre-war England squash international and still distinctly brisk at 35, was bowling, right-arm fast, with a stiff sea breeze at his back. Harrison wasn't the sentimental sort to begin with, and, roared on now by the crowd, he tore in to bowl the first ball of what proved to be the penultimate over of the day to Williams, with five minutes to go and nine runs needed to win. Williams raised his bat and extended the pad. There appeared to be some midwicket exchange of pleasantries between batsman and bowler before Harrison let fly again, and Williams managed to get enough on it to send the ball skidding past square leg for four. A bouncer followed. Williams squatted far underneath it. It became almost a *pas de deux,* with Harrison consistently aggressive, straight and fast, and the tall but still painfully gaunt tailender relentlessly defending. Another reflexive jab of Williams's bat off Harrison's last delivery produced a similar result, the ball flying off the edge to pierce the unguarded midwicket area and cross the rope for four. The scores were now level.

It had been a long day, and, Harrison aside, the Sussex seamers had clearly begun to fail in speed and accuracy. Jim Langridge, slow left arm, consequently threw the ball up to Roper to begin what everyone knew had to be the last over. Roper met it with a forward lunge of irreproachable correctness. The next two balls each brought sustained shouts for lbw, much of the noise emanating from the direction of long leg, but both were declined by the umpire. Roper extended his bat to the fourth ball, too. It took the inside edge and would have dropped like a stone into the hands of point, had one been present, and in his absence the batsmen crossed for a single. The Australians had won, and the small but vocal crowd had just witnessed 'some of the most thrilling and sporting cricket that has ever been seen on our historic old ground', in the words of the *Evening Argus*.

Already drained by a schedule of near-daily competitive cricket since their first coming-together as an organised unit in mid-April, some of the Australians were not best pleased to then find themselves pressed into service as part of the Empire XI visiting Northern Ireland in the middle of September. As Cec Pepper later said, 'One thing I didn't count on was the fact that after a long hot [*sic*] summer of five Tests up and down England I'd find myself picking daisies in a field outside Belfast.' The drawn two-day match at Wallace Park, Lisburn, from 11–12 September took place on a pitch that proved to be a paradise for bowlers one day, and for batsmen the next. The home side went in first and scored exactly 100, with the England duo of Pope and Pollard taking five wickets apiece. Miller himself then scored 71 in the Empire's reply, batting much like a boy enjoying a day out on the beach, with Pepper adding 27 in a stay of three overs before sprinting down the pitch to the Stormont civil servant and cheerfully part-time spinner Jimmy Boucher, to be comprehensively stumped – actually, more of a case of the batsman simply running headlong back from the middle to the dressing room, with the actual breaking of his wicket merely a necessary formality along the way. Pepper had been so far out of his ground by that stage that no one bothered to appeal. Pollard and Pope did some further damage in the second innings, but somehow inevitably it then rained again, with the visitors still 44 runs short of their target.

At 11 the next morning, the Empire XI went back into the field for a two-innings match against Ulster at the lovely Ormeau ground in Belfast. The home side made 117 and the visitors replied with 179/5 declared, Miller content with a two-over cameo of 15 and Pepper, having made 35 in 15 minutes, then losing his footing when coming down the track at the point where village cricket fields are apt to be most treacherous, where the mown part of the pitch meets the long grass, and skying a catch to cover as he lay flat on his back as a result. The Irishmen then somewhat whimsically declared their second innings at 84/5, setting their opponents a target of 23, which they reached off nine deliveries. There was an agreeably non-partisan crowd, and, on the basis of giving them more of what they had come to see, Miller and his partner Pepper were invited to stay and put on an exhibition. They duly did so, each hitting a few sixes into the leg-side oak tree before Miller gave himself out, caught behind, only to be persuaded to stay at the crease by the absence of any appealing, but then made sure of the matter by swinging across the line to the next ball, to be bowled all ends up by the local farmer and occasional seamer Jack Bowden (not to be confused with the Irish hockey international of the same name). In the event it was to prove the only representative match of Bowden's career, but he had something to tell his grandchildren about.

There was a dinner afterwards at the city's Grand Central Hotel, which contained all the customary good cheer associated with a late-summer's Friday night in the Ulster capital. Pepper was thought by one local journalist to have asked a lot of 'unbelievably stupid' questions about recent Irish history, but perhaps this judgement spoke more of the journalist than it did of Pepper, whose points were probably born of genuine curiosity and lack of education on the subject, not stupidity at all. Years later, Miller remembered that the teams had 'done wonders for the annual turnover of the Guinness company', and that a threatened speech by a Belfast city alderman had been forestalled only when George Pope had advised him of the mutual disinclination among both sets of players present to be treated to an address of a lofty or sententious nature, although Miller later admitted that Pope's actual choice of words 'might have been more colourful'. A party or parties unknown took the opportunity of the dinner going on downstairs to visit the Australian players' hotel rooms on the upper floors and relieve them of some of the souvenir tankards presented to them earlier by the Irish Cricket Association, an act Miller understandably thought to be 'bumping along the bottom of all decency'.

A few nights later, back at Lord's, Pelham Warner rose to his feet in his role as president of the British Empire XI to note that a playing record for the season of 45 matches, of which 28 were won and only four lost, was one that any team, professional or amateur, might be proud of. On top of this, the total of £6,350 raised for a variety of war-relief funds was a 'most worthy emolument, which I shall distribute with the greatest pride and happiness'. Notwithstanding his somewhat frosty image, Warner took a close personal interest in the recipients of his teams' charity. In October 1945, he quietly added a further private gift of £500 (£7,500 today) to the Red Cross.

* * *

Just 24 hours after their last-gasp win at Hove, the Australian Services were back on their bus for the day-long journey to the Acklam Park ground in Middlesbrough. Their opponents were a Combined Counties XI largely composed of northern-based amateurs, and in the event it proved a somewhat lopsided affair as sporting contests go. Batting first, the Australians declared at 268/5, and their hosts were then all out for 77, Jack Pettiford taking 6-20 with his bag of leg spin. Pettiford was a particular master of the googly, but of many other variants, too, some of which may have existed only in his opponents' heads. 'If the batsman thinks it's spinning, it's spinning,' he liked to remark. There was a moment when Pettiford had bowled Yorkshire's old-timer Arthur Booth that seemed to prefigure Shane Warne. The ball had dipped late into the leg side, almost comically wrong-footing the batsman as he fell to his right, before ripping diagonally back across to hit the off bail. Booth himself later referred to this dismissal as 'the greatest spectacle I ever saw' – or to be pedantic, didn't entirely see – on a cricket field. And the batsman knew whereof he spoke, going on to take 111 wickets at an average of just 11.61 the following season to head the national bowling averages. As the 1945 series progressed it was increasingly said of Pettiford that he could bowl every kind of spinner in the book, as well as several that were his own invention, and that he rarely tried the same thing twice. 'He was a handful,' Arthur Booth ruefully confirmed.

The next day, 16 September, the Australians lost a rare Sunday fixture by 28 runs to a North Yorkshire and South Durham league side at Darlington. Their RAAF colleagues were meanwhile in action 300 miles away at Hastings, where they were officially designated the home team for the visit of Northamptonshire. The scorebook records only that the visitors won, although to be fair the Australians were by then suffering a whole series of absences, illnesses and early homeward departures such that they could put only five fit men in the field. Their line-up had a somewhat makeshift feel to it as a result, with the hurried recruitment of half a dozen able-bodied spectators to the cause, one of whom turned out to be an unescorted German prisoner on day work-release, and who later conscientiously left the ground to report back to his camp. It was noted that the Northants and future England opener Dennis Brookes made a century. That effectively concluded the Australians' summer tour, which had combined both high-class cricket and a degree of sorely needed sports-assisted therapy for a war-weary public. After that there was just time for a final, well-lubricated dinner – another of the themes of the tour – at a gaming club discreetly tucked away in a side street off London's Edgware Road, where Walter Hammond was thought to have a financial interest. Lindsay Hassett established that at 32 he still retained the spring in his step with which he had begun the series by performing his party piece of leaping over a billiards table from a standing start. He had proved himself a universally popular figure wherever he went in Britain, and duly succeeded the retired Don Bradman as his country's full-time captain from January 1949 until his final return to Britain in the summer of 1953, when he was invited to put on a top hat and morning suit to attend the coronation of Queen Elizabeth II in Westminster Abbey, but lost the Ashes series one-nil to Len Hutton's England.

The Australian manager, Keith Johnson, paid generous tribute to his team's hosts in a statement released later in the month. 'I would like to say "thank you" to the cricket administrators, the cricketers and to the great cricketing public of Britain,' he remarked. 'The matches this season will always be a pleasant memory to us, and if we have in any way contributed to the rehabilitation of English cricket, then it was our honour and our pleasure ... In thanking all the people who helped us,' Johnson added, 'I would particularly refer to Sir Pelham Warner, our guide, philosopher and friend. To him, we owe the honour of the first opportunity of playing at Lord's and our subsequent important games.'

These effusions were handsome on Johnson's part, but perhaps did not entirely reflect the views of all his team. Cecil Pepper, for one – again proving the aptness of his surname – later noted, perhaps jokingly, that on his return to Australia he had seen fit to adjust the provisions of his last will and testament specifically so that it made reference to 'His Lordship' Pelham Warner. There 'wouldn't be a penny' for him in the revised document, he said. The sheer exhaustion among the touring party had been intense, and some of its members had had increasing difficulty motivating themselves as the summer progressed. Taking the five Victory matches in isolation, Miller led the visitors' batting averages with a total of 443 runs at 63.28, with Cristofani, Stanford, Hassett and Pepper following behind. Charlie Price, the left-arm spinner who had appeared in only two of the internationals, led the bowling list, although Cristofani, Pepper, Ellis, Miller and Graham Williams each took more individual wickets. It's of course absurd to judge a tour of that sort purely by its numbers. The Australians left Liverpool on 3 October on board the partly converted troop ship RMS *Stirling Castle,* and 19 days later arrived in Bombay for a further nine matches, taking them as far afield as Lahore in the north and Madras in the south, over the next four weeks. According to General Sir Ivan Mackay, the Australian high commissioner to India who flew in from Delhi to meet the 14 cricketers and five officials, the party uniformly looked to him in 'fine fettle', Reuters reported, with 'not a single outbreak of any seasickness' among the passengers. Keith Miller pronounced himself raring to play again. He had spent some of the long sea voyage reading D.H. Lawrence's *Lady Chatterley's Lover*, and the rest of it making the better acquaintance of some of the 300 brides on board returning to men whom they scarcely knew and whom they had met in brief wartime encounters, a number of them proving amenable to this early test of their wedding vows with a famous Australian cricketer. Perhaps no excursion with Cecil Pepper among its number could ever be truly incident-free, however, because a footnote to the same Reuters report of 24 October added: 'Sgt. C.G. Pepper told our correspondent that he had not yet signed a contract to play for an English League Club. He said that he would take time to consider the matter after he returned home to Sydney.

'A London message states that an official of the Rochdale (Lancashire League) Cricket Club expressed "some surprise" when informed of Pepper's statement.

'"It is true that Pepper has not yet signed on the dotted line", the official noted, "but he has still entered into an agreement before leaving England to play here for three seasons, and the terms were settled."

'The Rochdale source added that he had only a few days earlier received a letter posted at Gibraltar in which Pepper again clearly stated his intention to join them.'

In the event, Pepper did go on to play in the Lancashire League, but for Burnley, not Rochdale, and starting only in April 1949, not 1946.

* * *

It was in many ways a strange and obviously transitional environment the Australians were leaving behind them in October 1945. Some of the roistering and collective high spirits of the summer's tour were almost like a fortress against the gloom. Keith Miller later recalled that the country he encountered in 1945 had been 'knocked about' during the previous six years, but that there was 'plenty of fun to be had if you knew where to look for it', in his own case tempered only by the fact that 'everyone was going on about the end of the war in Europe, but for all I knew I was still about to be pushed out to fight the Japs in the Far East'.

It's not unusual for a large, industrialised nation to be socially and economically polarised between the haves and have-nots, but in the case of Britain in 1945 it almost begins to look like a form of schizophrenia. On one hand, there was the 'self-satisfied officer class at the top of the batting order', Miller remembered. Or perhaps it was more like a Venn diagram, with some individuals in their discrete group and other groups intersecting.

Of the latter, there were the ranks of those who one way or another had done well out of the war, and its accompanying restrictions and shortages – the 'froth and scum' of society, Miller called them, as represented by the 'pimps, spivs, pedlars, Shylocks and dodgy little characters who used to send their cards up to the dressing room inviting you to invest in their get-rich-quick schemes'. There were the cricketers and the cricket-watching public themselves, as well as the great majority of people who just wanted to resume some semblance of their old lives as they once knew them. And overlying it all like a suffocating blanket was the rigid consciousness of status and rank that in those days never seemed far removed from British life as a whole.

'I once went down to Waterloo station,' Keith Miller recalled. 'Going somewhere on my own, can't remember where. And here were these lines of poor ragged Tommies straight off the troop train, coming home from the war, and as they shuffled past there was an officer in full service dress, riding breeches, polished black boots and handlebar moustache shouting orders at them. In the midst of this stream of knackered-looking blokes, some of them bandaged up or on crutches, this man carrying on like they were on the drill square gave you one of those flashes where you see the two sides of life.'

Miller couldn't help but notice that a 'very British' sign had greeted the homecoming soldiers as they walked or limped past him on their way along the platform. It was not so much one of welcome or congratulation, but which instead read: 'ALL RETURNING FORCES ARE REMINDED THAT THEY ARE STILL SUBJECT TO KING'S REGULATIONS.'

The set-piece national celebrations aside, there was also evidence of a certain modest revival of public spirits, or at least a loosening of the ties of the communal wartime corset sufficient to encourage a few individual outbreaks of revelry. As the Sheffield housewife Edie Rutherford wrote in her diary on the day Miller and his fellow cricketers were on their torturous journey to play Surrey at Kingston: 'I shall go to London on Saturday of next week, for [a friend's] wedding. Husband says I'm mad to go for such a slight thing, but I'm content to be mad me, if the events of the last six years have been sane. I intend now to let up on personal restrictions after years of denying myself. If I can get a bed, I'll stay overnight too.'

In that same week, there was a street party in Canterbury Road, Leyton, to 'Commemorate the Cessation of all Worldwide Hostilities', and advertised with the understandable if optimistic slogan: 'May Universal Peace Now Reign For All Time!' The proceedings kicked off with a children's fancy-dress parade, 'with prizes distributed by The Rev. J.E.C. Seago', followed by a conjuring and ventriloquism display, and the projection of an unnamed silent film, 'with noises provided by the Audience'. Under the benign eye of Rev. Seago and his committee, there were also flags, flashes of bunting, sack races, donkey rides, tombola and coconut shies, and smiling church ladies pouring tea. At 8pm, the programme noted, it was a case of 'And So To All The Children Good Night and God Bless!', following which there was a further two hours of 'Dancing, Community Singing and Refreshments (Ad-Lib)', with musical accompaniment by a sort of proto-DJ called 'Gramo' – in reality a local 18-year-old apprentice fitter named Bert Spangler, alternatively accompanying himself on banjo, or dropping a knitting needle-sized stylus on a huge, mock-teak radiogram with a long electrical cord passing over the street and through the window of a nearby scout hut, and playing a repertoire of popular swing and big band numbers, until the ritual moment when everyone suddenly froze in place for the national anthem prompt at 10pm. Apart from Gramo himself, the night's other principal presenters mostly consisted of Wodehousian names like Reginald Smith-Bampfylde, Mr Orion Rochester, Miles Chudwell, Miss Arabella Rutherford and the Hon. Peregrine Holmes, JP.

And these, it should be remembered, were the irreproachable but then far from exclusive east London suburbs. As Keith Miller observed, it sometimes appeared that British life was 'just a bit topsy-turvy' at around the time the Germans and Japanese successively surrendered, and seemed to some people, like Miller himself, to resemble nothing so much as an extended family 'with all the wrong people in charge of it'.

The Britain of summer 1945, of Miller being paid a few shillings a day to entertain overflow audiences, and Pelham Warner's laborious exchanges with George Pope, might strike us as ludicrously archaic by modern standards. Life on and off the cricket field was quantifiably harder, for one thing. Even in summer, London seemed permanently winter-bound and sulphurously foggy, very much still the Victorian city, haunted by the past. As Edie Rutherford wrote in her diary that September: 'My hairdresser sisters were closed last week while they went to town for a holiday. But London's scars distressed them, especially the amount of bombed churches. Admitted food was hard to get and complained bitterly about the swarming Americans.'

Other visitors were similarly disappointed to find both London and most other cities still looking distinctly shabby, and even now bathed only in a murky half-light when the country's power stations cut their output by half at nine o'clock each night. Others commented on the unappealing mixture of bureaucracy and poverty of the sort experienced by the cricketer Joseph Hazel, who returned home that summer after three years as an inmate of the Japanese camp system, only to spend much of his time corresponding with organisations like the Inland Revenue over matters such as his permissible travel expenses, or what back pay might be due following his ordeal.

'There was a distinct mood of bloody-mindedness, which wasn't so much there in 1939,' another repatriated POW, the Glamorgan cricketer and Welsh rugby international Wilf Wooller, later said. Wooller long recalled an incident when he had watched a uniformed private soldier run up to a passing post office delivery van in the streets of Cardiff late one Friday afternoon in August 1945. The soldier had asked the postman if he would accept an already stamped and addressed letter he was carrying with him, and the postman refused to touch it, telling the man to retrace his steps to the nearest pillar box and, should one not be available, to present himself at the door of the town's main post office when it opened for business at nine the following Monday morning. 'Somehow that summed up the pettiness that lay over most people's lives at the end of the war,' Wooller said, remarking on the 'bolshie attitude' that seemed to accompany the nation's victory.

Apart from that, Wooller most remembered the baffling events that followed the decision to put Britain's clocks back, not once but twice, in the summer and early autumn of 1945, only for them to go forward again the following spring. 'No one really ever explained the rationale for all this buggering-about,' Wooller said. 'The impression was that it was all part of the bigger trend of confusion and administrative nonsense – a general cock-up – at the time, whatever the choice of government.' Perhaps at the end of the day it was a case of 'Meet the new boss/Same as the old boss', as the future songwriter and social critic Pete Townshend, born in May 1945, would put it.

Of course, there were also positive and often enthusiastically seized-upon developments in 1945 as a whole. Apart from the communal celebrations breaking out over Britain in May and August, it was widely recognised that London and many of the country's other bomb-ravaged towns had been providentially offered the chance to rebuild. To many people, such places had been far from a communitarian Eden, let alone the playground of Bright Young Things clad in tassled dresses, cloche hats and Old Etonian spats evoked by the cast of Evelyn Waugh's 1930 novel *Vile Bodies*. Most British town centres of the time were distinguished less by their air of raw energy and racy promise than by their rows of undifferentiated red-brick houses packed together as tight as dominoes ready to fall, where indoor plumbing was far from universal, family members took a bath with bowls and pitchers in front of the kitchen stove, being 'on the phone' was a distinct novelty, and many middle-class homes featured postage-stamp-sized rooms patched together by crumbling plaster walls. For the most part, these were conditions that had changed little since Charles Dickens's day, although even that great chronicler of Victorian slum life might have been struck by some of the sanitary facilities in British homes and workplaces, let alone at the nation's public sports venues or places of entertainment. While none of this changed overnight, there was at least a pre-existing proposal for the nation's physical renewal that someone in authority had studied while the war was still in progress. The result was the Town and Country Planning Act of October 1945 and its matching Redistribution of Industry Act later that autumn, which between them gave local authorities powers of compulsory purchase over blitzed and derelict sites at 1939 prices, and at least in theory encouraged them to rebuild homes and businesses – more than a third of which had been destroyed by Luftwaffe action in central London alone – along more congenial lines.

In the event, some if not all of those living in the areas of greatest need would be dead before most aspects of the scheme were realised, and even their children and grandchildren would wait in vain to reap the benefits, while many of the aggressively linear housing blocks that actually ensued were of an ugliness that seemed almost wilful, the product of a sadistic, relentlessly 'modern' master plan. But there was at least an opportunity there to be grasped to drag much of the nation's infrastructure into the 20th century, if some 50 years after the fact, and a certain strategy by which to do so.

To read the letters and diaries of ordinary Britons in 1945 is to be exposed to a certain optimism, even if tinged by the bitter experience of recent events. The second half of the year was far from a time of uninterrupted debauchery as a suddenly rejuvenated nation as one kicked up its heels in a communal display of high spirits. But there was a definite sense of expectation to the place as a whole, and here and there already a few pockets of a new prosperity: television broadcasts resumed, more cars were on the roads, people's meals, although still rationed, showed a welcome advance from the wartime staple of Woolton Pie and the inevitable carrots. As one small but vivid snapshot of the times, Keith Miller remembered venturing down into the Piccadilly Circus underground station shortly before he left Britain for the summer, and seeing alongside the stark, utilitarian lighting some recently installed tubes that glowed in shades of red, yellow and violet. It was the first public installation of neon anyone had seen in London, and, to Miller, 'like gazing into the future'.

The cricket matches played in the summer of 1945 were clearly an important part of this broader public sense of renewal, and even at times of euphoria. The five Victory matches may not have been an official Ashes series, largely because the Australian board had groundlessly thought their side might not be strong enough to compete with England, but for the most part they were highly accomplished affairs which combined cricket's all-important sense of the pastoral and contemplative with moments of drama whose intensity was often magnified by the torpor which preceded it. With the exception of the drawn fourth Test – and even there Miller hit an imperious century – the internationals were all glorious displays of technical brilliance and fluctuating fortune, and even to those who never normally went near a cricket ground a source of pride, something to celebrate, an excuse to have a party. The weather aside, it was a magnificent series: 15 days of nearly unbridled sporting excitement, with enough collective goodwill among the teams to last a lifetime.

* * *

The Australian Services spent the remainder of 1945 in India and present-day Pakistan, where they lost one of the three unofficial Tests and drew the remainder. Jack Pettiford, Lindsay Hassett and Keith Carmody scored the most runs, and Cecil Pepper took an impressive number of wickets, with Miller for once subdued in both categories. Stan Sismey was forced to have an emergency operation on his back. Arriving home in Australia shortly before Christmas, the Services continued their tour by playing each of the domestic Sheffield Shield sides, ending with a three-day match against Tasmania in Hobart at the end of January, where Pepper took a further nine wickets and a capacity crowd of 3,500 appeared for the middle day's play. By then the Services had been in nearly continuous action for nine months, and several of the players had been away from their homes for five years. Only Hassett and Miller went forward as international cricketers, although there had been high hopes for Pepper up until the moment he self-destructed by apparently offending Don Bradman in the game at Adelaide. There was particular satisfaction at the news on 30 December that Warrant Officer Graham Williams, the POW who had returned to play competitive cricket that summer, had been awarded the MBE, not so much for his captivity per se, but for his services in teaching his fellow prisoners. Keith Miller was one of those who thought Williams's honour to be the bare minimum warranted under the circumstances. 'It would have been a knighthood if he'd been English,' he said.

In keeping with lesser mortals, some of the cricketers of 1945 fared better than others when it came to their post-war lives. A consistent theme throughout was one of poverty. Few of the game's most illustrious names lived to see, let alone to personally enjoy, even a fraction of the wealth available to their modern successors. As Len Hutton once remarked, 'You'd be walking out to bat in front of 30,000 people, and one part of your mind was worrying about the gas bill waiting for you back home.' The poor cricketer, and the poor cricketer's family, remained a sad reality of the game until at least the late 1970s, and arguably beyond even then. A top professional English player of the 1940s might have been earning a basic £500 (now £7,500) for his five months' work each summer, a figure that with bonuses and incentives may have reached £700–£800, or as much as £1,000 in exceptional cases. If the man in question was lucky enough to find winter employment, or to be selected to go on an overseas tour, his annual salary would still only have put him in line with that of a mid-level clerk serving in some worthy but minor administrative capacity in a provincial town hall.

The Australian Services captain **Lindsay Hassett** clearly continued in his nation's tradition of pocket-sized batting heroes, finishing his career with 3,073 runs at an average of 47 from his 43 Tests. He served as Bradman's deputy on the all-conquering 'Invincibles' England tour of 1948, and as we've seen returned in sole charge on the team's next visit five years later. Puckish though not without the necessary touch of grit when called for, Hassett retained his good humour even after his side had been destroyed by the Surrey and England duo of Jim Laker and Tony Lock, the latter deploying his trademark 'double-whirl' bowling action to devastating effect, to lose the final Test of the 1953 series at the Oval. 'Not bad,' Hassett privately allowed, 'considering Tony threw us out.' As a captain, he was said to have always attended to the particular, but never to lose sight of the context in which it took place. In retirement, Hassett ran a sports goods business and occasionally commentated on cricket, until the point around 1980 when he said he could no longer stand the more aggressive approach that had developed in an Australian team built around the likes of the Chappell brothers, Dennis Lillee, Jeff Thomson and Rod Marsh. After that, he moved to the small New South Wales seaside town of Batehaven to indulge his love of fishing, and died there on 16 June 1993 at the age of 79. The news reached England on the eve of the second Test between Allan Border's side and England at Lord's, where the pavilion flags flew at half-mast in his honour.

Hassett's nominal superior by virtue of military rank, **Stan Sismey**, continued to carry the shrapnel in his back as a souvenir of being shot down off the coast of Algeria in 1942, sometimes joking that all the metal affected the compasses of aeroplanes he flew in. Discharged from the RAAF in July 1946, Sismey went on to serve as a state selector, worked as a banker both in Australia and in his wife's native Scotland, and died in 2009 in the small New South Wales town of Taree, just down the Wool Road from where he was born nearly 93 years earlier. **Dick Whitington** became a prominent author and journalist, writing at some length of his distaste for South Africa's ban from Test cricket in the 1970s, and working as an employee of the Packer family prior to his death at the age of 71. The leg-spinning **Jack Pettiford** was one of the last of the 1945 crop still to be an active player by the time he retired from the game in 1961, having appeared alongside the likes of Godfrey Evans and Doug Wright at Kent, where he enjoyed a 1959 benefit season that raised £2,900, but died in October 1964 at the early age of 44. **Jim Workman** died in 1970; the former POW **Keith Carmody**, credited as the inventor of the umbrella field while captain of Western

Australia, in 1977; and **Bob Cristofani**, the man whose name had come through the static to the newly liberated E.W. Swanton in the Thai jungle, in 2002, either at his retirement home in Hampshire, or 10,000 miles away in Canberra; the UK National Archives say the former, and *Wisden* the latter.

The great all-rounder and contrarian **Cecil Pepper** went on to a long and comparatively lucrative career in the Lancashire League, supposedly making him the best-paid cricketer in England, before – surely the definitive case of a poacher turned gamekeeper – donning an umpire's white coat to officiate in English first-class matches for 16 seasons, a role which in no way curtailed his affinity for the barbed remark while in the middle. When Pepper died in March 1993, aged 76, he left behind an estate worth £135,000 (£350,000 today), which was divided equally between his adult son and a woman he had met a few weeks earlier.

Pepper's roommate on tour **Reg Ellis**, a left-arm spinner good enough to have clean bowled Walter Hammond in the second Victory match at Sheffield, and to take a ten-wicket haul in the late-season game at Scarborough, was the last surviving member of the Services team at the time of his death in June 2015, at the age of 97.

As we've seen, **Keith Miller** was above all others the living embodiment of cricket's reawakening – and perhaps also of Britain's revival – from the despair of war. It does no more than to state the often-repeated truth to say that he was clearly a magnificent all-rounder, a natural performer who was in his element in the packed English grounds of 1945, and a force of nature to boot. If some malign alien invader were to destroy all we know of cricket, only Miller surviving, it's a fair bet that we could clone from him every essential detail and quality of the game. It's not outside the realms of logic to think of an Australian team consisting of him, another seamer, a couple of batsmen, and perhaps a wicketkeeper giving a game to most other first-class sides of their day. 'There were no rations in an innings by Denis Compton,' Neville Cardus famously wrote of England's sun-drenched home Test series with South Africa in 1947, a line which could apply just as well to Miller's own role in the rain-soaked series two years earlier.

Above all, Miller hated the thought of wasting time – one of his habits was to give a hurrying clap to his fellow fieldsmen between overs – and clearly intended to live life while he could. Shortly after separating from the RAAF, he went on to marry his American fiancée Peg Wagner, in Boston, on 21 September 1946. They would raise four sons and remain together until 1999, at which point, Miller, with some abruptness, elected to move in with a younger woman who worked as a hospital secretary in Melbourne, apparently in the belief that she could look after him better in his final years. It has to be said that there was some suggestion that he may have taken a relaxed view of his wedding vows to Peg even prior to that date. As well as the rumoured – and quite possibly apocryphal – affair with the young Princess Margaret, Miller was widely thought to lead a vibrant social life that revolved around his consuming passions of sport, music and sex. In that last context, Godfrey Evans once assured me that he had come downstairs into the dining room of an English country hotel where they were staying at the time of the 1989 Ashes series, to find Miller alone there but for an 'extremely attractive lady of about 23, built along Barbara Windsor lines, sitting on his lap', and that by way of introduction, 'Keith calmly unbuttoned his companion's blouse, which she wore without a bra' and invited the former England stumper to 'admire the goods' thus on display. 'It was one of the more surprising moments of my life,' Evans was later forced to admit, no small accolade.

Outrageous, and perhaps untypical, though the story may be, it suggests a picture of Miller which is at odds with the fundamentally upright Australian-in-excelsis figure of legend: a crimson-faced and lubricious roué, then approaching his 70th birthday, who suffered cruelly from both ill health and various family disappointments in old age. As the preceding pages have, perhaps, shown, at his best Miller had been a superbly versatile cricketer, gifted by the gods, who at all times played with the awareness that there was more to life than cricket: women, horses and music being only the most obvious rival attractions. Despite professing his indifference to the accountancy of the game, he finished with figures of 14,183 first-class runs at an average a fraction below 50, and 497 wickets at 22 apiece. But Miller's countless worldwide admirers would always remember him less for his playing statistics than the way he could suddenly break into a grin while in the middle, casually flicking back his mop of hair before bounding in off his deceptively short run to send one scorching past the tip of the batsman's nose, or, conversely, unleashing a textbook drive off the full face of the bat, followed in short order by the rifle crack of the ball hitting the boundary board.

In his post-playing years, Miller worked for Vernons Pools and augmented his income as a characteristically plain-spoken commentator and journalist, once ruffling the feathers of England's captain Ted Dexter on the latter's 1962/63 tour of Australia by writing that he seemed to have 'had his eye on a pretty woman [Dexter's fiancée and future wife Susan, who was in Australia on a modelling assignment] as much as the cricket' – an allegation that almost makes one wonder whether a printer's error might have been involved – and later calling for the removal of the 'boring' Allan Border as Test captain. Miller was widely compared to the swashbuckling actor Errol Flynn, and it's true that both men combined youthful matinee-idol looks, a winning smile, and a hearty, self-mocking laugh with formidable professional skills that allowed them to make something supremely hard look ridiculously easy in their respective trades. In both cases, a certain self-indulgence also took its toll in later years. Miller died in October 2004 at the age of 84. A state funeral packed St Paul's Cathedral in Melbourne to the rafters, where one of the speakers, the former Australian Test opener Bill Brown, perhaps best captured the departed when he described him as a 'man's man, and a ladies' man as well'. The two had played together on Bradman's tour which had ravaged England in 1948, a series in which Miller's unpredictable genius with the ball was joined by the more smoothly calibrated Ray Lindwall at the other end. They took 142 first-class wickets between them that summer and aroused the contrary feelings among the British public of extreme apprehension at seeing either one of them roll up his sleeves to come on to bowl, with the unmitigated pleasure of the knowledge that they were witnessing the very finest at their art the game had to offer.

* * *

Walter Hammond led England on a tour of Australia meant to further cement Allied goodwill over the winter of 1946/47, with Bill Edrich as his senior professional. It was a hastily arranged and, on purely competitive grounds, disastrous series for the visitors, who lost three of the five Tests and drew the remainder. Nor was it especially successful in advancing Anglo-Australian relations in general. As we've seen, things got off to a poor start as early as the first day of the first Test at Brisbane, where the England captain addressed his Australian counterpart as a 'fucking cheat' following the latter's disinclination to walk when apparently caught in the slips by Jack Ikin.[10] It did not help Hammond's mood that Bradman went on to score 187, while at the other end, Lindsay Hassett, registering his first Test century, made 128. Hammond set off in a car that night to drive the first half of the way to the team's next engagement in Sydney. His passengers were Len Hutton and Cyril Washbrook, who spoke among themselves while their captain brooded in silence throughout the 400-mile journey.

For Hammond, things only seemed to deteriorate from there. In the tour's second Test at Sydney, Australia were able to declare

10 In a subsequent tour match in England, Jack Ikin had reached the 90s when Bradman instructed Keith Miller to bowl. Miller refused, pointing out that Ikin had been one of the heroes of the Tobruk campaign of 1941–42, and that the least they could do was to allow him to reach his century. At that, Bradman irritably threw the ball to Ray Lindwall, who had no such scruples and dismissed the batsman with his score on 99.

at 659/8, after Bradman and Sid Barnes had each scored 234. ('At least now we know when the buggers are vulnerable,' Hutton had remarked, displaying his gift for gallows humour, while unwinding back at the team hotel.) In another England rout by an innings, there was at least a Bill Edrich century and a crisp 54 by Compton – a promising augury of their famous partnerships in 1947 – to point to. But set against this were Hammond's continuing shortcomings both as a captain and a batsman, with just 93 runs to show from his four Test innings thus far. At one point during Bradman's double century at Sydney, the Englishman had strolled over to greet him not with some congenial words of congratulation, but, in a further lapse from the intended spirit of the tour, to enquire how many runs 'the little bugger' meant to steal from them today.

In all, it was a sad twilight tour for Hammond, who played his 85th and final Test against New Zealand while on the way home to England in March 1947. The popular consensus of him was that of a dazzling youthful talent – deemed by Cardus to be the 'Nijinsky of cricket', almost spoilt by fortune – who later bloated in his final South African exile like Elvis Presley at Graceland. It's a caricature, if one with a grain of truth. A colleague at Denham Motors in Durban in the 1950s remembered that 'Wally kept in his desk a selection of postcard-sized photos, all pre-signed, presumably meant for the fans he expected to flock to the showroom where he worked. I rarely saw anyone do so.' In February 1965, the England team was playing a Test down the coast at Port Elizabeth, and happily agreed to pass round the hat in order to take their old skipper out to dinner. In recent years, Hammond had both lost his job and been involved in a serious car crash, events that possibly served to further darken a personality already prone to the choleric.

The England wicketkeeper John Murray remembered: 'We got to the hotel and there was Wally waiting for us. Everyone said a cheery hello and we told him we just had to nip in to another room to shake some hands, but that we'd be right out again and on our way to a slap-up dinner. When we got back 15 minutes later, Wally was gone. He left a note behind. It said he'd never been so insulted in all his life by our behaviour in making him wait for us. "I am a former captain of England, and you buggers have dishonoured the office" was the gist of it. He died just a few months later. All very sad.'

It's worth repeating again that Hammond, who was just 62 at the time he suffered a fatal heart attack, was by popular acclaim one of the greatest English batsmen of the 20th century. Perhaps he never quite aspired to be the happy warrior – unlike, say, Denis Compton – whom every boy in pads hopes to emulate. And perhaps it's also unfair to judge him from a modern perspective in which it's no longer fashionable to admire reticence in our sporting heroes. There were periods in the 1930s when Hammond was as complete a batsman as ever went to the crease, a player who on his day was also a useful seam bowler and an electrifying slip fielder who once held 78 catches in a season, ten of them in a single match. As an all-rounder, Hammond bestrode the inter-war years of world cricket in a way not even Bradman could challenge. As a captain and a human being, he sometimes struggled to make taking an interest in lesser mortals seem anything but a necessary chore. For all that, he was affectionately remembered by a small but loyal inner circle of friends who gained his trust, and respectfully by the tens or hundreds of thousands who came to admire a batting style that was a cross between the classicism of Hobbs and the almost robotic precision of Bradman. Hammond was by far the best-qualified candidate to lead England in 1945; the many personal letters Pelham Warner sent him during the summer anxiously enquiring into his health are a testament to the regard in which he was held at the highest level.

Hammond's eventual successor as Test captain, **Len Hutton,** overcame his wartime injury to score some 30,000 further first-class runs with a bat of a size usually only to be seen in schools cricket. As noted, he led England to victory against Australia both at home in 1953, and away 18 months later, before announcing his retirement. Hutton would continue to score runs at almost inhuman levels of efficiency after the 1945 series while, much like Hammond before him, never bothering to affect any particular 'people' skills with his teammates, nor for that matter ever enjoying the full confidence of certain England selectors who still preferred their captains to be drawn from the ranks of the nation's ancient universities. 'My face never fitted,' Hutton once remarked. He died in September 1990, at the age of 74.

With a small private income and a larger determination to enjoy himself, that cricketing sparkplug **Bill Edrich** played in the minor counties for his native Norfolk well into his fifties, did some desultory sales work for Hambro Life, travelled the world, continued to consume champagne in near-industrial quantities, and married five times. In 1947, he and his Test and county colleague Denis Compton famously signalled a return to an altogether happier and saner post-war state of affairs when they scored 3,539 and 3,816 first-class runs respectively, a record that will surely be impossible to beat so long as the English season retains its present shape. Cardus wrote of going to Lord's one summer's day to sit among 'a pale-faced crowd, existing on rations, the rocket-bomb still in the ears of most, and see[ing] the strain of anxiety and affliction passed from all hearts' as England went on to beat South Africa in, for once, blazing sunshine.

Edrich would surely have played far more than his 39 Tests but for his faux pas in having disturbed the sleep of the chairman of selectors when making his late-night return to his hotel room – possibly by way of the drainpipe, rather than the conventional front door – during the Manchester Test in 1950. Crawford White, writing in the *News Chronicle*, considered the Middlesex player, 'while unpopular in certain quarters', to have been the man best qualified to captain his country at that time. Edrich died as a result of falling backwards down a flight of stairs late on the night of St George's Day 1986, aged 70. Compton followed him exactly 11 years later, at the age of 78. Their teammate **Cyril Washbrook** faced the unusual situation of finding himself both an England selector and actually playing for his country in the third Test of the 1956 series against Australia at Leeds, where he scored 98, sharing a stand of 187 with Peter May that helped England to right the ship and then to win the match by an innings. Washbrook died in April 1999, aged 84. **Stewart 'Billy' Griffith** played three post-war Tests, scoring a century on his debut, and later serving as secretary of MCC for 12 eventful years which included the introduction of one-day cricket, the creation of the Test and County Cricket Board and the D'Oliveira Affair. He died in April 1993, aged 78. **Harold Gimblett**, the precociously gifted if emotionally troubled Somerset player who scored an impetuous 104 batting for the West of England at Lord's in July 1945, also played just three Tests, which seems ludicrously few for a man who, when in the mood, could destroy any bowling line-up in the world and who had announced himself with the legendary *Boy's Own* innings of 123, made with a borrowed bat, on his debut at Frome. Following a period of ill health, Gimblett took his own life in 1978, leaving behind a wife and a son. Like Crusoe Robertson-Glasgow, he was aged 63 at the time of his death.

The Lancashire and England bowler **Dick Pollard** died in December 1985, in the same small town where he was born 73 years earlier. **John Dewes**, who later taught at Dulwich College, where Nigel Farage was among his pupils, died in 2015, at the age of 88. His fellow 1945 debutant **Donald Carr**, after a distinguished career as a cricket administrator, died the following year, aged 89. **Luke White**, the third of the schoolboy prodigies to represent England in the 1945 series, died in 1990, also at the age of 63.

Sir Pelham Warner, without whose single-minded dedication the Victory matches could never have taken place, retired from his secretarial duties at Lord's at almost the same moment the Australian Services party left the country in early October 1945. Five years later, he was elected president of MCC at the age of 76 and continued speaking and writing about the game with his trademark note of authority and gentle humour, frequently invoking the golden age of late Victorian cricket he personally had adorned, until very nearly the end of his life in January 1963. Perhaps providentially, his death happened to fall on the eve of the formal ending of the game's gentleman and player status, an initiative he deplored. Some years later, MCC opened a stand in his name at Lord's.

Warner's sometime antagonist **George Pope** played only one official Test, against South Africa at Lord's in 1947, but finished his first-class career, which had always been a thing of fits and starts, with no fewer than 677 wickets at an average of only 19, and 7,518 runs scored at nearly 30. Like that other plain-spoken character Cecil Pepper, he went on to stand as an English county umpire for several years. Pope was strictly impartial in his judgements, but, again like Pepper, never saw the muttered aside (as in, 'That man down at cover might as well be sitting in a chair doing *The Times* crossword – bring him up to short leg, and give the ball some bloody air') as incompatible with his duties. It was said that he mellowed in his later years and became locally popular as an after-dinner speaker whose remarks were typically distinguished by their wry self-mockery and a total lack of discretion. He died in October 1993, at the age of 82.

Kent's veteran wicketkeeper-batsman **Leslie Ames**, who played in the first of the Victory matches at Lord's, later remembered the summer of 1945 as the most enjoyable of his 20 years as a professional cricketer. After having endured periods of either drab routine or mortal danger for so long, the general mood of the day had been one of mingled relief and guarded optimism, Ames recalled. 'Life didn't suddenly improve, either in sport or anywhere else,' he admitted. 'But we were still alive, and we were back playing the game we loved.'

After reflecting for a moment, Ames went on to compare the experience to waking up on the first day of spring after a hard winter. 'Maybe things could still go wrong, but at least we'd earned the right to hope again,' he added.

Source Notes

THIS BRIEF section shows at least the formal interviews, published works, and/or archive material used in the preparation of the book. Although I can't claim any intimate familiarity with that great cricketer, I was lucky enough to have come to know Keith Miller when he was in England during the 1989 Ashes series, thanks to an introduction by our mutual friend Godfrey Evans. I put on record here my profound admiration for Miller the sportsman and all-round force of nature, and leave it to others to judge whether his personal life invariably lived up to the same lofty standards. Evans himself was a human tornado that blew through my life for several years, and I miss him still. Several relatives or other interested parties also kindly put their ancestors' diaries or other material at my disposal. A warm thanks to all the individuals and clubs listed, who should find their names in the acknowledgements at the front of the book.

A key source for the early part of the book was the biography of Bill Edrich by the late Alan Hill, as listed in the bibliography, as well as my long-ago interviews of both Edrich and Denis Compton. The records of both the Imperial War Museum and Cricket Australia were invaluable in finding the service details of Edrich and others – notably Keith Miller – in this part of the text; I'm particularly grateful to Jane Rosen at the former institution. It's also a pleasure to acknowledge Roland Perry's fine biography of Miller, again as cited in the bibliography. I've more than once quoted from Perry's book, as credited, either verbatim or slightly edited for sense.

I was also fortunate enough, again through Godfrey Evans, to meet and ask questions of the inimitable E.W. Swanton. Swanton, while never one to exude millions of volts of synthetic charm, was extraordinarily kind and patient with me. I only wish I'd been slightly less clueless at the time when I had the opportunity to mingle convivially with men such as Swanton and Gubby Allen – or to have perhaps made more of the long evening when I found myself seated next to no less than Len Hutton at Evans's 70th birthday dinner – but I did my best. On a more contemporary note, I should warmly thank Neil Robinson of the MCC Library and Jon Surtees, head of media at Surrey CCC, both of whom answered all my enquiries on the 1945 season with unfailing patience and courtesy. I say without the least misgiving that the former's recent book *The Other Side of Trust* is a spy novel with which John Le Carré might not have been disappointed.

Further details on the fates of those cricketers who perished in the 1939–45 war can be found in the papers of the Imperial War Museum (IWM) London. The memory of Hedley Verity's last hours while in the hospital at Caserta is included in The Sound Recordings by James Blackburn (Catalogue No. 27065) held at the IWM. Other material in these early pages was provided by Alex Legge, who very kindly supplied me with photographs and other details of his grandfather Geoffrey Legge; and by David Robertson, David Pracy, Rob Boddie and Phil Britt, respectively of or associated with Kent CCC, Essex CCC, Sussex CCC and Warwickshire CCC; I am warmly grateful to all those listed.

Among newspapers I consulted were: the *Cambridge Evening News*, the *Daily Express*, the *Daily Telegraph*, *Kent Messenger*, *Liverpool Echo*, *Northampton Daily Echo*, *Oxford Times*, *The Times*, the *Western Evening Herald* and the *Yorkshire Post.* Other source material came from the London Library, CricInfo, the Cricket Archive site, the Public Record Office and the National Army Museum in London.

The diary account of Sapper Ernest Ridgers of his induction into the Royal Engineers and his encounters there with Denis Compton can be found in The Papers of Ernest Ridgers, Late of 665 Artisan Company, R.E., held at the IWM London. I was also lucky enough to have known David Blake of Hampshire and Free Foresters when we were at one time neighbours in Wickham, Hants, and who kindly put his family recollections at my disposal. The UK Ministry of Defence was able to provide a service record and other material relating to the great George Macaulay of Yorkshire and England.

The quote suggesting that Bill Edrich 'got his pleasure from short-time highs …' is from Alan Hill, *Bill Edrich*, p. 127. The figures relating to RAF losses variously due to bad weather and other factors can be found in the minutes of the War Cabinet of 19 August 1941, held in the UK National Archives (UKNA), reference no. CAB 65/19/20. The quote by E.W. Swanton beginning 'The Allied invasions [of Japan] were planned for early September …' can be found in Swanton's memoir *Sort of a Cricket Person*, as cited in the bibliography, pp. 135–6.

The account by Ernest Toovey following the sinking of HMAS *Perth* can be found in the National Archives of Australia, War Record no. B4747, Toovey, Ernest Albert; E.W. Swanton's quote beginning 'About three one morning …' is from his book *Sort of a Cricket Person*, p. 180. The instructions regarding the proper use of the UK's wartime ration were reported in the *Sunday Graphic* of March 1945. The ordeal of the soldier-cricketer Joseph Hazel can be read in The Papers of Lt. Col. E.J. Hazel (Document 3750) in the IWM London. The helpful instructions to American servicemen stationed in the UK noting 'The British are often more reserved …' can be found in the file marked 'Intelligence for American Forces in Great Britain', June 1942, and modified in August 1945, held in the US War Department Archives.

The quote by R.C. ('Crusoe') Robertson-Glasgow beginning 'While the fate of the world was being determined …' was included in his annual notes in *Wisden*, both in 1946 and *passim*. The description of the physical infrastructure of English first-class cricket grounds, and of the straitened circumstances of their host clubs, can be found in the same edition of the almanack, as can the comments by E.W. Swanton beginning 'It was perhaps the very fact of our so occupying ...'

In an effort to capture the essential mood of the time I also re-read both Ronald Mason's *Sing All a Green Willow*, as cited in the bibliography, and *Herbert Farjeon's Cricket Bag* (London: Macdonald, 1946), and am delighted to have the opportunity of expressing my thanks to two authors whose cricket writing was the treat of an otherwise healthily austere childhood.

For a number of the match reports in the first half of the 1945 season I turned to the pages of the 1946 *Wisden*, edited by Hubert Preston, as well as to the peerless Cricket Archive service; I'm grateful to Jim Hindson at the latter. I doff my cap, too, as any student of the 1945 season should, to Mark Rowe and his book *The Victory Tests*, as cited in the bibliography. It's an estimable piece of work, if, perhaps, one sometimes labouring under its author's note of social indignation at the reigning state of affairs in the Britain of that era. Simon Garfield's book *Our Hidden Lives* is equally important for any writer striving for a sense of how ordinary men and women lived in the final days of war and the first ones of peace, and I've occasionally quoted from it here, as indicated, once or twice lightly amended for sense.

As well as the above, I again consulted the files at the Imperial War Museum, which contain journals and scrapbooks of sportsman-combatants in the war; the Cabinet Papers (PREM 11) of the UK National Archives; and the correspondence files of 1942–45 of the National Archives and Record Service, Washington DC. It's a great pleasure to again acknowledge the help given by the secretaries, staff or volunteers of Essex CCC, Hampshire CCC, Kent CCC, Leicestershire CCC, Middlesex CCC, Northamptonshire CCC, Surrey CCC, Warwickshire CCC, Worcestershire CCC and Yorkshire CCC. It was a particular thrill to again visit the County Ground, Hove (my thanks to Jon Filby and Rob Boddie), where I first watched county cricket while incarcerated at a local prep school 50-odd years ago.

The quote by Edie Rutherford beginning 'I find folk are grumbling more now …' is from Simon Garfield, *Our Hidden Lives*, as is the same party's quote beginning 'Talking on Friday to a friend due for demob …' The quote by Pat Bell beginning 'Old Father Thames is at least good …' is contained in The Papers of Mrs P. Bell, Department of Documents, file no. 86/46/1, IWM London. The minutes of the Cabinet meeting of 15 April 1945, and the paper entitled 'Directive by the Prime Minister and Minister of Defence' are in the UK National Archives, reference no. CAB 66/64/50. The figures relating to Britain's national debt compared to her GDP in mid-1945 are available on the website www.economicsheep.org.

The description of the 'heartwarming' scene at Hove, 'looking as if nothing had changed', even if 'the weather was dreadful' is from Laetitia Stapleton, *A Sussex Cricket Odyssey*, as cited in the bibliography. The letter from Pelham Warner to George Pope dated 30 April 1945 is from the archives of the MCC Library at Lord's, where I'm especially grateful to Neil Robinson and his colleagues. The exchange between Warner and Basil Allen on the subject of Walter Hammond is included in David Foot's book *Wally Hammond: The Reasons Why*, as cited in the bibliography, p. 101. The quote describing Hammond the car salesman as 'never in any sense a grafter …' is from the same source.

The letter from Pelham Warner to S.C. 'Billy' Griffith dated 23 April 1945 is similarly contained in the files of the MCC Library at Lord's. The quote beginning 'After seeing this exhibition I feel we ought to shoot every German …', lightly edited for sense, is from Maureen Waller, *London 1945* (London: John Murray, 2004), pages 113–114. The carefully nuanced words of Herbert Morrison remarking 'After considering the views put to me, I am personally not convinced …' are contained in the minutes of the War Cabinet's Memorandum of 1 May 1945, held in the UK National Archives, file no. CAB 66/65/29. The minutes of the UK War Cabinet meeting of 4 May 1945 are from the same source. Noël Coward's remarks beginning 'A wonderful day from every point of view …' are included in Tom Pocock, *1945: The Dawn Came Up Like Thunder* (London: Collins, 1983), p. 102.

The letter from Pelham Warner to William Shakespeare of 11 May 1945 is in the files of the MCC Library at Lord's. The flying exploits of Flt. Lt. Percy MacKenzie, DFC, were reported in the *London Gazette* of 23 February 1943. Keith Miller's remarks about the 'unreality' of life in 1945 form part of the author's interview with Miller of August 1989. The obituary notice for Cecil Pepper, quoting the *Manchester Evening News* correspondent, is in the 1994 edition of *Wisden Cricketers' Almanack*, p. 1,350. The inimitable line describing the posture of certain Australian players in the Lord's dressing room as being 'like stunned mullets' is from Mark Rowe, *The Victory Tests*, as previously cited, p. 43. Lindsay Hassett's comments on the ensuing match, beginning 'By the time we had dismissed the formidable English batting ...' were published in the *Melbourne Argus* of 21 May 1945. The description of the somewhat threadbare facilities of the ground at Leyton is from Alan Gibson, 'Leyton and the Commentary Box', included in the anthology *The Penguin Cricketer's Companion* (London: Penguin, 1981); I'm most grateful to Rupert Rushbrooke for the gift. The correspondence between Pelham Warner and George Pope of 24 and 31 May 1945 is included in the files of the MCC Library at Lord's. The arrangements for the matter of parliamentary candidates wearing their military uniform while campaigning were discussed in the Cabinet meeting of 9 May 1945, the minutes for which are in the UKNA, file no. 66/66/6.

At one time Godfrey Evans also provided an introduction to, among others, Leslie Ames, Alec Bedser, John Dewes, Reg Hayter, Howard 'Hopper' Levett, Cyril Washbrook and Doug Wright; it was perhaps the greatest pleasure of an already lucky life to be able to loiter with some of the above in the downstairs dining room (and conveniently adjacent bar) of the old Cricketers Club in Blandford Street, London. I was also fortunate enough in November 1999 to interview Harold Pinter, when the Nobel Laureate told me of the regrettable incident of the girl's bottom he pinched in the collective euphoria of VE Day, with such disastrous results for himself.

I'm indebted for much of the material covering the period June–July 1945 to the late Len Hutton and Keith Miller, as well as the aforesaid Godfrey Evans, who – thanks to the vagaries of army deployment – while not a direct participant in the Victory series, was closely acquainted with the English cricket scene of the time. Donald Carr once kindly put his recollections of the 1945 season at my disposal. I should also again particularly thank Neil Robinson and his colleagues at the MCC Library at Lord's, as well as the late Sir Oliver Popplewell, Jon Surtees of Surrey CCC, Nick Tudball and Nigel Hancock of the Cricket Society, and those great players the late Bill Edrich, Neil Harvey, Micky Stewart and Sir Garry Sobers, all of whom spoke to me of their youthful experiences of the era. I consulted both *Wisden Cricketers' Almanack* and the Cricket Archive website throughout.

The account of General Eisenhower's visit to Lord's was provided by the late Brigadier General Robert Stack, US Army, Eisenhower's military aide, whom I knew at one time at our mutual family home in Tacoma, Washington. The letter from the Colne CC secretary to Pelham Warner beginning 'I thank you for your telegrams …' is courtesy of Neil Robinson at the MCC Library, Lord's. The account of The Army v British Empire XI match at Westcliff on 16 June 1945 can be found in *Wisden Cricketers' Almanack 1946*, p. 206. The provisions for post-war lighting on British streets were discussed in the Cabinet meeting of 22 June, Cabinet Papers file no. CAB 66/66/43, UK National Archives. Winston Churchill's remarks in the minute beginning 'The Prime Minister recalled that, when he agreed to meet President Truman and Marshal Stalin …' are from the same source.

Fred Trueman's evocative description of conditions at Bramall Lane, Sheffield, are found in his book *As It Was* (London: Macmillan, 2004); it does nothing to detract from that great fast bowler and raconteur to suggest that the passage in question may possibly owe something to a ghost writer. The comment by Edie Rutherford beginning 'A pouring wet day again ...' is from *Our Hidden Lives*, as previously cited. Further details on the fickle British climate of 1945 can be found in the review 'A Century of London Weather' posted by the UK Met Office on their site metoffice.gov.uk. C.B. Fry's remark beginning 'Thought you might like to know what that one did, Lindsay ...' is from Mark Rowe, *The Victory Tests*, as previously cited, page 110.

Gubby Allen's account of the 'handled the ball' incident at Lord's on 30 June 1945 is a composite of the version published in E.W. Swanton, *Gubby Allen: Man of Cricket* (London: Stanley Paul, 1985) and Allen's own remarks to me in May 1989. The adventures of the young cricketer Hubert Webb and General Montgomery are included in The Papers of Hugh [*sic*] Webb, Document 19653, held at the IWM London. Webb would play 15 first-class matches, including a single appearance for Hampshire, before going on to a distinguished career as a professor of neurology; he died in November 2010, at the age of 83.

The letter from George Pope to Pelham Warner beginning 'Following my telegram to yourself re. the Test Match ...' is contained in the files of the MCC Library at Lord's, where I'm again grateful to Neil Robinson and his colleagues. The remarks by John F. Kennedy about the UK general election of July 1945 were published in the *New York Journal-American* of 24 June 1945. Kennedy's subsequent remarks beginning 'Mr Churchill and his men have let ...' are from the *New York Journal-American* of 3 July 1945. John Dewes's statement insisting 'I admired [Hammond] to the ends of the earth ...' formed part of my interview with Dewes at Dulwich in May 1988. The concluding remarks about the third Victory match of 14–17 July 1945 are contained in *Wisden Cricketers' Almanack 1946*, p. 175. The letter sent by Pelham Warner that same week to Charles Leatherbarrow beginning 'I apologise for again worrying you ...' is from the collection of the MCC Library at Lord's. The description of the atomic bomb test beginning 'All present seemed to sense immediately ...' is from a memorandum by Leslie Groves to the US secretary of war Henry Stimson, dated 18 July 1945, and forms part of the Manhattan Engineer District Records, file no. RG77, held in the US National Archives.

The letter from Pelham Warner to Walter Hammond beginning 'I hope to Heaven your lumbago is going ...' is similarly from the collection of the MCC Library at Lord's.

For advice or source material in the final chapters of the book I'm particularly indebted to Mike Atherton, the late Donald Carr, the late John Dewes, the late Ted Dexter, the late Len Hutton, the late Keith Miller, Peter Perchard, Micky Stewart, the late Doug Wright and the late and irreplaceable John Woodcock.

The description by Chester Wilmot about the 'quite alarming' conditions at the fourth Victory match at Lord's is included in Mark Rowe, *The Victory Tests*, as previously cited, p. 177. The letter from Pelham Warner to the new British prime minister of 4 August 1945 beginning 'The Committee of M.C.C. would be greatly honoured ...' is from the collection of the MCC Library at Lord's. The remark by Ross Stanford beginning 'Pope was bald ...' is also quoted in Rowe, *The Victory Tests*, p. 181. Keith Miller's views on the same ball-altering technique, which if nothing else would seem to partly explain Miller's preferred well-lacquered pompadour hairdo, formed part of our interview of August 1989.

The minutes of the UK Cabinet meeting of 10 August 1945 are held in the Cabinet Papers, file no. CAB 128/1/3 at the UK National Archives. The remarks by Himmler insisting 'By the end of the year, the Jewish question will have been settled ...' are found in Helmut Krausnick, *Anatomy of the SS State* (New York: Walker, 1968), p.123. The description of the London street scenes on VJ Day is partly from Maureen Waller, *London 1945*, as previously cited, p. 315. The minutes of the Cabinet meeting of 20 August 1945, reference no. CAB 128/1/7, are held in the UKNA. The remark by the Australian player Dick Whitington insisting he walked 'disconsolately from the ground to the accompaniment of organised hooting from the Old Trafford members …', an incident, it has to be said, not similarly recalled by others present, is included in Mark Rowe, *The Victory Tests*, as previously cited, p. 202. Walter Hammond's words of appreciation for the departing Australian Services cricketers are similarly included in *The Victory Tests*, p. 220.

The press report beginning 'A London message states that an official of the Rochdale (Lancashire League) cricket club …' was published on page 1 of *The Advocate* (Tasmania) of 24 October 1945. The diary entry by Edie Rutherford beginning 'I shall go to London on Saturday …' is included in Simon Garfield, *Our Hidden Lives*, as previously cited, p. 89. Edie Rutherford's subsequent diary note beginning 'My hairdresser sisters …' is from *Our Hidden Lives*, p. 101.

The account of the England players meeting Walter Hammond at their Port Elizabeth hotel in February 1965 was given to me by my late friend and peerless wicketkeeper-batsman John Murray, of Middlesex and England, whom I continue to think of as one of the two or three greatest men I've had the pleasure to know.

Once again, I consulted *Wisden Cricketers' Almanack 1946* throughout.

Bibliography

Arlott, John, *Arlott on Cricket* (London: Willow, 1984)

Birley, Derek, *A Social History of English Cricket* (London: Aurum, 1999)

Burumsa, Ian, *Year Zero: A History of 1945* (New York: Penguin, 2013)

Cardus, Neville, *Autobiography* (London: Collins, 1947)

Foot, David, *Wally Hammond: The Reasons Why* (London: Robson, 1996)

Frindall, Bill, *The Wisden Book of Cricket Records* (London: Headline, 1993)

Garfield, Simon, *Our Hidden Lives* (London: Ebury Press, 2004)

Green, Benny (ed.), *The Lord's Companion* (London: Pavilion Books, 1987)

Hammond, Walter, *Cricket My World* (London: Stanley Paul, 1948)

Hill, Alan, *Bill Edrich: A Biography* (London: André Deutsch, 1994)

Howat, Gerald, *Len Hutton* (London: Heinemann, 1988)

Judt, Tony, *Postwar* (New York: Penguin, 2005)

Kilburn, J.M., *A History of Yorkshire Cricket* (London: Stanley Paul, 1970)

Kynaston, David, *Austerity Britain 1945–51* (London: Bloomsbury, 2007)

Mason, Ronald, *Sing All a Green Willow* (London: Epworth Press, 1967)

Miller, Keith, *Cricket Crossfire* (London: Oldbourne Press, 1956)

Peebles, Ian, *Spinner's Yarn* (London: Collins, 1977)

Perry, Roland, *Keith Miller* (London: Aurum, 2006)

Press Association, *100 Years of Cricket* (Lewes: Ammonite Press, 2008)

Preston, Hubert (ed.), *Wisden Cricketers' Almanack 1946* (London: Sporting Handbooks, 1946)

Prittie, T.C.F., *Cricket North and South* (London: Sportsman's Book Club, 1955)

Robertson-Glasgow, R.C., *46 Not Out* (London: Hollis & Carter, 1948)

Rowe, Mark, *The Victory Tests* (Cheltenham: SportsBooks, 2010)

Sandford, Christopher, *The Final Innings: The Cricketers of Summer 1939* (Cheltenham: The History Press, 2019)

Stapleton, Laetitia, *A Sussex Cricket Odyssey* (Havant: Ian Harrap, 1979)

Swanton, E.W., *Sort of a Cricket Person* (London: Collins, 1972)

Warner, Pelham, *Cricket Between Two Wars* (London: Chatto & Windus, 1942)

Wilde, Simon, *Number One* (London: Gollancz, 1988)

Williams, Charles, *Bradman* (London: Little, Brown, 1996)

Wynne-Thomas, Peter, *The History of Lancashire County Cricket Club* (Bromley: Christopher Helm, 1988)

Index

Adams, Gunner Sidney 31
Albert, Ernest 270
All England Tennis Club 150
Allen, Basil 88
Allen, Sir Gubby 166, 212, 230, 269, 275
Altham, Harry 82
Ames, Leslie 159-160, 196, 267, 273
Andrews, Jack 175
Annaly, 5th Baron, *see also* White, Hon. Luke 82, 180
Arkwright, Francis 42
Arlott, John 241
Armstrong, Tommy 191
Atherton, Mike 276
Attlee, Clement, Prime Minister 137, 155, 204, 206-207, 217, 220, 231-232

Badcock, Ted 239
Bailey, Trevor 83, 199, 213
Bairstow, Jonny 167
Barber, Major Tom 58-59
Barber, Wilf 214
Barling, Tom 220
Barnes, Sid 262
Barratt, Fred 233
Barritt, S.A. 140-141
Bartlett, Hugh 34-35
Beckett, Samuel 31
Bedser, Alec 159, 227, 273
Bedser, Eric 227
Bell, Pat 78, 272
Bennett, Bob 69
Bernays, Robert 194
Bishop, Ian 158
Blackburn, James 269
Blake, John 39-41, 43
Blake, David 58, 270
Blake, Peter 168

Blunt, Roger 132
Bompas, William 46
Boomerang Club 230
Booth, Arthur 166, 191, 247
Border, Allan 258, 261
Boucher, Jimmy 244
Bowden, Jack 245
Bowell, Norman 42
Bowes, Bill 31, 46, 84, 159-160, 170, 192, 214
Bowley, John 46
Bradman, Sir Don 22, 25, 82, 95-96, 121, 124, 248, 256-257, 262-264
Bremner, Colin 235
Broad, Lt. Gen. Sir Charles 148
Brookes, Dennis 116-117, 247
Brooks, Paul 82-83
Brown, Bill 261
Brown, Freddie 31, 46, 84, 213, 243
Budd, Lloyd 147
Butterworth, John 41-42

Cadogan, Alexander 217
Cahn, Sir Julien 90, 92
Calthorpe, Freddy 233
Cardus, Sir Neville 47, 241, 259, 263, 265, 193
Carr, Donald 266, 274, 276
Chalk, Flt. Lt. Gerry 29-30
Chappell brothers 258
Cheetham, Bert 122, 127, 183, 201
Christopherson, Sir Stanley 104, 158
Chudwell, Miles 252
Churchill, Sir Winston 48, 80-81, 154-155, 174-175, 195, 204-205, 274
Clarke, Bertie 108-109
Coldrick, William 194
Colne Cricket Club 86, 135-136, 140-142, 172, 202, 274
Compton, Denis 37-38, 60, 73, 159, 166, 221-222, 259, 264, 268
Compton, Leslie 166
Constantine, Lord Learie 81, 132-133, 229
Copson, Bill 112
Coward, Sir Noël 110, 205, 272
Cowdrey, Colin 93
Cox, 'Young' George 83
Coxon, Alec 177, 237
Crabtree, Harry 152

Cranston, Ken 80, 83, 199
Creber, Arthur 196
Cristofani, Robert 117, 136-139, 145, 175, 185, 190, 192, 201, 225-226, 249, 258
Crouch, Maurice 80
Curtin, 'Honest John' 94-95

Daugherty, E.A. 57
Davies, Jack 240
de Gaulle, General Charles 40
Derbyshire 65-67, 86, 112, 123, 134, 146, 191-192, 202, 217
Dewes, John 82-83, 180-183, 185, 193, 199, 211, 213, 273, 275-276
Dexter, Ted 94, 261, 276
Dönitz, Grand Admiral 119
Donnelly, Martin 131-132, 229, 237-238

Ealing 140-168
Earls-Davis, Michael 152
Edrich, Bill 17-20, 39, 47, 100, 115-117, 125, 129, 142, 162, 164, 175, 181, 183-185, 205, 213-218, 236, 262-263, 265, 268, 270, 274
Edrich, Justin 17
Eisenhower, Dwight D. future US president 147-149, 274
Ellis, Reg 97-98, 108, 145, 159, 235, 239, 249, 259
Essex cricket 19, 26, 35-36, 105, 137, 152, 233
Evans, Godfrey 30, 38-39, 59, 79, 90, 114, 133, 143, 179-180, 231, 258, 260, 268, 273-274

Fagg, Arthur 30, 190
Farage, Nigel 266
Farjeon, Herbert 242, 271
Farnes, Ken 26, 99
Fell, Desmond 146
Fishlock, Laurie 202, 219, 225, 238-239, 236
Fleming, Ian 40
Foot, David 88, 180, 272
Fry, C.B. 156, 162-163, 275

Garfield, Simon 271-272, 277
Gibb, Paul 123
Gibson, Alan 133, 273
Gillingham, Rev. Frank 105
Gimblett, Harold 35-39, 132, 193, 196, 266
Gloucestershire cricket 67, 86-88, 213, 233
Gordon, Sir Home Seton Montagu 67, 241, 240

Göring, Hermann 20
Gover, Alf 128-129, 153
Grace, W.G. 32, 103
Grace, Fred 152
Graveney, Tom 87-89, 94
Gregory, Ross 99
Gregory, Bob 200
Griffith, Stewart 'Billy' 34, 102, 113-115, 135, 152, 183-186, 222, 225, 266, 272
Griggs, Jim 77
Groves, Leslie 276

Hammond, Mrs. Dorothy 25
Hammond, Sybil 195
Hammond, Walter 18, 25, 35, 63, 87-92, 100, 122-124, 127, 161, 163, 169, 177, 179-184, 193-195, 202, 208-209, 223-226, 229-231, 239-240, 248, 259, 262-264, 272, 276-277
Hampshire cricket 39, 41-42, 58, 64, 67, 115, 146-147, 151, 162, 175, 241, 259, 270
Hardstaff, Joe 159
Harfield, Bernard 64
Harris, Sgt. Charlie 196
Harrison, Eddie 200, 243
Harvey, Neil 100, 274
Hassett, Lindsay 61, 96, 101, 124-125, 163, 199, 208, 223, 225-226, 231, 239, 248-249, 256-258, 262, 273
Haultcoeur, Guy 30
Hawke, 7th Baron 72
Hayter, Reg 273
Hazel, Lt. Col. Joseph 50, 253, 270
Henson, Lt. Col. Hugh 85-86, 172
Hill, Alan 268, 270
Hirohito, Emperor 210-211
Hitler, Adolf 18, 64, 73, 80, 103-104, 119-120, 133, 156, 161, 196, 215, 223
Hobbs, Sir Jack 65, 151, 199
Hobson, Harold 137
Hodgetts, Harry 95
Hogan, Ben 19
Holmes, Flt. Lt. Albert 17
Holmes, Celia 138
Holmes, Errol 64-65, 159, 180
Holmes, Hon. Peregrine 252
Hooper, K.E. 159
Horowitz, Celia 161-163

Hough, Gerald 133
Hunt, Robert 152
Hutton, Sir Len 26, 35, 82, 122, 161, 177, 182-183, 191, 202, 224-225, 237, 257, 262-265, 269, 274, 276, 236

I Zingari 82, 239
Ikin, Jack 124, 262

Jackson, Sir Stanley 74-75
Jackson, Vic 90-91
James, Ken 237-238
Jenkins, Roy 137
Johnson, Keith 145-146, 170-171, 198, 224-225, 235, 248
Johnston, Brian 92-93, 242

Kay, John 223
Kennedy, John F., future US president 174-175, 275
Kent cricket 19, 26, 29-30, 39, 57-58, 104, 123, 133, 190, 196, 212-213, 228, 240, 258, 267, 269
Kerr, Colonel Rowan Rait 75, 105
Khan, Imran 76
Kilburn, Jim 237, 241
Knight, David 108
Krausnick, Helmut 276

Laker, Jim 64, 93, 257
Lancashire League 86, 134, 215, 249-250, 259
Langridge, James 201, 244
Langridge, John 228
Larwood, Harold 26, 233
Laski, Harold 155
Leatherbarrow, Charles 171-172, 186, 188, 210, 212-213, 275
Lee, Kenneth 162
Legge, Geoffrey 26
Leveson-Gower, Sir Henry 236-238
Levett, Howard 'Hopper' 196, 273
Lewis, Claude 131
Leyland, Maurice 152
Lillee, Dennis 258
Lindwall, Ray 100, 262
Lock, Tony 93, 150, 240, 257
Lord's Cricket Ground 19, 22, 27, 31, 36, 54, 57, 59-60, 62-63, 66-67, 74, 82-86, 94, 102, 104-106, 111, 113, 115, 117-120, 123, 126, 130-132, 134-136, 140-

143, 147-149, 157-160, 162, 166-167, 171-173, 180-182, 185-187, 192-193, 200-206, 209, 211-213, 221, 229-231, 237, 240, 258, 265-267, 272-276
Lyttelton, John 66

Macaulay, George 26-27, 270
MacDonald, Tom 91
Mackay, General Sir Ivan 249
MacKenzie, DFC, Flt. Lt. Percy 115-116, 273
MacKinnon, F.A. 158
MacLeod, Alister 41-42
Mallett, Tony 213
Mallyon, Capt. John 61
Marsh, Rod 258
Mason, Ronald 242, 271
Matthews, Austin 196, 237
Maxwell, Cecil 240
May, Peter 93, 151, 210, 266
MCC 11-12, 46, 55, 60-61, 66, 74, 80, 82, 89, 103-107, 112, 119, 134, 136, 150, 158-159, 169, 172-173, 229, 236-237, 266-267, 272-276
McLachlan, Elma 130
Miller, Keith Ross 'Nugget' 21-25, 43-47, 52-55, 70, 95, 98, 100, 108-109, 117-118, 122, 125-126, 130, 142, 145-146, 156, 161, 164, 177-179, 181, 183, 185-186, 189, 191-192, 196-197, 206, 208-210, 218-221, 224-226, 229-230, 235, 238-239, 243-246, 249-252, 255-262, 268, 273, 276
Mitchell, Arthur 214
Montgomery, General, later Field Marshal, Bernard 167-168, 203, 204, 275
Moore, Denis 213
Morey, Clare 197
Morrison, Herbert 107, 272
Murray, John 263, 277
Mussolini, Benito 104

Nelson, Robert 57
Nottinghamshire cricket 90, 124, 146, 196, 233-234, 240
Nutter, Bert 215-216

Orwell, George 48

Palmer, Charles 213
Parker, Jack 237
Parks, Harry 200-201
Partridge, Reg 211
Paynter, Eddie 180

Pearce, Captain Tom 'T.N.' 105, 152-153
Pennock, James 46
Pepper, Cecil 117, 120-121, 125-131, 144, 163, 192, 211-212, 235, 239, 244-245, 248-250, 256, 259, 267, 273
Pettiford, Jack 108, 117-201, 209, 224, 246-247, 256, 258
Phillipson, Eddie 224
Pierpoint, Fred 228
Pinter, Harold 110, 273
Pocock, Tom 273
Pollard, Dick 159, 161, 164, 184-186, 196, 224, 244-245, 266
Pope, Alf 192, 212
Pope, George 65-66, 84-87, 112, 123, 134, 140-141, 149-150, 159, 164-165, 171-173, 180, 186-188, 192, 202, 208, 210, 212, 224, 244-246, 267, 272-275
Popplewell, Sir Oliver, O.B. 151, 274
Pracy, David 269
Preston, Norman 111, 271
Price, Charlie 128, 138, 144, 234, 249, 235
Princess Margaret 260
Prior, Jim 151
Pritchard, Tom 238-239
Prittie, Terrence 46

Ramblers Cricket Club 82
Raven, Simon 151
Reeves, Neville 178-179
Ridgers, Ernest 38, 269
Rimell, Anthony 151
Roberts, Bill 69-70, 142, 159, 185, 224
Robertson, David 269
Robertson, Jack 59, 125, 127, 180, 202
Robertson-Glasgow, R.C. 'Crusoe' 60, 66, 242-243, 270
Robins, Sqn. Ldr. Walter 73-74, 88, 236
Robinson, Ray 209
Robinson, Ellis 214
Rochdale 79, 249-250, 277
Rochester, Mr. Orion 252
Roper, Mick 95, 167, 214, 234-235, 243-244
Rose, Kenneth 202
Rowan, Leslie 231
Rowe, Mark 271, 273, 276-277
Rutherford, Miss Arabella 252
Rutherford, Edie 77-78, 156, 251-253, 272, 275, 277

Seago, Rev. J.E.C. 251-252
Seeley, Gerald 42
Sellers, Brian 237
Shakespeare, William 75-76, 79, 111-115, 159, 171, 192, 202, 273
Sismey, Stan 98-99, 127, 130, 185, 203, 208, 221, 235, 256, 258
Smith-Bampfylde, Reginald 252
Sobers, Sir Garry 274
Spangler, Bert 252
Squires, Stan 175-176
Stack, Brigadier General Robert 149, 274
Stanford, Ross 98, 120, 125, 190, 201, 207-208, 214, 224, 249, 276
Stapleton, Laetitia 81, 272
Stewart, Micky 274, 276
Stimson, Henry 276
Stuart-King, Jasper 152
Sunnucks, Peter 228
Surridge, Stuart 227-228
Surrey cricket 12, 19, 26, 31, 34, 64-65, 67, 82, 93, 128, 133, 150-151, 159, 167, 175-176, 200, 202, 215, 219, 227-228, 237, 243, 251, 257, 269, 274
Sutcliffe, Billy 213
Suttle, Ken 143-144
Sussex cricket 34, 38, 67, 81, 102, 116, 122, 143-144, 146, 162, 168, 199-200, 227-228, 244, 269
Swanton, E.W. 'Jim' 32-33, 45, 54-55, 62, 71, 226-227, 241, 259, 268-271, 275

Tallon, Don 34
Tedder, Arthur 147-148
Tennyson, Lord Lionel 19, 64
Thomson, Jeff 258
Toovey, Ernest 33-34, 270
Townshend, Pete 253
Trott, Albert 229
Trueman, Frederick 19, 26, 93, 156, 274-275
Truman, Harry S., US president 190, 205
Turnbull, Elizabeth 220
Turnbull, Major Maurice 29, 219

Valentine, Bryan 212
Verity, Hedley 27-29, 99, 219, 269
Voce, Bill 124, 233-234
von Greim, Ritter 20

Wagner, Peg, the future Mrs. Keith Miller 22-23, 260

Walker, Don 42
Waller, Maureen 272, 276
Warner, Sir Pelham 'Plum' 61-66, 72-74, 84-88, 102-103, 111-115, 134-136, 140-142, 148-150, 156, 159-160, 166, 169, 171, 186-189, 192-193, 198, 200, 203-207, 210, 220, 230, 246, 248, 264, 266-267, 272-276
Washbrook, Cyril 68-69, 95, 142, 213-214, 226, 236, 238, 262, 265-266, 273
Webb, Hubert 168, 275
Wellard, Arthur 36
Wellings, Evelyn 'E.M.' 241
Wheatley, Garth 82
White, Crawford 265
White, Hon. Luke, *see also* Annaly, 5th Baron 82, 180-182, 202, 266
Whitehead, John 177
Whitington, Dick 117, 121-122, 163, 225, 258, 276
Wilkinson, Ellen 195
Williams, Eddie 226
Williams, Graham 33, 97, 118, 122, 126-127, 177, 243, 249, 256-257
Williams, Spen 97
Wilmot, Chester 203, 276
Wisden Cricketers' Almanack 27, 42, 82, 102, 109, 120, 128, 142, 158, 165, 176-177, 186, 203, 223, 225, 228-229, 237, 239, 270, 277
Witherington, Denys 31
Wood, Arthur 237-238
Woodcock, John 276
Wooller, Wilf 32, 253-254
Woolley, Frank 19
Workman, Jim 120, 185, 198, 208, 221, 258, 235
Wright, Doug 123, 125, 185, 258, 273, 276
Wyatt, Bob 194, 214, 236

Yorkshire cricket 12, 26-27, 31, 46, 72, 93, 159, 161, 166, 169, 177, 191-192, 199, 214-215, 237, 247, 270